Towards More Effective Global Drug Policies

Caroline Chatwin

Towards More Effective Global Drug Policies

palgrave
macmillan

Caroline Chatwin
University of Kent
Canterbury, UK

ISBN 978-3-030-06356-6 ISBN 978-3-319-92072-6 (eBook)
https://doi.org/10.1007/978-3-319-92072-6

Softcover re-print of the Hardcover 1st edition 2018

Cover design: Fatima Jamadar

Printed on acid-free paper

This Palgrave Macmillan imprint is published by the registered company Springer International Publishing AG part of Springer Nature
The registered company address is: Gewerbestrasse 11, 6330 Cham, Switzerland

Contents

1
Introduction

A Crossroads for Global Drug Policy?

This book begins from the premise that we are at an interesting juncture for global drug policy. Many theories of policy process propose that policy continues for long periods in a state of relative stasis, before undergoing significant change at key moments. Kingdon (1984), for example, developed a multiple-streams framework which conceptualises the policy process as composed of: problem definitions; a policy 'soup' of potential ideas and solutions; and political actors and agendas. Usually, these 'streams' operate separately from each other, but in occasional and short-lived 'windows of opportunity', the defined problems, proposed solutions and political will combine to allow rapid and significant change to occur (Zahariadis 2007). In a similar fashion, Baumgartner and Jones (1993) developed 'punctuated equilibrium' theory which argues that "political processes are generally characterized by stability and incrementalism, but occasionally they produce large-scale departures from the past" (True et al. 2007: 155).

Many researchers working in the drugs field have sought to apply these theories, as well as other models of policy process, to

C. Chatwin, *Towards More Effective Global Drug Policies*,
https://doi.org/10.1007/978-3-319-92072-6_1

developments in global and national drug policy. Ritter and Bammer (2010), for example, argue that many models of policy process are applicable to the drugs field, and that our deepest understanding will probably come from efforts to combine elements from different models. They provide the example of change in the legal status of cannabis in Western Australia as an effective example of utilisation of a 'window of opportunity'. Lenton (2004) further explains how support from the general public for cannabis policy change in Western Australia, and his own timely proposal for cannabis reform, successfully combined with an opposition party review of drug policy to produce an effective change in legislation. Another example is provided by cannabis re-classification in the UK in 2004 when the support of the general public and the police, combined with much publicity for an experiment in cannabis decriminalisation in the London borough of Lambeth and expert evidence from an Advisory Council on the Misuse of Drugs report (ACMD 2002), to facilitate the change in classification of cannabis from class B to class C.

The changes described above are national in nature, but multiple-streams or punctuated equilibrium theory could also describe the nature of change in global drug policy debates. The 2010s, thus far, have been marked by "unprecedented momentum for drug policy reform" (Hetzer 2016: 1) and Fordham and Jelsma (2016: 1), recently suggested that we were at a "critical juncture, an opportunity for an honest evaluation of global drug policy and how to address the most pressing challenges going forward". A critical juncture—"a situation of uncertainty in which decisions of important actors are causally decisive for the selection of one path or institutional development over other possible paths" (Capoccia 2016: 1)—certainly seems to match the criteria for the creation of a policy window or provide the conditions for a punctuation of the status quo. This section explores the evidence that we are currently at a critical juncture for drug policy, tracing a path from long-standing dissatisfaction with dominant drug policy approaches to the recent United Nations General Assembly on global drug policy in 2016.

The growing appreciation of the failure of a war on drugs or zero tolerance approach to the control of illicit substances has long roots. In 1993, Elliott Currie (1993: 3) commented on the depressing failures of

US drug policy: "Twenty years of the 'war' on drugs have jammed our jails and prisons, immobilized the criminal justice system in many cities, swollen the ranks of the criminalized and unemployable minority poor, and diverted desperately needed resources from other social needs. Yet the drugs crisis is still very much with us. More recent drug policy research indicates that little has changed: for example, Shiner (2003) and Small et al. (2005) link repressive drug policy with burgeoning imprisonment rates; Beyers et al. (2004) associate abstinence-based policies with higher levels of drug use and MacCoun and Reuter (2001: 1) brand the drug problem in the US as "worse than that of any other wealthy nation". Finally, a significant body of research has warned of the adverse effect of intolerant drug policy towards people who inject drugs on the levels of HIV and AIDS (Bastos and Strathdee 2000; Maher and Dixon 1999; Moore and Dietze 2005), prompting Wolfe and Malinowska-Sempruch (2004), in an evaluation of the global response to the illegal drug issue, to call for a greater focus on harm reduction and HIV prevention.

In the 2010s these critiques of American and global drug policy have further matured. Obama's administration avoided the term war on drugs, embarked on a programme to pardon and shorten the prison sentences of hundreds of federal inmates, and spoke out in favour of treating marijuana as a public health issue (Lopez 2017). Gomis (2016) argues that American drug policy is at a critical juncture brought about by a recent opioid crisis, its efforts to legalise or regulate cannabis in many states, and its system of mass incarceration which is increasingly being viewed as both unfair and unsustainable. Increasingly, however, dissatisfaction with the way illegal substances are being controlled is being expressed on a global basis and against global systems of drug control. Take, for example, the Global Commission on Drugs, which was founded in 2011 and is currently chaired by Ruth Dreifuss, the former President and Minister of Home Affairs of Switzerland. The Commission brings together an influential and wide-reaching panel of world leaders and intellectuals from around the globe, united in their mission to create drug policies based on scientific evidence, human rights, public health and safety.

In 2011 they published their first report (Global Commission on Drug Policy 2011), calling for an end to the "criminalization, marginalization and stigmatization of people who use drugs" and pronouncing the global war on drugs a resounding failure. In 2014, a further report (Global Commission on Drug Policy 2014) proposed five pathways to drug policies that work, including: focusing on public health; ensuring access to controlled medicines; decriminalising the personal use and possession of illicit substances; exploring alternatives to punishment; and promoting longer-term socioeconomic development. These and other efforts have brought global focus onto the failure of a war on drugs approach to control of the illicit drug situation, and have also illuminated the many unintended and harmful consequences of a fiercely law-enforcement orientated global drug policy (for example, human rights abuses, mass-incarceration, increased levels of violence and corruption, environmental harms). Efforts such as these have ensured a mounting pressure to move away from a war on drugs approach to the global drug situation.

At the same time that failings of existing policies are being brought into sharp focus, increasingly imaginative alternatives are being experimented with in the public arena. An obvious example of this is provided by the proliferation of attempts to decriminalise, regulate or legalise cannabis, and sometimes other substances, around the globe. Europe has long played host to tolerant cannabis policies with the well-established Dutch coffeeshop system, as well as more ad hoc situations such as the sporadic free cannabis market that sprang up in Copenhagen's free city of Christiaina, or the UK's experiment in 2001 with de facto cannabis decriminalisation in the London borough of Lambeth. In 2001, Portugal took European drug policy tolerance to new limits with a piece of drugs legislation rooted in the effort to primarily reduce drug related harm such as death and disease, rather than reducing the number of drug users per se.

It is more recently adopted systems, however, which have really pushed the boundaries of existing global drug legislation. In November 2012, voters in Colorado and Washington supported a proposal to fully regulate the cannabis market within respective state borders. Now relatively well-established, both markets are firmly organised around a commercial system designed to bring profit to the government and benefit to wider society—for example, in Colorado a significant proportion of cannabis taxes are fed directly into the state's education and school-building funds. Meanwhile in Uruguay in 2013, a decision was taken by the then President, Jose Mujica, and without wide-spread public support, to fully legalise and regulate the Uruguayan cannabis market. Progress since then has been relatively slow with home cultivation and cannabis grower clubs being legalised in 2014, but state licensed pharmacies only beginning to sell cannabis in 2017, and then only on a very localised scale. In contrast to the commercialised markets created in Colorado and Washington, Uruguayan cannabis regulation has been described as more paternalistic in nature with prices kept to a minimal level and users being required to register as such with the national government (Room 2013).

Room (2013) describes these American and Uruguayan changes as in direct contradiction of the terms of the international drug conventions which govern global drug policy, and argues that we must thus seek to review the specifics of global drug legislation to ensure it remains an accurate reflection of policy that is implemented across the globe. This issue grows more pressing as new areas have either introduced their own systems of cannabis regulation, or announced their plans to do so in the near future. In the US, for example: Washington DC announced its intentions to create a regulated cannabis market in 2014; followed in 2015 by Oregon and Alaska; in 2016 by California, Maine, Massachusetts and Nevada; and most recently (at the time of writing), in 2018, Vermont. Elsewhere, Canada, Jamaica, Israel and Norway have all recently announced plans to regulate or decriminalise their cannabis markets, and Guatemala, Mexico, Italy and Morocco are all considered likely to shortly announce plans of their own (TNI 2016).

A further factor contributing to the development of alternative strategies of global drug policy is the increased profile of Latin American leaders and institutional organisations in the debate. In 2013, the Organisation of the American States (OAS) produced an influential report—'Scenarios for the drug problem in the Americas 2013–2025' (Organisation of American States 2013)—which sought to lay out a series of narratives about what *could* happen in the future in terms of alternative styles of drug policy, working forwards from different conceptual starting points. This report represents the first time an international institution has critically analysed the war on drugs and officially outlined potential new approaches. It implies the need to put all options on the table (Robelo 2013) when considering the future of drug policy. Importantly, it provides a counter-point to the dominant Western discourse about the need to focus drug control efforts around supply reduction and law-enforcement above all else. It promotes understanding of how a more even representation of the global problems caused by both illicit substances and the policies enacted to control them, can lead to different strategies and policy implementations.

Significant Latin American influence on the global drug policy debate also came in 2012, in the form of calls from the leaders of Mexico, Colombia and Guatemala—three countries that have suffered disproportionate levels of drug-related violence and other collateral damage (Bowling 2011) in the war on drugs and the focus on supply reduction above all else—to bring forward the next United Nations General Assembly Special Session (UNGASS) to discuss global drug policy. Originally scheduled for 2019 or 2020, Latin American leaders successfully brought UNGASS forward to 2016 stating that "revising the approach on drugs maintained so far by the international community can no longer be postponed", and the UN should "conduct an in-depth review analysing all available options, including regulatory or market measures, in order to establish a new paradigm that would impede the flow of resources to organized crime groups" (cited in Fordham and Jelsma 2016: 1).

UNGASS 2016 thus became somewhat of a rallying call for those feeling the need for global drug policy reform, and was seen by some as a critical juncture (or window of opportunity) for reacting to the failure of the war on drugs and the proliferation of actual and imagined alternative systems of control. As Fordham and Jelsma (2016: 1) suggest: "UN special sessions are rare and crucial moments in UN-level policy making and are designed to ensure a coherent UN System-wide response to global problems of major concern to the international community". In the build up to UNGASS 2016 there was an unprecedented mobilization (Hetzer 2016) of the drug policy reform movement, boosted by the concentrated involvement of civil society organisations and coalescing around issues such as human rights, acknowledging the failure of the war on drugs approach and searching for alternatives, as well as coupling drug policy to sustainable development targets.

Yet, UNGASS 2016 itself, and the Outcome Document (UNODC 2016) it produced, were seen by many of those involved in the reform movement as a disappointment. Immediate reactions centred around the "turgid restatement of 'business as usual'" (Rolles, cited in Transform 2016) and the "lowest common denominator consensus position that is almost entirely disconnected from reality" (Fordham, cited in Transform 2016). Responders such as these, who had been at the forefront of civil society reform efforts, were dismayed by the swift agreement of the Outcome Document (UNODC 2016) before UNAGSS 2016 debates took place in earnest. Immediate attention was focused on the lack of acknowledgement of the failure of the war on drugs approach and the lack of consideration for either the need to reform the terms of the international drug conventions or to set up an expert advisory group overseeing the future development of global drug policy. In sum, it felt like the window of opportunity had snapped shut without the significant change in approach to global drug policy that many had hoped for.

Based on this evidence, it could be argued that the critical juncture for global drug policy has passed and the decision has been made to continue with the status quo. A more considered view, however, has since emerged from the drug policy reform movement, recognising the many gains in terms of human rights, sustainable development, involvement of civil society, and increased reference to public health, that have emerged as a result of UNGASS 2016. Furthermore, UNGASS is now thought to have strengthened the drug policy reform movement into a "formidable global social movement…leading to sustainable and seismic breakthroughs at national, regional and ultimately UN levels" (Fordham 2016: 1). As we move towards the next UN High Level Meeting on drugs in 2019 further work can be done towards drug policy reform goals and viable alternatives can continue to be explored and evidenced.

Perhaps then it is overstating the case to suggest that we are at a critical juncture for global drug policy: Kingdon's (1984) streams have not yet fully aligned to create the right window of opportunity and change continues to take place at a slow and incremental level, rather than occurring all at once in a punctuation to the equilibrium (Baumgartner and Jones 1993). The period remains, however, an important one as pressure for reform continues to mount, particularly as an increasing number of countries and territories implement innovative systems of cannabis regulation. "Change is slow to come to the UN. But with citizens across the world pushing for reform, and with countries moving ahead with novel drug policies, sooner or later the UN too will have to change to reflect new realities on the ground, or risk becoming an irrelevant and ignored force in global drug policy control" (Hetzer 2016: 1). When it does, it will be important to have a wide-ranging and well-evidenced suite of alternatives ready to provide a counterpoint.

A Public Criminology Approach

This book borrows from a broad interpretation of a public criminology perspective. This is a concept that requires further explanation, as public criminology has become somewhat of an "umbrella" (Loader and Sparks 2010: 774) term meaning very different things to different people. It is not a new idea, but one which has, perhaps, newly found fertile ground amongst scholars in the twenty-first century. Interest in it arises from a general feeling that, despite the rise of interest in the study of criminology at university and the rise of criminology focused journals, conferences and academic fora, criminology as a discipline has failed to have critical and engaged policy impact on our reactions to crime and the development of criminal justice systems. "Despite its accumulated theoretical and empirical heft, the discipline of criminology has had distressingly little impact on the contours of public policy towards crime and justice" (Currie 2007: 175). Matthews (2009: 341) describes an "inverse relationship" between the proliferation of academic activity in this field and the policy relevance of the contributions.

For many, the term public criminology has come to mean engaging directly with the public. This important part of the concept encompasses both agenda setting and research dissemination. For example, members of the general public, as well as NGOs and civil society, might create partnerships with academics and have input to the development of research agendas in general and research questions for specific projects (Currie 2007). In turn, academics might strive to attract the "public spotlight" (Uggen and Inderbitzen 2010: 742) by making their research accessible to a general audience, by ensuring that it is newsworthy and by engaging in non-academic mass media and new media communication forms (Carrier 2014). I do not dispute that these are worthy goals, both for criminology in general and the exploration of drug control policies in particular, but this is not the conceptualising of public criminology that I am claiming for this book. Rather, I am drawing on the work of Uggen and Inderbitzen (2010), Currie (2007), Loader and Sparks (2010) and Matthews (2009, 2016) to produce a book that aspires to be "distinctive for [its] breadth of interests and strong communication skills … [that] can aid in uncovering and publicizing harm or inequity without necessarily redressing it, and might attempt to do so from a value-neutral perspective" (Uggen and Inderbitzen 2010: 737).

The starting point for justifying the validity of this type of work lies with Burawoy (2005: 4) who identified a need to develop (or re-develop) a public sociology with the central aim of engaging "multiple publics in multiple ways". He argued that those conducting academic research in the field of sociology could broadly be divided into four different categories: policy sociology which focuses on specific solutions to problems and is commissioned by clients; professional sociology which provides evidence and expert advice to support official policies; critical sociology which aims to challenge the dominant discourse and push the discipline forward into new areas; and public sociology which allows the general public to engage in ongoing dialogue with academic experts and play an important role in defining and responding to important social issues. With particular relevance for the development of this book, however, he states that: "Public sociology aims to enrich the public debate about moral and political issues by infusing them with sociological theory and research" (Burawoy 2004: 1603).

Burawoy's (2005) work outlining the different categories of sociology has prompted similar debates in other social science areas, and has been mapped into the criminological discipline by Uggen and Inderbitzen

(2010) who also advocate different categories of criminologist along the same lines of policy, professional, critical and public. Furthermore, as Burawoy et al. (2004: 104) call for the promotion of sociological dialogues "about issues that affect the fate of society", so Uggen and Inderbitzen (2010) argue that harmful and/or ineffective policies should be challenged and subjected to open debate by criminologists. The arguments outlined here about using theory and research to enrich public debates have also been the focus of other criminological scholars who have sought to contribute to the development of this side of public criminology.

For example, Currie (2007) identifies an encroaching 'marginality' of criminological research and suggests an important role for scholars who seek to synthesise and analyse the available evidence, and to explain and interpret it in an accessible way. As he outlines, criminologists (and academics from other disciplines) are good at designing and conducting original research studies, and then publishing their findings in peer reviewed academic journals, but are less good at producing and contextualising their findings in a way that can contribute meaningfully to wider public debates. Similarly, Loader and Sparks (2010: 778) have developed the concept of 'democratic under-labourer' to suggest that the role of the public criminologist is to open up the debate in a contentious area, to challenge entrenched public opinion and political postures, and to be "bearers and interpreters" of their own hard-won knowledge. In sum, the public criminologist should aim to "contribute to public discussions of crime control issues in an argumentative and intelligent way by being sceptical and critical of the taken for-granted assumptions and common sense notions that pervade such discussions" (Crepault 2016: 802).

Matthews (2009, 2016) has also taken up and developed this side of public criminology in his work. He promotes a criminology that does not compartmentalise into the categories suggested by Burawoy (2005) and confirmed by Uggen and Inderbitzen (2010). Instead, he calls for a "joined up criminology" (Matthews 2016: 1), which "links theory, method and intervention with the aim of developing a coherent critical realist approach" (Matthews 2009: 341). Cullen (2011) outlines the need to move on from a 'nothing works' attitude towards crime and criminal justice in general, and instead seek to focus on what does work. Taking a critical realist approach to this question of what does work will also involve using theories and hypotheses (Matthews 2009) to explore how it works and why it works. Collectively, these ideas about the need to infuse public debate with academic research and theory, to synthesise research and effectively communicate it to a diverse audience, to be critical and sceptical of common knowledge assumptions, and to explore what works and why, have formed the guiding framework for the development of this book.

Many of the ideas outlined above about developing a public sociology or a public criminology, could also be applied more specifically to developing a public drug policy. The idea that a war on drugs approach to the control of illicit substances has been ineffective, or that it has contributed to harmful and unintended consequences, for example, will not be of surprise to academic scholars and experts working in the field. A lot of time and energy has been expended by a great number of credible and experienced academics on explaining these matters to law-enforcers and policy makers without much impact in terms of global or national drug policy change. The control of illegal drugs is a moral and political issue that is of interest to the general public and which, at the same time, impacts heavily on society in general. It thus provides a good fit with Burawoy's (2005) central thesis about the kind of issue to which public sociology is most suited. Furthermore, academics working in this area are well placed to add valuable information to the national (and, importantly, international) conversation about drugs and drug control, in line with Uggen and Indertitzen's (2010) criminological take on the development of a public academia.

Two further facets to the debate have pertinence specifically to the illegal drugs issue. Firstly, Burawoy (2005) and Currie (2007) both emphasise the important role that Non Governmental Organisations (NGOs) and civil society in general can play in providing the link between academia and wider society, encompassing both the general public and the policymaking elite. On the international stage, and in the run up to UNGASS 2016, civil society has played an increasing role in the global drug policy debate, synthesising available research and disseminating it in an accessible format. Secondly, Matthews (2016) has highlighted the need for a global response to criminologically interesting problems. Furthermore, Burawoy (2005) notes the irony that while the global south has generally well developed public sociologies (in comparison to the global North), an Americanised or Westernised style of sociology, that is not particularly public in its approach, has gained disciplinary dominance. These themes are also directly applicable to the area of drug policy. Recent years have seen the entry into global drug policy debates of the global South in a direct challenge to the existing hegemonic interpretations of the issue by the global North.

To conclude, then, this book seeks to synthesise and analyse the breadth of information available on the global drug issue and to present it in an accessible and intelligent format. It aims to enrich and enhance the existing debate by challenging common sense assumptions and by opening up the field to a wider audience. It aspires to link theory and practice to produce suggestions about what we ought to do, underpinned by explorations of how and why we ought to do it. In doing this, it draws heavily throughout on work and commentary provided by civil society, acknowledging the important and increasing role they play in global drug policy debates. Finally, it seeks, as far as is possible under the hegemonic dominance of research culture by the global North, to emphasise and dwell on the transformative nature of the global South's contributions to global drug policy debates.

Structure of the Book

The overall aim of this book is to provide five steps towards the development of more effective global drug policies. Each chapter outlines one of the steps we need to take: (i) acknowledge the failure of a war on drugs approach to drug control and the harm it has caused; (ii) recognise the primary importance of addressing the harm that stems from and is associated with drug use and drug control policies; (iii) encourage the development of innovative strategies of drug control; (iv) ensure that drug policy innovations are evaluated and evidence on their effectiveness is shared widely; and (v) broaden the horizons of the drug policy debate.

Chapter 2 argues that, despite the increasing evidence against the effectiveness of a 'war on drugs' strategy in global drug policy, contemporary policy decisions continue to be shaped by this framework. It begins by outlining the history of international drug control and the emergence of a war on drugs heavily promoted by the US, before exploring the failure of this approach to meet its aims: for example, to significantly reduce the number of people who use drugs and/or the availability of illegal drugs. In further detail, it explores the growing evidence of the unintended consequences of pursuing a war on drugs strategy. In terms of drug consuming countries, it presents evidence of harm in areas such as arrest and incarceration rates for drug offences, the role of race in determining drug offence outcomes, and the failure to develop adequate alternatives to the law enforcement approach. In terms of drug producing countries, it presents evidence of harm in areas such as the corruption of governments, the increased levels of violence and homicide, environmental issues, human rights abuses, and the problem of displacement. It particularly focuses on the relatively recent inclusion of the global south in debates about the harmful unintended consequences of global drug policy, and the enhanced understanding of them that this has provided.

Recent attempts to publicly move away from the term war on drugs are documented, but the discussion of two case studies suggests little has changed in terms of underlying attitudes. The first case study evidencing the enduring popularity of the war on drugs strategy is provided by the global response to dealing with New Psychoactive Substances (NPS) and Human Enhancement Drugs (HED), which has almost universally been to implement war on drugs style emergency legislation. The second features the failure of successive United Nations Assemblies on this topic (including UNGASS 2016) to move away from a zero-tolerance approach. It concludes that, if we are to see progress in global drug policy, we need to not only accept the limitations of a 'war on drugs' approach and acknowledge the many harms that it has produced, but also to develop and implement alternative strategies that are not based exclusively in the law-enforcement sphere.

This theme is taken up in Chapter 3 which establishes the need to develop alternative strategies to the war on drugs which are based around reducing drug-related harm rather than the use of drugs per se. It includes critical discussion of existing alternative strategies and offers suggestions about how to move increasingly towards them. It begins by discussing harm reduction strategies that seek to reduce the health, social and economic harms of drug use to individuals, communities and societies, and which have largely developed in response to the challenge of reducing the unintended harms caused by illegal drug policy. The first half provides a brief history of the concept of harm reduction, draws on detailed examples of harm reduction initiatives (e.g. methadone maintenance, needle exchange, drug consumption rooms, pill and powder testing facilities, etc.), and ends with a presentation of the concept's limitations. Specifically, it suggests the need for harm reduction strategies to also address the harm that is done by poverty and societal and/or material inequality, and to provide a more proactive approach to tackling human rights abuses around the globe. It advocates the need to commit to creating drug policies that are fundamentally rooted in harm reduction and public health, rather than seeking to add these elements on to existing policies as the need arises.

The second part of the chapter addresses the extent to which alternative strategies of drug policy have been accepted and developed around the globe, and argues that they remain very much of secondary status to law-enforcement or war on drugs approaches. In support of this argument it provides an in-depth case study of Portugal—one of the only countries to base national drug policy around the principle of harm reduction in a radical policy shift which occurred in 2001. A further case study outlines the historical difficulties experienced in writing harm reduction drug policy strategies into official drug control documentation, and highlights the dominance of relevant discourse by actors from the global North. Finally, it suggests that national and international bodies concerned with the control of illicit drugs need to recognise that alternative forms of drug control can exist as part of a system of overall prohibition and play their part in championing and encouraging their wider development and adoption.

A vital part of increasing both confidence in alternatives to drug control and a wider range of interventions from which to choose, is concerned with encouraging the development of innovative strategies of drug policy control. Chapter 4 thus argues that it is only through experimentation with innovative policy options that we will discover effective and appropriate drug policy solutions. International systems of drug control should therefore seek to encourage a more diverse range of drug policy options. This chapter begins by outlining complex debates around room for manoeuvre within the international drug control treaties. Essentially it argues that, while these treaties were written with considerable flexibility, there are other significant forces (e.g. the International Narcotics Control Board) that have been consistently applied against the development of innovative policy responses.

It offers a detailed exploration of different examples of policy innovation, focusing mainly on historical and more recent developments in the decriminalisation and regulation of cannabis. Specifically, this section encompasses Spanish cannabis social clubs, Jamaican decriminalisation for medical and religious purposes, Dutch coffeeshops, and the fully regulated markets created in some US states and in Uruguay. Furthermore, it advocates the benefits a diversity of policies can bring, in terms of developing a range of geographic and context specific strategies, to a field where 'universal' solutions should not be readily expected. Finally, it emphasises the limitations that have been placed on the development of innovative policies around the globe by inflexible interpretation of the international drug treaties, and briefly explores some of the options for international treaty reform.

Chapter 5 further argues that drug policy innovations are only useful in a system that also allows for their evaluation, and which has the resources to disseminate the results widely. It begins by critically exploring the rise of evidence based policy debates in general, and their applicability to the complex or 'wicked' field of drug policy in particular. The second section explores the extent of cross-national comparative drug policy data collated around the globe, outlining the problematic nature of undertaking comparisons in this area. It further elaborates on the difficulties of defining 'success' in the drugs field when there is little agreement about whether success, for example, is indicated by reduced overall drug *use* or reduced overall drug *harm*. Finally, it makes suggestions about how we could develop better metrics for evaluating drug policy efforts, and emphasises the important role that soft policy transfer and lesson-drawing can play. In particular, it emphasises the significance of civil society efforts in this area.

Finally, Chapter 6 argues that we need to broaden the horizons of the drug policy debate in four key areas. The first part of this chapter relates to the Westerncentric nature of criminology debates in general and extends this perspective to the drug policy field. As outlined in chapter one, it suggests that the views of producer countries and the global South in general have often been absent from global drug policy debates. In order to produce a more effective global drug policy, this problem must thus be overcome and effective strategies must be implemented within a global framework that considers the problems of both producer and consumer countries, and which designs strategies that can encompass them both. The second part draws on multi-level governance theory to emphasise the importance of including the local level, as well as national and international levels, in the development of global drug policy. This connects with ideas expressed in chapters three and four about the need for culturally and geographically contextualised strategies and the absence of 'universal' solutions.

A broadening of the range of substances usually included in global drug policy debates is the subject of the third section. Evidence is presented to document the increasing tendency, amongst academics, to consider legal substances such as alcohol and tobacco alongside illegal substances in debates about the harm that they can cause. This section also encompasses a discussion of the rise in popularity of new drugs (NPS and HED), and the impact these have had on existing knowledge about drug prevalence, drug markets, drug policy and drug harms. Finally, the chapter argues that the impact and far-reaching consequences of technological advances such as the internet need to be routinely included in debates: considering wider drug scene developments and landscapes will allow a better understanding of the kinds of policy that will be effective.

The book concludes by exploring the current opioid crisis emerging in the US and other areas of the global North. It argues that this example provides evidence of a continuation of the status quo with respect to a new and alarming facet of the global drugs issue and offers an outline of how responses would differ were the steps suggested in this book to be taken. Given the continued dominance of existing drug control strategies, it explores the many obstacles to developing alternative approaches. Finally, it suggests that the future nature of global drug policy change is likely to remain incremental and largely driven by the development of local-level responses to new and emerging issues. To move towards more effective global drug policies, a more flexible international approach is required.

References

ACMD. (2002). *The classification of cannabis under the misuse of drugs act 1971*. Home Office. https://www.gov.uk.

Bastos, F., & Strathdee, S. (2000). Evaluating effectiveness of syringe exchange programmes: Current issues and future projects. *Social Science and Medicine, 51,* 1771–1782.

Baumgartner, F. R., & Jones, B. D. (1993). *Agendas and instability in American politics*. Chicago: University of Chicago Press.

Beyers, J., Toumbourou, J., Catalano, R., Arthur, M., & Hawkins, J. (2004). A cross-national comparison of risk and protective factors for adolescent substance use: The United States and Australia. *Journal of Adolescent Health, 35,* 3–16.

Bowling, B. (2011). Transnational criminology and the globalisation of harm production. In M. Bosworth's & C. Hoyle's (Eds.), *What is criminology?* Oxford: Oxford University Press.

Burawoy, M. (2004). Public sociologies: Contradictions, dilemmas, and possibilities. *Social Forces, 82,* 1603–1618.

Burawoy, M. (2005). 2004 presidential address: For public sociology. *American Sociological Review, 70*, 4–28.

Burawoy, M., Gamson, W., Ryan, C., Pfohl, S., Vaughan, D., Derber, C., et al. (2004). Public sociologies: A symposium from Boston college. *Social Problems, 51*, 103–130.

Capoccia, G. (2016). Critical junctures. In O. Fioretos, G. Tulia & A. Sheingate (Eds.), *The Oxford handbook of historical institutionalism*. Oxford: Oxford University Press.

Carrier, N. (2014). On some limits and paradoxes of academic orations on public criminology. *Radical Criminology, 4*, 85–115.

Crepault, D. (2016). The rise of partisan pedagogy: How stakeholders outside of the academy are answering the call to public criminology. *British Journal of Criminology, 57*, 789–807.
Cullen, F. T. (2011). Beyond adolescence-limited criminology. Choosing our future—The American Society of Criminology 2010 Sutherland address. *Criminology, 49*(2), 287–330.
Currie, E. (1993). *Reckoning: Drugs, the cities and the American future*. New York: Hill and Wang.
Currie, E. (2007). Against marginality: Arguments for a public criminology. *Theoretical Criminology, 11*, 175–190.
Fordham, A. (2016). The drugs consensus is not pretty—It's been ripped apart at the seams. *Huffington Post*, 3 May 2016. http://www.huffingtonpost.co.uk.
Fordham, A., & Jelsma, M. (2016). *Will UNGASS 2016 be the beginning of the end for the 'war on drugs'?* TNI. https://www.tni.org.
Global Commission on Drug Policy. (2011). *War on drugs: Report of the global commission on drug policy*. http://www.globalcommissionondrugs.org.
Global Commission on Drug Policy. (2014). *Taking control: Pathways to drug policies that work*. http://www.globalcommissionondrugs.org.
Gomis, B. (2016). *US drug policy; Clinton vs. Trump*. Global Drug Policy Observatory Situation Analysis, October 2016.
Hetzer, H. (2016). *UNGASS outcome: Missed opportunity for UN, but global reform movement grows & continues to push for better drug policies*. Drug Policy Alliance. www.drugpolicy.org/blog.
Kingdon, J. (1984). *Agendas, alternatives, and public policies*. Boston, MA: Little Brown.
Lenton, S. (2004). P'ot, politics and the press—Reflections on cannabis law reform in Western Australia. *Drug and Alcohol Review, 23*, 223–233.
Loader, I., & Sparks, R. (2010). What is to be done with public criminology? *Criminology and Public Policy, 9*, 771–781.
Lopez, G. (2017). *How Obama quietly reshaped America's war on drugs*. Vox media. https://www.vox.com.
MacCoun, R., & Reuter, P. (2001). *Drug war heresies*. Cambridge: Cambridge University Press.
Maher, L., & Dixon, D. (1999). Policing and public health: Law enforcement and harm minimisation in a street-level drug market. *British Journal of Criminology, 39*, 488–512.
Matthews, R. (2009). Beyond 'so-what?' criminology: Rediscovering realism. *Theoretical Criminology, 13*(3), 341–362.

Matthews, R. (Ed.). (2016). *What is to be done about crime and punishment? Towards a 'Public criminology'*. London: Palgrave Macmillan.

Moore, D., & Dietze, P. (2005). Enabling environments and the reduction of drug-related harm: Re-framing Australian policy and practice. *Drug and Alcohol Review, 24*, 275–284.

Organisation of American States. (2013). *Scenarios for the drug problem in the Americas 2013–2025*. https://www.oas.org.

Ritter, A., & Bammer, G. (2010). Models of policy-making and their relevance for drug research. *Drug and Alcohol Review, 29*, 352–357.

Robelo, D. (2013). *Breaking the Taboo: Why the OAS report on alternatives to drug prohibition is such a big deal*. Drug Policy Alliance. www.drugpolicy.org.

Room, R. (2013). Legalizing a market for cannabis for pleasure: Colorado, Washington, Uruguay and beyond. *Addiction, 109*, 345–351.

Shiner, M. (2003). Out of harm's way? Illicit drug use, medicalisation and the law. *British Journal of Criminology, 43*, 772–796.

Small, W., Wood, E., Jurgens, R., & Kerr, T. (2005). Injection drug use HIV/AIDS and incarceration: Evidence from the Vancouver injection drug users study. *HIV AIDS Policy Law Review, 10*, 5–10.

TNI. (2016). *UNGASS 2016: Watershed event or wasted opportunity?* https://www.tni.org.

Transform. (2016). *Diplomacy or denialism? The language that the UNGASS outcome document overlooked*. www.tdpf.org.uk.

True, J. L., Jones, B. D. & Baumgartner, F. R. (2007). Punctuated-equilibrium theory: Explaining stability and change in public policymaking. In P. A. Sabatier (Ed.), *Theories of the policy process*. Boulder, CO: Westview Press.

Uggen, C., & Inderbitzen, M. (2010). Public criminologies. *Criminology and Public Policy, 9*, 725–749.

UNODC. (2016). *Outcome document of the 2016 United Nations General Assembly Special Session on the world drug problem. Our joint commitment to effectively addressing and countering the world drug problem*. New York: United Nations. http://www.unodc.org/documents.

Wolfe, D., & Malinowska-Sempruch, K. (2004). *Illicit drug policies and the global HIV epidemic. Effects on UN and national government approaches*. New York: Open Society Institute, International Harm Reduction Development.

Zahariadis, N. (2007). The multiple streams framework: Structure, limitations, prospects. In P. A. Sabatier (Ed.), *Theories of the policy process*. Cambridge, MA: Westview Press.

2

Step One: Acknowledge the Failure of a War on Drugs Strategy and the Harm it has Caused

The first step in any attempt to improve global drug policy must be to acknowledge the failure of the currently dominant approach to the control of illicit substances. This chapter charts the rise of prohibition as the centrepiece of global drug policy and explores its development into a fully-fledged 'war on drugs' championed, primarily, by the United States. It offers evidence of the failure of this approach and details the unintended and negative consequences that global adherence to such a policy principle has produced. Importantly, it contends that, despite increasing dissatisfaction with a 'war on drugs' approach, in reality the international drug control apparatus clings to the status quo and does not acknowledge these failures and harms. Without doing so, global drug policy cannot hope to move forward to a position of increased effectiveness.

The Rise of Prohibition Based Drug Policy

Until the early 1900s, few countries had any form of national drug legislation, but this situation was to change radically from the date of the first Opium Convention held at Shanghai in 1909. Thirteen powers

C. Chatwin, *Towards More Effective Global Drug Policies*,
https://doi.org/10.1007/978-3-319-92072-6_2

came together (although it is generally recognised that the US provided the main driving force behind the meeting) and formed an aim to subject international drug policy to strict control measures. This aim was realised three years later in 1912 at The Hague Opium Convention which saw the birth of an international approach to drug policy as well as the emergence of prohibition as the accepted way of dealing with drugs (Bruun et al. 1975). The 1912 Hague Convention also led to the creation of the Advisory Committee on Traffic in Opium and other Dangerous Drugs and designated the general supervision of opium trafficking to the League of Nations.

Between the 1912 Hague Convention and the symbolic 1961 Single Convention on Narcotic Drugs, numerous drug-related international meetings were held, and further international commitments were made by individual countries. In 1925, regulation of drug distribution was organised at the Geneva Convention and, in 1931, a Limitation Convention was held to restrict opium manufacture to the amounts required for scientific and medical purposes. Further working bodies were created to deal with the increasing regulation of the drug trade at this time. 1929 saw the creation of a Permanent Central Narcotics Board (PCB), a Drug Supervisory Body (DSB), the International Health Office in Paris, and the Health Committee of the League of Nations.

After the Second World War, the United Nations (UN) replaced the League of nations and assumed primary responsibility for drug control. To simplify the wealth of international cooperation and legislation that now existed in the matter of drug control, a Single Act was created to encapsulate international commitment: the Single Convention on Narcotic Drugs 1961 bound its signatories to a prohibitive approach towards the control of drugs and made them acknowledge the need for international cooperation, committing signatories to the recognition that "addiction to narcotic drugs constitutes a serious evil for the individual and is fraught with social and economic danger" (United Nations 1961: 1). In line with this principle, the manufacture, import, export and possession of substances such as cannabis, cocaine and opium, must be prohibited, and are usually criminalised. Ultimately, the aim of this policy of prohibition is to deliver a 'drug free world' operating under the assumption that "criminalization deters drug use, and therefore reduces harm to health" (Mena and Hobbs 2010: 61).

Since the implementation of the 1961 Single Convention on Narcotic Drugs, international cooperation in the field of illicit drugs has continued to expand under the guidance of the UN. In 1971, the Convention on Psychotropic Substances was adopted, extending existing policy to synthetic psychotropic substances such as amphetamines and ecstasy. A further international drug control convention against Illicit Traffic in Narcotics and Psychotropic Substances was held in Vienna in 1998. This time, a commitment was made to focus on the demand side of the drug problem, as well as on the more traditional supply side (Leroy 1995).

The 1998 Convention was the first to require states to establish the offence of possession for personal use under criminal law, an extension of harmonisation from the trafficking of drugs to the possession of drugs for personal consumption. The requirement in relation to possession of drugs, however, is not as strict as for drug trafficking. It is subject to the proviso of constitutional limitations of the state or, in other words, up for interpretation by national governments (Dorn and Jamieson 2000) and is the result of political compromise (Bewley-Taylor et al. 2014). It is possible to avoid the imposition of criminal sanctions on those possessing drugs purely for personal use by arguing that, as existing legal systems do not provide sanctions for drugs use, it would be inappropriate to provide them for possession for personal use. Equally, where criminal sanctions do exist, it can easily become the norm to divert those possessing drugs for personal use to treatment or social facilities (Dorn and Jamieson 2000).

This “room for manoeuvre” (Bewley-Taylor and Jelsma 2011: 9) in the interpretation of the international treaties has contributed to the development of a variety of contrasting, and often competing, global strategies for dealing with the possession of illicit drugs for personal use. The next section, however, will argue that it is the most stringently prohibitive systems that have gained global dominance, while those that focus their attention away from law enforcement have found themselves side-lined as radical ‘alternatives’ to the global drug policy approach. Indeed, since the 1980s, the UN drug-control machinery has promoted the ‘Vienna Consensus’, preaching that all must adopt a united front in the battle against the danger presented by illicit drugs. The International Narcotics Control Board (INCB), charged in 1968 with a watchdog role scrutinising compliance with the international conventions, has, since the 1980s, evolved its role towards guardianship of this strictly prohibitive interpretation (Bewley-Taylor and Trace 2006). These developments have made the relaxation of drug policy controls generally more difficult.

The Emergence of a War on Drugs

The policy of prohibition has, since the outset, been championed most forcefully and most consistently by the US, as demonstrated by their heavy involvement in the implementation of an international system of drug control and their commitment to ensuring it is enforced throughout the world. American national drug policy was significantly escalated under President Richard Nixon to that of a 'war on drugs', an extreme and entirely law-enforcement based version of prohibition that used moralising and fear-mongering rhetoric to justify the use of the most severe sanctions in an effort to curb the drugs trade at all costs. Under Richard Nixon, drugs were designated public enemy number one within the US, a state of national emergency was declared, mandatory sentences were introduced for drug related crimes, and a huge increase in federal funding was provided for the 'fight' against drugs (Woodiwiss 1988). The Drugs Enforcement Agency (DEA) was also created and initiated Operation Intercept against cannabis production and trafficking in Mexico, the first of a series of attempts to wage the drugs war against countries that were supplying illegal substances to the US.

Successive American presidents continued to intensify Nixon's initial declaration of war. Ronald Reagan, in reaction to a public hysteria about the crack-cocaine epidemic ravaging the US in the 1980s, declared illegal drugs to be a national security threat and used this mandate to implement a zero tolerance programme of tough measures to be used against drugs and drug users. His presidency saw a huge increase in funding for drug policy and a significant increase in the use of incarceration for those convicted of drug offences. It also saw the launch of the infamous 'just say no' campaign headed up by Nancy Reagan and now widely believed to have been responsible for spreading a legacy of nationwide fear and ignorance about drugs (McGrath 2016;

Owen 2016). In turn, George Bush senior completed the shift in the focus of war efforts to the countries that supply drugs and channelled more American money and effort into curbing drug production (Bullington 2000). Illegal drugs were now firmly established in the minds of Americans as an external threat (Youngers and Roisin 2005) and an Andean Initiative was launched to make Bolivia, Colombia and Peru the new frontline of the drugs war. Much of Andean Initiative strategy involved US military training and support to empower Latin American forces to conduct their own counterdrug initiatives. These trends were largely continued by Clinton who authorised further increases in US drug spending and helped to launch Plan Colombia, which focused military efforts more specifically on curbing the Colombian cocaine trade.

Although the 'war on drugs' approach originated in the US, its effects have been felt around the world, much of which has adopted the terminology and convictions of a zero tolerance approach. As already briefly outlined, much of the war on drugs strategy involved waging war on the producers of drugs via military campaigns beginning with Operation Intercept against cannabis and cocaine production in Mexico, continuing under Reagan's Andean Initiative, and culminating in Plan Colombia against cocaine trafficking and organised crime. A connecting feature of each of these campaigns was to recruit the governments of drug producing countries to the war on drugs approach and the implementation of zero tolerance national drug strategies. This aim was achieved through the provision of funds for an escalation of drug control efforts, the implementation of targets on which other aid and support would become dependent, and a wholesale exportation of an American style of drug control. Such as exclusive focus on the drugs war necessitated the designation of significant funds, often diverted away from other important issues such as the reduction of poverty or the provision of education (Bowling 2011) and inflicting other domestic harms. Plan Colombia for example required 1% of Colombia's GDP every year, involved a significant amount of environmental damage via the pervasive aerial crop spraying programmes employed to limit coca leaf production and central to the overall plan, and saw 57,000 deaths related to expanding drug markets and confrontations between organised drug traffickers and the government (Mejia 2015).

Further international support for a war on drugs has been courted by successive American governments via two main methods: coercion of less powerful countries by threatening to withhold aid and impose other sanctions if drug reduction targets were not met, and the relentless promotion and strict oversight of the international drug control regime. Nixon's 1974 Narcotics Control Trade Act allowed drug producing countries and countries through which drugs were transported to be subjected to American sanctions, such as withholding aid and increases in duties and tariffs, if they failed to cooperate with the war on drugs approach. This bullying (Woodiwiss and Bewley-Taylor 2005) approach was used against many countries—Burma, Afghanistan, Colombia, Nigeria, Guatemala, Haiti, Venezuela, Mexico—even the Netherlands with its coffeeshop system for the semi-legal provision of cannabis made a brief appearance on a list of emerging threats (Jelsma 2011).

Elsewhere, cooperation was 'encouraged' by ensuring that strengthening and maintaining a strictly prohibitive stance through the international drug conventions remained a top priority for the United Nations. Woodiwiss and Bewley-Taylor (2005) describes how this was achieved by prolific American funding of drug control and the aggressive promotion of an American drug control agenda within which law-enforcement and the reduction of drug supply featured heavily. In 1990, for example, the United Nations, at their General Assembly, declared the period from 1991 to 2001 to be a decade against drugs, aiming to significantly strengthen the UN drug policy apparatus during this time. Jelsma (2015) describes how this represented an acceptance of US 'war on dug' strategies and helped their proliferation around the world as the UN applied pressure against any incidences of drug policy reform and encouraged the militarisation of counter-narcotics efforts in general. At the next general assembly in 1998, despite evidence of some cracks in the Vienna Consensus surrounding global drug policy and little evidence of success, the goal of a drug free world within 10 years was agreed. In 2008, the World Drug Report (UNODC 2008: 1) referred to the "undeniable success" of a hundred years of international drug control which had been instrumental in containing illicit drug use to less than 5% of the adult population. A later general assembly endorsed the ongoing goal of a drug free world and extended it for a further

10 years. By this time, however, there were growing systemic tensions (Bewley-Taylor 2012a) within international systems of drug control and an increasing disillusionment with a 'war on drugs' style approach.

Failure of War on Drugs

Accounts of the failure of the 'war on drugs' strategy have been consistently presented since its inception: for example, Duke and Gross (1982), Nadelmann (1989), MacCoun and Reuter (2001), and Global Commission on Drug Policy (2011). Hakim (2011) reports that three out of four Americans now believe the policy of the past 40 years to have been a failure. Proponents of this view point in the main to the failure of the 'war on drugs' strategy to have achieved its principle aim of creating a drug free world, or, failing that, a world in which the production and consumption of drugs are significantly reduced. Instead, the evidence suggests that the number of drug users has grown significantly since the 1960s and remains at a consistently high level: the most recent World Drug Report (UNODC 2016b) estimates that about 5% of the global adult population (a quarter of a billion people) used an illegal drug at least once in 2015. Looking specifically at 1998–2008, the decade in which the aim of a drug free world was supposed to have been achieved, the Global Commission on Drugs (2011) report that global use of opiates increased 34.5%, cocaine 27%, and cannabis 8.5%. Felbab-Brown (2008) further reports the emergence of new drug use markets—for example, in Brazil, South Africa, Eastern Europe and China—during this time period. Zhang and Chin (2015) document an increase in the total number of people who are registered as being dependent on drugs in China from 901,000 in 2001 to 2,475,000 in 2013; Galeotti (2015: 2) brands Russia the "world's leading heroin-using nation per capita"; and Miraglia (2015) charts an increasing trend for cocaine use in Brazil rising from 0.7% of the general population reporting use in 2005 to 1.75% of the general population in 2015.

Evidence on drug production levels, the prices and purity of available drugs and the scale of the overall black market confirm these trends. The decade in which drugs were supposed to be eradicated (1998–2008) saw potential global opium production increase by 78% and potential global cocaine production by 5% (UNODC 2010). Werb et al. (2013: 1) conducted an audit of longitudinal measures of price and purity in different global regions and found that "with few exceptions and despite increasing investments in enforcement-based supply reduction efforts aimed at disrupting global drug supply, illegal drug prices have generally decreased while drug purity has generally increased since 1990". Finally the illegal drugs trade represents a huge financial market estimated to be worth $320 billion worldwide in 2011 (Haken 2011).

Despite this failure to meet the lofty aims of a drug free world, the containment argument, put forward by Antonio Maria Costa (2008), then head of the UNODC, maintains that systems of international drug control have been successful in the sense that they have limited the use of drugs to less than 5% of the global population: if prohibition were not in place as a drug control strategy, he contends, then the problem would be far worse than it is now. Strictly prohibition oriented policies can therefore be defended regarding their reduction of harm to health which would be much higher if drugs were not criminalised (Mena and Hobbs 2010). At the same time, and in the same report, however, Costa (2008) also acknowledges the unintended consequences that the pursuit of a 'war on drugs' has brought about: the creation of a thriving and profitable criminal market; policy displacement from a health based approach to a law enforcement based one; the geographical displacement of drug production and trafficking to new, previously unaffected, areas; substance displacement to less controllable and more dangerous substances; and the stigmatisation and marginalisation of drug users around the world. Much focus has since been placed on these 'unintended consequences' of global drug policy practices. Bowling (2011), inspired by the work of Jock Young (1971) on drug control and deviancy amplification, has described global drug control policy as an example of *iatrogenic* harm whereby drug problems have worsened, not in spite of prohibition policies but, in some cases, because of them. In other words, the countries which have implemented these policies have not only failed in their attempts to reduce harm via the eradication of drugs but have also themselves become the producers of harm.

Unintended and Harmful Consequences: Consumer Countries

As cited in the introduction, in the early 1990s Currie (1993) encapsulated the unintended consequences that a war on drugs approach had already had for the US and, by extension, other countries that are characterised as net consumers of drugs. For example: overloading the criminal justice system; criminalising and stigmatising vulnerable members of society; exacerbating existing social issues such as poverty and unemployment; and representing a huge financial drain on resources that could be directed elsewhere. Today, many of these consequences continue to be significant contributory factors in incidences of social harm. Kebjaj et al. (2013) report on significant increases in the number of people being arrested and incarcerated for drug offences which leads to an overall increase in the number of people, particularly young people, being criminalised, and clogs up the courts and the prisons (Shiner 2003; Small et al. 2005), as well as proving to be an expensive process. In 1980 fewer than 50,000 people were imprisoned for drugs offences in the US but by 2007 this had increased to over 500,000 (Felbab-Brown 2008). The link between contact with the criminal justice system and race is now well documented (Alexander 2010; Provine 2007) resulting in disproportionate numbers of young black men being sanctioned for drug offences: "the most notable accomplishment of this latest war effort has been the wholesale incarceration of young men, and especially minority males, at extraordinary rates for their involvement in drug use and sales" (Bullington 2000: 126).

In addition to the above, a war on drugs has significant unintended social consequences on the health of drug users and, by extension, wider society. The World Drug Report (2016) estimates that 29 million people who use drugs suffer from some kind of disorder as a result of their use and 12 million are people who inject drugs (PWID) facing the extra harms that can be caused by intravenous drug use. It describes the impact of drug use on health as "devastating" (World Drug Report 2016: 11) with an estimated 207,400 drug-related deaths in 2014. Kilmer et al. (2015) highlight the fact that drug overdoses are now responsible for more deaths than traffic accidents in the United States. As this evidence suggests, the users of drugs face many health problems that arise as a direct result of drug consumption. The important point here, however, is that these already significant problems are often *exacerbated* by a zero tolerance approach to drugs.

Policies that view drugs as a dangerous threat, and their users as criminals above all, create an attitude of stigmatisation and marginalisation towards people who use drugs that can make it difficult to come forward and ask for help or access treatment and other relevant services, and which can lead to associated problems such as unemployment and homelessness. Furthermore, very strict policies which allow treatment rather than punishment only for those who can completely and immediately abstain from drug use, or which prohibit the kind of paraphernalia that can allow drugs to be used more safely (e.g. clean needles), or which seek to limit the available information about drugs, can all intensify the risks taken by those who have become dependent on their use. Finally, the escalation of sanctions for becoming involved in the supply of drugs pushes control into the hands of experienced and organised criminals, and serves to make the market a more dangerous and violent place, leads to excessive price increases that have significant impact for an already impoverished population, and encourages the wholesale corruption of substances with harmful impurities added in an effort to make them more profitable. A substantial body of research has, for example, supported the position outlined here, with particular reference to the adverse effect of repressive drug policies on levels of HIV/AIDS and hepatitis B and C within the population of people who inject drugs (Bastos and Strathdee 2000; Burris and Strathdee 2006; Maher and Dixon 1999; Moore and Dietze 2005).

A further social consequence of a zero tolerance approach to drugs is the fact that much of the acquisitive, opportunistic crime committed by drug users stems from the illegal nature of the substances on which they are dependent and the unnaturally high prices demanded for them by the black market. Drugs such as opium, cannabis and cocaine can be easily and cheaply produced, at a fraction of the cost they sell for within the black market, but attract extremely high prices due to the risks that are undertaken in their production and distribution. Prohibition can also increase levels of violence as those involved in drug markets have no legal way to sort out their disputes (Goldstein 1985). Werb et al.'s (2011) systematic review of the evidence in this area finds that, contrary to popular belief, an increase in law enforcement efforts does not lead to a reduction in drug availability and market related violence, and can instead actually lead to increases in violence. Pryce (2012: 102) thus concludes: "prohibition has the unintended social consequence of actually increasing crime levels, making society less secure".

Pryce (2012) in her work on the politics of drug prohibition, also outlines ideological and economic costs that come as a result of a war on drugs approach to drug control. In terms of ideological costs, an escalation of prohibitive strategies can lead to increased powers for law enforcement agents concerned with detecting and punishing drug related crime. This can facilitate public acceptance of significant increases in police power leading to increases, for example, in the normative use of invasive surveillance techniques throughout wider society, and their particular application against communities who have come to be associated with the drug trade. It also contributes to the further marginalisation and stigmatisation of people who use drugs. Economic harms meanwhile coalesce around the considerable costs of funding the drugs war which are borne by society in general: in 2009 the annual cost of drug prohibition for the US was estimated to be $44 billion (Pryce 2012). The harmful consequences outlined in this section can be seen most starkly in the USA where prohibition has been stringently interpreted but can also be observed to a greater or lesser extent in most other nations characterised as net consumers of drugs.

Unintended and Harmful Consequences: Producer Countries

There are even more devastating consequences for countries which are characterised as the traditional producers of drugs. Bush senior conceptualised the drugs issue as a problem that was external to the US: "Drugs are seen as a threat to the United States coming from outside its borders, an enemy against which a war must be waged"

(Youngers and Roisin 2005: 4). This emphasis on reducing the supply of drugs via war against countries which produce drugs is a strategy that has been adopted wholesale throughout the Western world. In general terms, it has resulted in the production of a great deal of harm in countries that are already vulnerable because of, for example, fragile state institutions and endemic poverty.

Countries with fragile state institutions and weak criminal justice systems, perhaps due to political conflict, are "vulnerable to infiltration and corruption by organised crime" (West Africa Commission on Drugs 2014). Pryce (2012) describes how the harm done by organised crime in general, and drug trafficking groups in particular, is exacerbated by the political consequences of drug prohibition and misguided intervention from countries like the US which has funded corrupt anti-drug trafficking institutions (Klein 2011) and helped to create private drug control armies and militarisation of drug control in general (Isacson 2005). Furthermore, the suppression of the drugs trade has helped to exacerbate poverty related issues by depriving poor countries of a valuable income revenue and by diverting limited resources towards drug prevention above other issues such as disease and food and water shortages. In a study of the drug trade in Afghanistan, Felbab-Brown (2015) describes how cutting off access to the opium poppy economy has helped terrorist organisations to gain footing by styling themselves as protectors of this valuable trade.

Another issue associated with the drug trafficking trade is violence. A case in point is Mexico which is a producer and exporter of marijuana, heroin, cocaine and methamphetamine (Hope 2015). Pryce (2012) reports that 28,000 have died in Mexico's drug war in the last 4 years, at a rate of 30 a day. A report into the drug trade in the Americas (Organisation of American States 2013a: 75) highlights drug-related violence as the most significant threat to the "well-being and prosperity" of those living in the region, and attributes a large part of that violence to drug prevention strategies. For example, it reports that drug policy successes in Colombia resulting in a 10% increase in the international price of cocaine would also result in a 1.2–2% increase in the homicide rate. Interestingly, the same report highlights the fact that deaths related to the drugs trade and its suppression far outweigh deaths related to the use of drugs. For example, in Mexico, approximately 60,000 people died as a result of the drugs trade between 2006 and 2012 while 563 died from drug overdose during the same period (Organisation of American States 2013b).

Further harms are produced in terms of damage to the environment, for example through the use of crop spraying programmes that aim to eradicate cannabis, coca and opium poppy crops by dispersing toxic chemicals over wide tracts of agricultural land. For many years crop spraying formed a cornerstone of 'Plan Colombia' aimed at eradicating drug production in Colombia. Crop spraying causes significant environmental damage to land which can be long lasting and which can contaminate water sources and other crops which are intended to be eaten. Its effectiveness remains in question as, despite some reduction in the overall number of hectares used in coca cultivation, the value of the country's cocaine production and trafficking business continues to be worth about 1.2% of Colombia's GDP (Mejia 2015). Furthermore, where crop eradication is not accompanied by the effective provision of alternative livelihoods for those involved in its production, often some of the world's poorest and most vulnerable people, the result can be political unrest and regime instability (Felbab-Brown and Trinkunas 2015).

Running through all the harms documented above is the central issue of erosion of human rights: "The unintended consequence of the belief that drugs are evil has been a less than scrupulous global attitude to human rights and liberties, an erosion of the values of the societies which prohibition is designed to protect" (Pryce 2012: 93). Continuous external pressure to reduce the drug problem has also contributed to the development of systems of drug control in some producer countries whereby extrajudicial killings have become the norm. Amnesty International (2011) has reported on the routine shooting of child cannabis farmers in Iran; Hope (2015) documents the 682 civilians killed as a result of counter narcotics operations in Mexico since December 2012; and according to an investigation by the Philippines Daily Inquirer (2016) there were 1278 drug-related killings in the first 100 days of President Duterte's government of the Philippines. An investigation into coercive treatment for people who use drugs in Cambodia, Laos and Thailand found that basic health needs were not being met and abuse is pervasive (International Harm Reduction Development Programme 2010). A report on the use of the death penalty for drug related offences found that there are at least 33 countries that stipulate the death penalty as a possible punishment for drug-related offences, and at least 10 of these have the death penalty as a mandatory sanction (Gallahue and Lines 2015). In recognition of the seriousness of this sanction, an International Centre on Human Rights and Drug Policy was established in 2009 to monitor activity in this area.

Significant amplification of the harm described above occurs when the end result of a concentrated effort to eradicate drugs, for example through 'Plan Colombia', results in displacement of the production from one region to another: "The drug trade, it seems, is more like a balloon than a battlefield. When one part of a balloon is squeezed its contents are displaced to another" (Youngers and Roisin 2005: 5–6). Felbab-Brown and Trinkunas (2015) provide examples of this by outlining how counter narcotics efforts in Thailand and Iran in the 1970s and Pakistan in the 1980s pushed poppy cultivation to Afghanistan; how a focus on the Andean region during the 1980s and 1990s pushed coca production to Columbia with transit through Mexico; and how law enforcement activity in Mexico during the 2000s drove trafficking organisations to weaker Central American states. The most recent example of drug trade related displacement is West Africa which has now become a significant transit route to Europe and North America for illicit drugs produced in South America and Asia (West Africa Commission on Drugs 2014). Gberie (2015) describes how, as a result of this displacement, Guinea and Mali have seen increased rates for the consumption of drugs, rising levels of drug-related political corruption and an exacerbation of poverty.

The Endurance of a War on Drugs Approach

These failures outlined above, together with the harms produced by illicit drug policy as practised in both consumer and producer countries, have led to an increasing disillusionment with a 'war on drugs' approach. The Obama administration made concerted efforts to move away from the terminology and promised to tone down war on drugs rhetoric. There is increasing evidence of American based criticism of a zero tolerance approach towards the control of drugs (Beyers et al. 2004; Greene 1999; Rhodes et al. 2005; Shiner 2003; Small et al. 2005). Yuri Fedetov, on his appointment as executive director of the UNODC in 2010, stated that: "drug use is a health problem, not a crime, drug users are affected by a disease, addiction, and instead of punishment, what they need is treatment, care and social integration" (Fedetov 2010, cited in Pryce 2012: 139). As outlined in the introduction, several American states and Uruguay are experimenting with legal systems of cannabis regulation. Furthermore, the voices of producer country governments are increasingly heard in global debates on drug policy, pushing forward alternative responses that do not rely on implementing 'war like' tactics within their borders.

These developments may be interpreted as suggesting that we are already, globally, moving away from war on drugs approaches and that a first step in improving global drug policy has already been undertaken. This final section of the chapter uses two case studies to explore the evidence that this is not, in fact, the case, and asserts that the war on drugs approach is an enduring one. The first case study extracts evidence of war on drugs approaches in global policy by examining the different approaches that have been taken to a new facet of the drugs issue—the recent rapid development and dissemination of New Psychoactive Substances (NPS). The second focuses on a failure of the international drug control system to acknowledge the lack of success of a war on drugs approach or the unintended consequences it has brought about within its official discourse represented by the international conventions and the UNGASS 2016 Outcome Document.

Policy Developments Arising from the Proliferation of New Psychoactive Substances (NPS)

A first example of the enduring principle of a 'war on drugs' approach to drug policy is provided by the study of recent global policy responses to NPS, also variously known as 'designer drugs', 'synthetic drugs' and/or 'legal highs' (Perrone 2016). NPS are chemical compounds that have been newly and recently created, although some were synthesised many years ago with new evidence of sale and use. Others have been *designed* to mimic the effects of existing illegal drugs such as cannabis, MDMA, cocaine, LSD and heroin, and originally emerged outside the confines of current national and international systems of drug control. The design and manufacture of such substances is not a new phenomenon per se (Sumnall et al. 2011), but the speed with which such substances have emerged over the last decade, the role that the internet has played in facilitating their marketing and distribution, and their increasingly transnational nature (Measham 2013; Seddon 2014) have led to a significant "increase in their range, potency, profile and availability" (Winstock and Ramsey 2010: 1685).

Over the last ten years, NPS have fuelled the rapid and significant development of new policy responses (Chatwin et al. 2017; Chatwin 2014; Measham and Newcombe 2016; Stevens and Measham 2014). This is, at least in part, because NPS tend to emerge rapidly, and sometimes in tandem, making it difficult for existing reactive systems of drug control to keep pace with them. Under systems that modify or adapt existing laws and processes, once legislation is passed to prohibit a named substance or group of substances (generic control), compounds can be easily moderated to create others not covered by the legislation (van Amsterdam et al. 2013). This results in what has been termed a 'cat and mouse' (Measham et al. 2011) process between policy makers and manufacturers, whereby changes in legislation prompt the creation of new substances, which necessitates further changes in legislation, and so on.

Increasingly, demands have thus been placed on national and international drug control systems to adapt existing drug laws to make them more effective in responding to NPS (Measham 2013). The UN (UNODC 2013) has admitted that it is unable to cope with the plethora of new substances and, in 2013, the EU put forward proposals to increase their powers to deal with new substances more quickly (Chatwin 2017). Birdwell et al. (2011), Coulson and Caulkins (2011) and Hughes and Winstock (2011), all predicted that the development of substances and markets that do not fit neatly into existing systems of drug control would necessitate the development of new approaches. In sum, "new policies were needed to meet a drug problem that was in a state of flux and arose from a dynamic and rapidly evolving drug market" (Wolfgang Gotz, director of the EMCDDA, cited in Travis 2014: 1). If a war on drugs approach to drug policy has been recognised as a failure, then we could expect to see the implementation of policies in regard to this new facet of the drugs issue that were not exclusively law enforcement orientated and which took care to reduce the unintended consequences of drug policy in general.

Evidence to date, however, strongly suggests that the new policies that have been developed have been conceptualised primarily from a law enforcement perspective tending to further escalate existing sanctions, and thus could be viewed as an extension of a war on drugs approach (Reuter and Pardo 2016, 2017). Traditionally, drug legislation lists individual substances which are to be controlled, but systems have also been developed, often in response to NPS, which allow chemical compounds that are structurally similar (generic model), or which are perceived to have similar effects (analogue model) to existing controlled substances, to be controlled automatically at any one time. This creates an important shift from legislating against substances that have been *proven* to cause harm, to ones that are *presumed* likely to cause harm.

Other countries have responded to NPS by introducing emergency legislation that allows a substance to be immediately banned for a specific time period without undertaking the lengthy legislative procedures necessary to bring a substance under permanent control. One of the most time consuming facets of bringing a new substance under control relates to the risk assessments which are undertaken to establish the level of harm associated with it. If this part of the process is eliminated, controls can be implemented before a substance becomes widely available, but it also means that substances which may not be harmful might also be brought under control. This is particularly problematic as the criminalisation of drugs in general is often justified by referring to the harm they cause. Finally, a handful of countries have taken a further step away from legislation based on harm towards legislation based on the presumption of harm, by establishing a system whereby any substance meeting certain criteria (e.g. psychoactivity) will be subjected to a 'blanket ban': Ireland, Poland, Romania, New Zealand, Australia and the UK (Barratt et al. 2017).

Individually and collectively, the range of responses discussed above display a tendency to increase sanctions progressively and to classify

NPS as illegal drugs on "precautionary grounds" (Hughes and Winstock 2011: 1895). Stevens and Measham (2014: 1226) have applied the phrase "guilt by molecular association" to describe the situation where bans are being implemented, not because of any proven harm of the substance itself, but because of a presumption of harm based on similarities with other prohibited substances. Blanket ban legislation, prohibiting anything perceived to have a psychoactive effect provides the ultimate example of this: it represents a fundamental shift from drug prohibition against substances which are *known* to be harmful, towards the prohibition of any substance which *might* be harmful. Measham and Newcombe (2016) have thus revised the characterisation of the relationship between NPS development and policy change from 'cat and mouse' to 'hare and hounds', whereby the speed of policy change itself becomes one of the important drivers of future NPS innovations. This means that a 'modest and localised' (Reuter 2011: 4) facet of the overall drug problem has led to fundamental changes in the way that we control drugs at both the national and the international level (Chatwin 2017).

With reference to recent UK legislation effecting a blanket ban against psychoactive substances, it is notable that a number of exemptions for substances as pervasive as chocolate and caffeine had to be issued. In further critique of UK legislation against psychoactive substances, Stevens et al. (2015) remind us that not all banned substances are harmful, (e.g. lavender oil, morning glory seeds), that many have legitimate uses (e.g. nitrous oxide, petrol, glue), and that the psychoactive effects of substances about which very little is known can be hard to determine in general. Barratt et al. (2017), critiquing similar Australian legislation, build on these arguments to draw out the dangers of equating 'psychoactive' with 'harmful and worthy of control': doing so makes the psychological effects of individual substances seem stable and unchanging, rather than subjective and varying. It also "disassociates them from the cultural contexts in which they are taken and thus disregards well-established work on the importance of contexts of drug use" (Potter and Chatwin 2018: 3).

Not only does the NPS driven policy change attest to a continuation of war on drugs approach, it also attests to a continued failure to consider the harmful consequences that may arise as the result of a law-enforcement focused policy. The potential harms directly caused by bringing new substances under legislative control are many including, but certainly not limited to: the potential criminalisation of the user; the increase in price of NPS; the decrease in purity and general quality control of NPS; the rise in law enforcement costs; the prevention of research and the collation of information about NPS; the development of other, potentially more harmful substances once an NPS has been banned; and the increased likelihood that organised criminals will become involved in the market. One example of NPS related research evidencing both the ineffective nature of law enforcement strategies and the harm that can be caused by those strategies is provided by Measham et al. (2011) in their work on mephedrone use in the UK: while mephedrone was legal in the UK it was the 11th most popular lifetime drug amongst clubbers, but once it was banned it moved up to the 4th most popular.

This case study thus provides evidence that, when faced with a new facet of the drug problem, despite mounting evidence of a failure of war on drugs approaches, the vast majority of governments and international bodies have implemented strictly prohibition and law enforcement oriented strategies, rather than using this development as a catalyst to creating new and alternative responses. Indeed, developments in this area have actually been used to significantly *extend* law enforcement approaches via the introduction of policy based on a presumption of harm rather than on a verification of harm. Furthermore, the unintended consequences of such approaches have not been acknowledged indicating that new policy directions may have the potential to cause rather than reduce overall harm.

International Drug Conventions and Official Drug Policy Discourse

As already discussed, recent years have seen an increased perception that the war on drugs approach to drug policy has failed and that it has caused unintended and harmful consequences around the globe. In addition, many countries have experimented with increasingly liberal systems of control of the possession of illegal drugs for personal use, particularly in relation to cannabis (discussed more fully in Chapter 4). These changes have resulted in calls (via UNGASS 2016, for example, as outlined in the introduction) for reform of the international drug conventions to reflect this shift in conceptualisation of the drugs issue. To date, these calls have not, however, had any impact: the international conventions remain unchanged and acknowledge neither the failure of the war on drugs nor the need for new approaches to address some of its harmful consequences. As they currently stand, the international drug conventions in themselves do not necessitate a war on drugs approach, which could be interpreted as meaning that they do not need to change despite a shift in approach. Nevertheless, a more detailed exploration of activity in this area uncovers a reluctance to relax international prioritisation of strictly prohibition oriented approaches and allow more liberal strategies of drug control.

The existing international drug policy framework has been particularly challenged by the implementation of national strategies which retain only a tenuous link with the aim of prohibition. Flexibility has always existed within the international drug control system (see Chapter 3 for a fuller discussion of this) meaning that some countries have long been able to argue that tolerance towards people who use drugs can be practised as part of an overall system of prohibition which channels its efforts into other more harmful areas. In the Netherlands, for example, toleration of the small-scale sale of cannabis via the coffeeshop system in the 1970s was justified as still operating within the terms of international drug conventions because it formed part of an overall strategy aiming to prohibit the use of more harmful drugs by separating the market for them from that of cannabis. People who wanted to use cannabis would be able to do so without coming into contact with the black market, and so would be protected from encountering other substances. Police time and resources would be freed up to concentrate on reducing the use of more harmful substances, and disrupting the production and supply of all drugs. The coffeeshop policy can thus be argued to represent a necessary and rational part of an overall strategy of prohibition. Furthermore, examples such as the Netherlands remained relatively isolated cases and did not detract significantly from the ethos of the international drug conventions and their general requirement for all signatories to acknowledge drugs as a significant danger and operate a policy of prohibition towards them.

More recently, however, tensions have mounted in this area because of two factors: as acceptance of the failure of the war on drugs has grown an increasing number of countries have sought to adopt more liberal strategies towards people who use drugs; and the liberal strategies have gone further in their tolerance of drug use than ever before. Bewley-Taylor et al. (2014: 6) describe a "second wave" of flexible interpretation of the treaties affecting Latin American countries, European countries, and various Australian states and territories. These changes have been termed 'soft defections' as states implementing them have, like the Netherlands, "exploited plasticity within the treaties, while technically, remaining within their legal boundaries" (Bewley-Taylor 2012a: 51) which do not explicitly specify the unanimous need for the criminalisation of drug use and drug users. A pertinent example here is the changes implemented in Portugal in 2001 which saw the removal of all criminal penalties for the possession of all illicit substances for personal use. These were justified as part of an overall strategy which wanted to divert resources to the more pressing issues of reducing drug supply and preventing drug related harm.

In the past decade, a third wave of reform has emerged exclusively around cannabis. Cannabis is widely perceived to be one of the less harmful illicit substances and is also the illegal substance most likely to be used around the globe. An appreciation of the failure of the war on drugs has also focused on a failure to respond proportionately in respect to substances with different levels of harm. Cannabis has thus become a fault line in the system (Bewley-Taylor 2012b): disagreement about how to most appropriately deal with cannabis has come to threaten the Vienna consensus which calls for all countries to maintain a hard line interpretation of international drug prohibition commitments, with respect to all substances. This disagreement is evidenced by the creation of fully regulated markets in Uruguay and some American states (e.g. Washington and Colorado). Jelsma (2015: 15) designates these as "systemic breaches" that clearly contravene the terms of the international conventions. In both Uruguay and participating American states, it is not just the use of cannabis which is tolerated; the entire market, encompassing production, supply, distribution and use, has been regulated. Furthermore, in some American states, the regulated, state controlled market, is fully commercialised in nature creating significant profit margins and contributing to the licit economy. These developments thus indicate the failure of the Vienna consensus and the urgent need for modernisation of the international drug control system to indicate the failure of the war on drugs and the validation of alternative approaches such as regulated cannabis markets.

The developments in cannabis policy and decriminalisation of drugs for personal use outlined above suggest dramatic changes in our understanding of the drugs issue and appropriate ways to respond to it in line with an appreciation of the failure of the war on drugs approach. If the international drug conventions do not necessitate a war on drugs approach, and these new approaches do not fundamentally contravene the terms of the conventions, as some have argued, then change is not needed. We can continue to adopt a flexible interpretation of prohibition as demanded by the treaties which naturally adapt to a change in global opinion. Arguably, however, this has not been the case. Some UN bodies have been broadly supportive of reforms: the United Nations Office on Drugs and Crime (UNODC) and the World Health Authority (WHO), for example, have expressed support for the decriminalisation of drugs for personal consumption (United Nations Development Programme 2015). The INCB, however, in its role as guardian of the treaties, has proved an "inflexible defender of the status quo" (Bewley-Taylor et al. 2014: 6), gradually toughening its stance against drug policy reform/relaxation since 1980: for example, it has avoided the term 'harm reduction', tried to prevent reform generally and consistently, and singled out countries with relaxed drug policies for criticism (Bewley-Taylor 2012b). It operates in secret with no mechanism for accountability (Csete and Wolfe 2007) and has been accused of "stifling the evolution of the drug control treaties" (Bewley-Taylor and Trace 2006: 12).

This last point can be further illuminated by considering the example of Bolivia and its attempts to decriminalise the indigenous practise of coca leaf chewing which is unequivocally prohibited by the international conventions. In 2009 in a climate of rising recognition of the failure of a war on drugs approach and increased leniency towards less harmful drugs such as cannabis, Bolivia sought to secure an amendment to the existing conventions to allow chewing of the coca leaf for cultural and indigenous purposes. The tabled amendment, however, caused controversy within the overall system and was blocked by a small minority of 18 countries highlighting the ease with which these kind of proposals can be overcome by those who are opposed to them. In 2012, Bolivia therefore resorted to denouncing the international treaties and then joining again with a reservation from the part of the treaty prohibiting the use of the coca leaf. This decision has been "strongly condemned" by the International Narcotics Control Board and accused of undermining "the integrity of the global drug control system" (Bewley-Taylor and Jelsma 2012: 16).

Although there are no intrinsic review mechanisms for the international drug conventions (Jelsma 2015), since the 1990s, the United Nations General Assembly Special Sessions (UNGASS) on drugs have functioned as a forum to discuss the future of the global drug policy regime. As previously stated, UNGASS 1998 agreed to pursue the goal of the eradication of illicit drugs by 2008; in 2009 this goal was revised to achieving the eradication of, or significant reduction in, illicit drugs in the next 10 years. The next UNGASS was due to be held in 2019, but was recently brought forward to April 2016 at the behest of the presidents of Colombia, Guatemala and Mexico, who called for an open and honest debate on the issues outlined above in light of significant recent changes in global drug policy.

In the run up to the special session there was much anticipation that it would be used to debate many general issues—human rights, harm reduction, prohibition—and would also be used as a platform to consider reform of the global drug policy regime itself: "The global treaty regime should somehow show more flexibility in order to allow this irreversible dynamic of reform to influence, adapt and modernise the system. That will be the main challenge for the 2016 UNGASS" (Vasconi 2013: 23). This aspiration was lent some support by the UN secretary general, Ban Ki-moon's call for a "wide-ranging and open debate that considers all options" (Ban Ki-moon 2013) in relation to drug policy. If a failure of the war on drugs approach was really accepted, then surely the outcome of UNGASS 2016 would be a radical shift in aims of global drug control? Jelsma (2015: 17), however, suggested that, to the contrary, "a concerted effort is being made to keep the contentious treaty revision issue off the UNGASS 2016 agenda and to preserve the facade of global consensus".

The 2016 UNGASS Outcome Document (UNODC 2016a) largely confirms Jelsma's viewpoint. Despite the considerable momentum for reform, the conclusions of UNGASS 2016 are largely a "profound disappointment" (Global Commission on Drug Policy 2016: 1), at least in terms of those hoping for reform of the international drug treaties. The Outcome Document reaffirms the goal of a "society free of drug abuse" (UNODC 2016a: 1) and recommends a continuation of the current approach. There is no formal acknowledgement of the failure of the current approach or the unintended harms and consequences that it has produced, and there is little to no explicit reference to the principle of harm reduction in drug policy (TNI 2016b). Anne Fordham (2016), the executive director of the International Drug Policy Consortium, highlights the role that Russia played within the UNGASS 2016 debates in renewing commitment to the 'war on drugs' by signalling their continuing intention to fight in this area. In sum, the legacy of UNGASS 2016 is that the status quo has been upheld and that despite increasing calls for drug policy reform, the continuation of a 'war on drugs' approach has been largely confirmed.

Conclusion

This chapter has charted the rise of the international prohibition of drugs and its development into a war on drugs approach. It has explored mounting evidence for the failure of this approach, together with the unintended and harmful consequences it is responsible for in both consumer and producer countries. Despite this evidence and recent changes in drug control in some global regions, it contends that a war on drugs approach endures, in global terms. While we continue to cling to extreme versions of prohibition that prioritise law enforcement efforts over all other types of intervention, we cannot expect progress in global drug policy, and we will continue to suffer from its unintended harms and consequences. In order to improve the way that we control the use of illicit substances, the first step ought, therefore, to be to accept the global failure of the 'war on drugs' strategy, and to acknowledge the many harms that it has produced. Such a step should go beyond skin deep declarations that the war is over, should be enshrined in official documents that deal with global drug strategies, and should be evident from an examination of the way that we deal with new drug challenges going forward. An official acknowledgement of the failure of the 'war on drugs' does not mean the end of prohibition—reducing the demand for and supply of illicit substances is still a worthy goal. There are, however, many ways of implementing prohibition based policies that do not make enemies out of the users, suppliers and producers of illegal substances, but which rather achieve their goals without producing further harm or contravening human rights legislation. These alternative systems of drug control will be explored in the next chapter.

References

Alexander, M. (2010). *The new Jim Crow: Mass incarceration in the age of colorblindness*. New York: The New Press.

Amnesty International. (2011). *Addicted to death: Executions for drug offenses in Iran*. London: Amnesty International.

Barratt, M., Seear, K., & Lancaster, K. (2017). A critical examination of the definition of 'psychoactive effect' in Australian drug legislation. *International Journal of Drug Policy, 40*, 16–25.

Bastos, F., & Strathdee, S. (2000). Evaluating effectiveness of syringe exchange programmes: Current issues and future projects. *Social Science and Medicine, 51*, 1771–1782.

Bewley-Taylor, D. (2012a). The contemporary international drug control system: A history of the UNGASS decade. In J. Collins & N. Kitchen (Eds.), *Governing the global drug wars* (LSE Special Report SR014). https://www.eprints.lse.ac.uk.

Bewley-Taylor, D. (2012b). *International drug control: Consensus fractured*. Cambridge: Cambridge University Press.

Bewley-Taylor, D., & Jelsma, M. (2011). *Fifty years of the 1961 single convention on narcotic drugs: A reinterpretation*. Series on legislative reform of drug policies. Transnational Institute: http://www.tni.org.

Bewley-Taylor, D., & Jelsma, M. (2012). *The UN drug control conventions: Limits of latitude*. Transnational Institute: https://www.tni.org.

Bewley-Taylor, D., & Trace, M. (2006). *The INCB: Watchdog or guardian of the UN drug control conventions?* The Beckley Foundation Drug Policy Programme.

Bewley-Taylor, D., Jelsma, M., & Blickman, T. (2014). *The rise and decline of cannabis prohibition*. Transnational Institute: http://www.tni.org.

Beyers, J., Toumbourou, J., Catalano, R., Arthur, M., & Hawkins, J. (2004). A cross-national comparison of risk and protective factors for adolescent substance use: The United States and Australia. *Journal of Adolescent Health, 35*, 3–16.

Birdwell, J., Chapman, J., & Singleton, N. (2011). *Taking drugs seriously: A demos and UK drug policy commission report on legal highs*. http://www.ukdpc.org.uk.

Bowling, B. (2011). Transnational criminology and the globalisation of harm production. In M. Bosworth & C. Hoyle (Eds.), *What is criminology?* Oxford: Oxford University Press.

Bruun, K., Pan, L., & Rexed, I. (1975). *The gentleman's club*. Chicago and London: University of Chicago Press.

Bullington, B. (2000). America's drug war: Fact or fiction. In R. Coomber (Ed.), *The control of drug use and drug users*. Amsterdam: Harwood Academic Publishers.

Burris, S., & Strathdee, S. (2006). To serve and protect? Towards a better relationship between drug control policy and public health. *AIDS, 20*, 117–118.

Chatwin, C. (2014). New psychoactive substances: New European policy landscapes. In G. R. Potter, M. Wouters, & J. Fountain (Eds.), *Change and continuity: Researching evolving drug landscapes in Europe*. Lengerich: PABST Publications.

Chatwin, C. (2017). Assessing the 'added value' of European policy on new psychoactive substances. *International Journal of Drug Policy, 40*, 111–116.

Chatwin, C., Measham, F., O'Brien, K., & Sumnall, H. (2017). New drugs, new directions? Exploring critical and social research priorities in NPS and HED debates. *International Journal of Drug Policy, 40*, 1–5.

Costa, A. (2008). *Making drug control 'fit for purpose': Building on the UNGASS decade*. Vienna: Commission on Narcotic Drugs.

Coulson, C., & Caulkins, J. P. (2011). Scheduling of newly emerging drugs: A critical review of decisions over 40 years. *Addiction, 107*, 766–773.

Csete, J., & Wolfe, D. (2007). *Closed to reason: The international narcotics control board and HIV/AIDS*. Toronto and New York: Canadian HIV/AIDS Legal Network and the International Harm Reduction Development (IHERD) Programme of the Open Society Institute.

Currie, E. (1993). *Reckoning: Drugs, the cities and the American future*. New York: Hill and Wang.

Dorn, N., & Jamieson, A. (2000) *Room for manoeuvre: Overview of comparative legal research into national drug laws of France, Germany, Italy, Spain, The Netherlands and Sweden and their relation to three international drugs conventions*. A Study of DrugScope for the Independent Inquiry on the Misuse of Drugs Act 1971, London.

Duke, S. B., & Gross, A. (1982). *America's longest war*. New York: Putnam and Sons.

Felbab-Brown, V. (2008). *Counternarcotics policy overview: Global trends & strategies*. Brookings: https://www.brookings.edu.

Felbab-Brown, V. (2015). *No easy exit: Drugs and counternarcotics policies in Afghanistan*. https://www.brookings.edu.

Felbab-Brown, V., & Trinkunas, H. (2015). *UNGASS 2016 in comparative perspective: Improving the prospects for success*. https://www.brookings.edu.

Fordham, A. (2016, May 3). The drugs consensus is not pretty—It's been ripped apart at the seams. *Huffington Post*. http://www.huffingtonpost.co.uk.

Galeotti, M. (2015). *Narcotics and nationalism: Russian drug policies and futures*. Brookings: https://www.brookings.edu.

Gallahue, P., & Lines, R. (2015). *The death penalty for drug offences: Global overview 2015*. London: Harm Reduction International.

Gberie, L. (2015). *Crime, violence and politics: Drug trafficking and counter narcotics policies in Mali and Guinea*. https://www.brookings.edu.

Global Commission on Drug Policy. (2011). *War on drugs: Report of the Global Commission on Drug Policy*. http://www.globalcommissionondrugs.org.

Global Commission on Drug Policy. (2016, April 21). *Public statement by the Global Commission on Drug Policy on UNGASS 2016*. New York: Global Commission on Drug Policy. http://www.globalcommissionondrugs.org.

Goldstein, P. J. (1985). The drugs-violence nexus: A tripartite conceptual framework. *Journal of Drug Issues, 15*, 493–506.

Greene, J. (1999). Zero tolerance: A case study of policies and practices in New York City. *Crime and Delinquency, 45*, 171–187.

Haken, J. (2011). *Transnational crime in the developing world.* Global Financial Integrity: http://www.gfintegrity.org.
Hakim, P. (2011). *Rethinking US drug policy.* Inter-American Dialogue: https://www.thedialogue.org.
Hope, A. (2015). *Plus Ca change: Structural continuities in Mexican counter-narcotics policy.* https://www.brookings.edu.
Hughes, B., & Winstock, A. R. (2011). Controlling new drugs under marketing regulations. *Addiction, 107,* 1894–1899.
International Harm Reduction Development Programme. (2010). *Detention as treatment: Detention of methamphetamine users in Cambodia, Laos and Thailand.* Open Society Institute.
Isacson, A. (2005). The U.S. military in the war on drugs. In C. A. Youngers & E. Rosin (Eds.), *Drugs and democracy in Latin America. The impact of U.S. policy.* London: Lynne Reinner Publishers.
Jelsma, M. (2011, January). *The development of international drug control: Lessons learned and strategic challenges for the future* (Working Paper). Geneva: Global Commission on Drug Policies.
Jelsma, M. (2015). *UNGASS 2016: Prospects for treaty reform and UN system-wide coherence on drug policy.* Brookings: http://www.brookings.edu.
Kebjaj, S., Shahidinia, N., Testa, A., & Williams, J. (2013). Collateral damage & the war on drugs: Estimating the effect of zero tolerance policies on drug arrest rates, 1975–2002. *The Public Purpose, XI,* 1–25.
Kilmer, B., Midgette, G., & Saloga, C. (2015). *Back in the national spotlight: An assessment of recent changes in drug use and drug policies in the United States.* Brookings: https://www.brookings.edu.
Ki-moon, B. (2013). *Statement: Secretary-general's remarks at special event on the international day against drug abuse and illicit trafficking.* United Nations. http://www.un.org.
Klein, A. (2011). 'Written evidence to the House of Lords' enquiry into the European drug strategy' in House of Lords. *The EU drugs strategy, oral and written evidence.* Home Affairs Subcommittee of the European Select Committee. http://www.parliament.co.uk.
Leroy, B. (1995). Assessing the legalisation debate. In G. Estievenart (Ed.), *Policies and strategies to combat drugs in Europe: Framework for a new European strategies to combat drugs.* Dordrecht: Martinus Nijhoff Publishers.
MacCoun, R., & Reuter, P. (2001). *Drug war Heresies.* Cambridge: Cambridge University Press.
Maher, L., & Dixon, D. (1999). Policing and public health: Law enforcement and harm minimisation in a street-level drug market. *British Journal of Criminology, 39,* 488–512.

McGrath, M. (2016, Tuesday, March 8). Nancy Reagan and the negative impact of the 'just say no' anti-drug campaign. *The Guardian.*

Measham, F. (2013). Social issues in the use of novel psychoactive substances: Differentiated demand and ideological supply. In P. Dargan & D. Wood (Eds.), *Novel psychoactive substances: Classification, pharmacology and toxicology*. London: Elsevier.

Measham, F., & Newcombe, R. (2016). What's so new about new psychoactive substances? Definitions, prevalence, motivations, user groups and a proposed new taxonomy. In T. Kolind, B. Thom, & G. Hunt (Eds.), *The Sage handbook of drug & alcohol studies*. London: Sage.

Measham, F., Wood, D., Dargan, P., & Moore, K. (2011). The rise in legal highs: Prevalence and patterns in the use of illegal drugs and first and second generation 'legal highs' in South London gay dance clubs. *Journal of Substance Use, 16*(4), 263–272.

Mejia, D. (2015). *Plan Colombia: An analysis of effectiveness and costs*. https://www.brookings.edu.

Mena, F., & Hobbs, R. (2010). Narcophobia: Drugs prohibition and the generation of human rights abuses. *Trends in Organised Crime, 13*(1), 6–74.

Miraglia, P. (2015). *Drugs and drug trafficking in Brazil: Trends and policies.* Brookings: http://www.brookings.edu.

Moore, D., & Dietze, P. (2005). Enabling environments and the reduction of drug-related harm: Re-framing Australian policy and practice. *Drug and Alcohol Review, 24*, 275–284.

Nadelmann, E. (1989). Drug prohibition in the US: Costs consequences and alternatives. *Science, 245*, 939–947.

Organisation of American States. (2013a). *Scenarios for the drug problem in the Americas 2013–2025*. https://www.oas.org.

Organisation of American States. (2013b). *The drug problem in the Americas.* https://www.oas.org.

Owen, T. (2016, March 6). Just say no: How Nancy Reagan helped America lose the war on drugs. *Vice News.*

Perrone, D. (2016). Designer drugs. In H. H. Brownstein (Ed.), *The handbook of drugs and society Chichester*. UK: Wiley Blackwell.

Philippines Daily Inquirer. (2016, October 16). *Story in numbers war on drugs.* https://www.newsinfo.inquirer.net.

Potter, G. R., & Chatwin, C. (2018). Not particularly special: Critiquing "NPS" as a category of drugs. *Drugs: Education, Prevention and Policy.* https://doi.org/10.1080/09687637.2017.1411885.

Provine, D. M. (2007). *Unequal under law: Race in the war on drugs*. Chicago and London: University of Chicago Press.
Pryce, S. (2012). *Fixing drugs: The politics of drug prohibition*. Basingstoke: Palgrave Macmillan.
Reuter, P. (2011). *Options for regulating new psychoactive drugs: A review of recent experiences*. London: UK Drug Policy Commission.
Reuter, P., & Pardo, B. (2016). Can new psychoactive substances be regulated effectively? An assessment of the British psychoactive substances bill. *Addiction*. https://doi.org/10.1111/add.13439.
Reuter, P., & Pardo, B. (2017). New psychoactive substances: Are there any good options for regulating new psychoactive substances? *International Journal of Drug Policy, 40*, 113–118.
Rhodes, T., Singer, M., Bourgois, P., Friedman, S., & Strathdee, A. (2005). The social production of HIV risk among injecting drug users. *Social Science and Medicine, 61*, 1026–1044.
Seddon, T. (2014). Drug policy and global regulatory capitalism: The case of new psychoactive substances (NPS). *International Journal of Drug Policy*. https://doi.org/10.1016/j.drugpo.2014.03.009.
Shiner, M. (2003). Out of harm's way? Illicit drug use, medicalisation and the law. *British Journal of Criminology, 43*, 772–796.
Small, W., Wood, E., Jurgens, R., & Kerr, T. (2005). Injection drug use HIV/AIDS and incarceration: Evidence from the Vancouver injection drug users study. *HIV AIDS Policy Law Review, 10*, 5–10.
Stevens, A., & Measham, F. (2014). The 'drug policy ratchet': Why do sanctions for new psychoactive substances typically only go up? *Addiction, 109*(8), 1226–1232.
Stevens, A., Fortson, R., Measham, F., & Sumnall, H. (2015). Legally flawed, scientifically problematic, potentially harmful: The UK psychoactive substance bill. *International Journal of Drug Policy, 26*, 1167–1170.
Sumnall, H. R., Evans-Brown, M., & McVeigh, J. (2011). Social, policy, and public health perspectives on new psychoactive substances. *Drug Testing and Analysis, 3*, 515–523.
TNI. (2016b). *The UNGASS outcome document: Diplomacy or denialism?* https://www.tni.org.
Travis, A. (2014, Monday, January 13). Legal highs: UK to opt out of new EU regulations regime. *The Guardian*.
United Nations. (1961). *Single convention on narcotic drugs*. http://www.druglibrary.org/schaffer/legal.

United Nations Development Programme. (2015). *Perspectives on the development dimensions of drug control policy*. www.undp.org.

UNODC. (2008). *World drug report 2008*. http://www.unodc.org/documents.

UNODC. (2010). *World drug report 2010*. http://www.unodc.org/documents.

UNODC. (2013, March). *The challenge of new psychoactive substances*. Global Smart Programme.

UNODC. (2016a). *Outcome document of the 2016 United Nations General Assembly Special Session on the world drug problem. Our joint commitment to effectively addressing and countering the world drug problem*. New York: UNODC. http://www.unodc.org/documents.

UNODC. (2016b). *World drug report 2016*. http://www.unodc.org/documents.

van Amsterdam, J., Nutt, D., & van den Brink, W. (2013). Generic legislation of new psychoactive drugs. *Journal of Psychopharmacology, 27*(3), 317–324.

Vasconi, C. (2013). *Where next for Europe on drug policy reform?* Expert Seminar June 20–21, Transnational Institute, Lisbon, Portugal.

Werb, D., Rowell, G., Guyatt, G., Kerr, T., Montaner, J., & Wood, E. (2011). Effect of drug law enforcement on drug market violence; a systematic review. *International Journal of Drug Policy, 22*(2), 87–94.

Werb, D., Kerr, T., Nosyk, B., Strathdee, S., Montaner, J., & Wood, E. (2013). The temporal relationship between drug supply indicators: An audit of international government surveillance systems. *British Medical Journal Open, 3,* 1–8.

West Africa Commission on Drugs. (2014). *Not just in transit. Drugs, the state and society in West Africa*. http://www.wacommissiondrugs.org.

Winstock, A., & Ramsey, J. (2010). Legal highs and the challenges for policy makers. *Addiction, 105*(10), 1685–1687.

Woodiwiss, M. (1988). *Crime, crusades and corruption: Prohibitions in the United States, 1900–1987*. London: Pinter.

Woodiwiss, M., & Bewley-Taylor, D. (2005). *The global fix: The construction of a global enforcement regime*. Amsterdam: Transnational Institute, Crime and Globalisation Programme.

Young, J. (1971). *The drugtakers: The social meaning of drug use*. London: McGibbon & Kee.

Youngers, C. A., & Rosin, E. (2005). The U.S. "war on drugs". In C. A. Youngers & E. Rosin (Eds.), *Drugs and democracy in Latin America*. London: Lynne Reiner Publishers.

Zhang, S., & Chin, K.-L. (2015). *A people's war: China's struggle to contain its illicit drug problem*. Brookings: https://www.brookings.edu.

3

Step Two: Recognise the Primary Importance of Addressing the Harm That Stems From and is Associated With Drug Use and Drug Control Policies

The control of illicit substances is often broken down into the supply side (concerned with reducing the production, distribution and marketing of illicit substances) and the demand side (concerned with reducing the use and availability of illicit substances). The war on drugs approach to the prohibition of illicit substances outlined in the previous chapter is firmly rooted in the supply side of the issue. Originating in the US, it primarily views drugs as a foreign problem ensnaring vulnerable people in consumer countries and supposes that solving the problem encompasses implementing strategies that, in one way or another, seek to disrupt the production, distribution and marketing of specific substances, often by employing the harshest penalties to engender an atmosphere of deterrence. An alternative way of approaching the drug issue is from the demand side, focusing on reducing the demand for drugs within consumer countries and supposing that if demand is reduced then supply will naturally fall off. This approach refocuses attention to Western consumer countries and relieves some of the pressure on producer countries from the global South which, arguably, have borne the brunt of war on drugs approaches.

C. Chatwin, *Towards More Effective Global Drug Policies*,
https://doi.org/10.1007/978-3-319-92072-6_3

Demand reduction can thus be seen as an alternative strategy of drug control in its own right. In general, demand reduction focuses on strategies such as education, treatment and prevention of initial drug use. These general demand reduction approaches are relatively well established, even within some of the more stringent national and international drug control policies, and are fundamentally aimed at reducing the prevalence of drug use within society—that is the primary goal that underpins them. They are therefore not the main concern of this chapter. The final suggestion of the previous chapter was that if we are to dislodge the enduring grip of the war on drugs approach, we need to develop robust alternatives. This chapter argues that these alternatives should coalesce around the primary desire to reduce the prevalence of drug related harm, rather than of drug use itself, although some will also eventually reduce drug use. Specifically, they should be concerned with: the reduction of harm to drug users in particular and wider communities in general, the promotion of a broad public health agenda, the application of human rights principles, and wider recognition that addressing social ills such as poverty and inequality will play an important role in the reduction of drug use.

This chapter charts the development of strategies that address the harm caused by and associated with drug use and drug control policies. The discussion begins by defining harm reduction and detailing its evolution into a broader public health agenda, explores the more recent concept of public good which seeks to also encompass and address issues of societal inequality within harm reduction, and emphasises the need to develop strategies that also address the harms arising from human rights contraventions, particularly in the global South and drug producing countries. In its final section, it argues that, despite the relatively well developed rhetoric on alternative systems of drug control, and despite the documented failures and harms of the war on drugs approach, there is a long way to go before alternative approaches are afforded the same acceptance and influence as law enforcement. Approaches that aim to reduce drug related harm remain limited in terms of geographical reach, are frequently relegated to add on status rather than forming underlying cornerstones of drug control, and are often conspicuously absent from official international drug policy documentation. To produce a more effective global drug policy, these limitations need to be addressed and harm reduction strategies should receive the level of attention and endorsement the war on drugs has enjoyed.

A Harm Reduction Approach to Drug Policy

People often think about public health as providing the counter-balance to law-enforcement within drug control as can be seen, for example, in debates about whether we should view the users of drugs primarily as criminals or as patients. All countries and territories build elements of public health into their national drug policies, by providing treatment and services for drug users and by attempting to educate potential drug users about the risks and harms that are associated with them. Public health strategies can, however, encompass a very wide range of practices which sometimes have a lot in common with a zero tolerance approach to drug control. Treatment, for example, can be coercive in nature and provided only with the end goal of complete abstinence from drugs in mind. This section details the development of a particular subsection of the public health side of drug policy—the harm reduction movement—which can very much be seen as an alternative kind of public health approach. It defines the nature of harm reduction, provides examples of its real world application, and evaluates its effectiveness.

Where public health initiatives have been implemented within an overall zero tolerance approach to drugs, they have typically focused on the aim of reducing drug use and helping as many people as possible to achieve abstinence. In the 1980s, however, the spread of HIV/AIDS emerged as a public health crisis. This issue was perceived as being connected to the use of drugs within society as levels of HIV/AIDS were particularly high within injecting drug using populations (Stimson 1995). Concerns about the potential for HIV/AIDS to spread from the drug using population to the general population (primarily by via unprotected sex) were widespread and provided a catalyst for a fundamental shift in the public health approach to drug policy in many Western nations. For the first time, achieving the less risky use of drugs, even without the underpinning goal of abstinence, was recognised as a worthwhile goal in its own right. If people who intravenously use drugs were helped to use them in a less risky manner, in this case by being provided with clean needles, the public health benefits to the general population would be significant. Essentially, the reduction of the prevalence of AIDS/HIV in society was seen as more of a priority than the reduction of drug use.

This shift in drug related public health policy can generally be referred to as the rise of the harm reduction movement, a broad brush term for "interventions, programmes and policies that seek to reduce the health, social and economic harms of drug use to individuals, communities and societies" (Rhodes and Hedrich 2010: 21). The overarching aim of a utopian (de Jarlais 1995) 'drug free society' is replaced by an acceptance that illicit drug use is part of our world, and by a goal of reducing the harm arising from the use of drugs (Lenton and Single 1998). These may be the primary harms caused by the use of drugs themselves, or, more usually, the secondary harms that are done to users and suppliers of drugs because of policies that have been put in place to control criminalised substances. An example of secondary harm is provided by the limitation of needles to prescription only, making it difficult for intravenous drug users to obtain them, and increasing the likelihood that they will put themselves at risk of developing HIV/AIDS, Hepatitis B and C, and other blood borne diseases. Newcombe (1992) argued that the definition of harm in harm reduction should not just encompass health (e.g. overdose) concerns, but also those relating to social (e.g. littering of used needles in common spaces) and economic (e.g. policing costs) issues.

Harm reduction aims to provide an amoral or neutral approach (Keane 2002) to the issue of illicit drugs shifting the focus from a judgemental and stigmatising perception of drug use and drug users towards an emphasis on the importance of reaching out to them and engaging them in some level of service provision (O'Malley 2009). For example, rather than focusing on abstinence as the primary goal of interaction between drug users and service providers, it seeks to engage drug users whatever their future intentions are towards drug use, and help them to use drugs in a less risky manner. If drug users prove unwilling or unable to cease drug use, they can still be supported in using drugs in a less 'harmful' way and the unintended consequences of drug policy initiatives can thus be alleviated. Essentially, harm reduction refuses "to make public care *conditional* on adherence to moralized norms around abstinence" (Race 2008: 418).

Harm reduction, as already suggested, is best thought of as an umbrella term for a variety of policies, programmes and interventions which share a desire to reduce the harm associated with the use of drugs and the policies implemented to control them (Lenton and Single 1998). The examples that follow will explore how these principles about the reduction of harm are applied in practice. The interventions most readily associated with harm reduction are the provision of substitution treatment and needle exchange programmes, both of which are entwined with a desire to prevent the spread of HIV/AIDS. Substitution treatment is most usually associated with the provision of a substance such as methadone in place of street heroin. Although providing people who are dependent on drugs with a similar substance can be viewed as counter-productive in terms of achieving the ultimate goal of abstinence, the harm reduction movement advocates that the regular provision of a 'safer' (because taken orally rather than injected) and more sanitised (free from impurities) substance can bring important benefits. For example, it removes the need for people who are dependent on drugs to engage with the criminal market and to organise their lives around securing the provision of their substance of choice, it reduces the need to rely on risky practices such as injection, and it decreases the harm that comes from the impurities often present in the unregulated street market.

Similarly, while the provision of clean needles for people who are dependent on street drugs such as heroin runs counter to a zero tolerance approach to drugs, it fits with the central aim of harm reduction: to enable people who wish to continue to use drugs, to do so in a less risky manner. The use of unclean needles is a major factor in the spread of blood borne viruses such as AIDS/HIV and Hepatitis B and C. The provision of clean needles allows those dependent on drugs to protect themselves and, by extension the wider population, from the transmission of these diseases. Opioid substitution treatment and needle exchange programmes are the most widely accepted forms of harm reduction in global terms: Harm Reduction International, reported in 2016 that 90 (out of 158 countries and territories reporting injecting drug use) now offer some form of needle exchange programme and 80 offer some form of opioid substitution treatment (Harm Reduction International 2016).

Some countries have experimented with further harm reduction measures which have never quite gained the popularity and widespread implementation of substitution treatment and needle exchange programmes. These countries have, in some instances, taken substitution treatment programmes a step further by providing heroin prescription programmes which allow people who are dependent on this drug to access regulated heroin rather than a proxy substance such as methadone. The UK, for example, has provided a service of heroin prescription since the 1920s, although this has been severely limited since the 1960s. This was emulated by Switzerland in the mid 1990s in an attempt to engage even those drug users who were not willing to give up the use of heroin for a 'safer' substitute, and has since spread to a handful of other countries e.g. Germany, the Netherlands and Canada. Following a similar approach, some countries have experimented with the provision of drug consumption rooms—safe, clean environments within which people can use drugs without fear of contact with law enforcement agents, with reduced personal risk (e.g. by accessing water, sterilisation equipment and clean needles) and without causing nuisance to others (e.g. leaving their used needles around or having to use in front of the general public). The global state of harm reduction report (Harm Reduction International 2016) documents 10 countries (8 from Western Europe, Canada and Australia) operating a total of 90 drug consumption rooms.

Also relevant here is the development of drug checking services which allow drug users to submit for official testing samples of the pills and powders they plan to consume. Reports establish whether or not the substance is what the users were expecting and the relative strength and purity of the sample. This empowers people who use these substances to use them in a more responsible manner, for example by reducing the amount consumed if the sample is very strong, or declining to consume altogether if the substance is not what was expected. A final example of harm reduction in practice is provided by the recent decision by some American states, in response to rising rates of drug overdose, to equip paramedics and police officers working in areas known for their drug using populations with naloxone, which can be used as an immediate and effective intervention to acute heroin overdose. This is not intended as a comprehensive list of harm reduction measures—other strategies, for example, include low threshold treatment services active within the communities they serve, the provision of condoms to enable safer sexual practices, the creation of internet discussion forums such as erowid or bluelight to disseminate accurate information about how to use substances responsibly, and efforts to decriminalise the possession of some substances for personal use. It serves, however, to provide example of harm reduction principles in practical application and attests to a common thread running throughout the interventions reviewed: a primary aim to reduce the harm done by drug use and drug control policies, rather than to reduce use itself.

Although much still needs to be done in terms of the evaluation of harm reduction measures, especially of the newer interventions such as drug consumption rooms, the evidence we have so far suggests that well-established harm reduction measures have been internationally accepted as an effective approach to the illicit drugs issue (Hunt and Stevens 2004). Most of the evidence relates to needle exchange programmes and substitution treatment programmes which were the first harm reduction methods to gain widespread acceptance. Hunt (2003), in his exploration of the evidence base for harm reduction measures, finds that needle exchange programmes are cost-effective, have a positive effect on HIV rates, and can be tailored to marginalised and vulnerable groups, particularly where they are combined with low-threshold outreach work. Most of the evaluation of substitution treatment has been in relation to methadone maintenance as a substitute for opiate use and Hunt (2003: 20) attests to a substantial evidence base "developed over almost 40 years and from across many different countries". Specifically, methadone maintenance programmes are found to retain people in treatment for longer than other treatment programmes, to be better at reducing opioid related crime, and to reduce the risk of mortality from opioid use.

Many harm reduction initiatives also aim to improve the social integration of dependent drug users so they do not remain marginalised from and stigmatised by wider society (Anderson and Jarvinen 2007), but effectiveness is less well-established in this area. Bourgois and Schonberg (2009: 299), while reviewing heroin prescription programmes, found that: "Soon after entering these programmes, outlaw addicts with life histories of crime, violence, vagrancy, and ill health (at great cost to society) often begin to lead comparatively stable, pacific, and healthier lives through the simple, cheap medical intervention of prescribing heroin". Their reading of the evidence suggests that participants in heroin prescription programmes are more likely to stay in treatment for longer, less likely to engage in poly drug use, less likely to engage in drug related crime and violence and, counterintuitively, more likely to achieve eventual abstinence from drugs, than those on methadone maintenance. There is therefore a positive base of research evidence for specific, usually long-standing, harm reduction based interventions, but there remains the need for continued and comprehensive evaluation, particularly of the newer measures, such as drug consumption rooms and pill and powder testing.

The Evolution and Limitations of Harm Reduction as an Alternative Strategy of Drug Control

At its outset, the emergence of harm reduction as a concept with applicability for the drugs issue was firmly rooted in the grassroots drug policy reform movement (Marlatt 1996) and was often associated with calls for the legalisation of drugs and public recognition that there might be benefits to (or rational reasons for) using drugs. As it has gained in popularity over time it has achieved mainstream recognition appealing to those on both sides of the drug policy debate: "Who, in their right mind, could oppose the notion of reducing harm" (Nadelmann 1993: 37). It has come to be described as a 'middle ground' between zero tolerance and legalisation (Inciardi 1999). As the principle of harm reduction has become more mainstream it has also had to develop to become more palatable to policy makers and the general public. This section charts the development of the harm reduction movement and documents some of its limitations.

In its earliest stages, harm reduction was primarily concerned with the health and welfare of drug users themselves. Measures that we might now think of as being self-evidently concerned with the reduction of drug related harm were in practice long before the term harm reduction became widely applied to drug policy initiatives. For example, Cook et al. (2010) document the use of narcotic maintenance clinics in the US from 1912 to 1923; the Rolleston report (1926) established substitution treatment programmes under a 'medicalisation' model in the UK; and Souleymanov and Allman (2016) report substitution treatment initiatives in Canada during the 1950s. It was not until the 1980s, however, and in direct response to the plight of drug using populations ravaged by HIV/AIDS, that these isolated incidences of harm reduction in drug policy were used as a catalyst for the development of a concerted harm reduction movement: "The reformulation of HIV transmission as an injection drug-related harm…spearheaded the harm reduction movement for illicit injection drug use" (Ezard 2001: 208). In exploring the role that social and environmental influences play in the health of drug using populations (Rhodes 2002), it quickly became evident that existing policies that marginalised drug users and denied them access to clean needles, were exacerbating their health related problems. Thus the idea that drug control policies could harm the health of drug using populations, over and above the harm caused by the use of drugs themselves, provided a catalyst for the development of harm reduction as a concept around which existing initiatives could coalesce and new endeavours could be promoted.

Initially, the promotion and implementation of harm reduction measures spread in a 'bottom up' manner, often advocated by drug policy reform groups or drug users themselves, before attracting the attention of mainstream public health providers, resulting in what

Roe (2006: 244) has termed "an unlikely coalition of public health authorities and activists". The grassroots or bottom up nature of the more widespread application of harm reduction measures is particularly evident in the Netherlands and the UK. In Amsterdam in the 1970s, a drug users' lobbying group, MDHG, were successful in lobbying first for a 'methadone bus' delivering to dependent drug users around the city, and then for the extension of this initiative in 1981 to an official Amsterdam wide methadone maintenance programme (Chatwin 2010). Similarly, in 1984, the Rotterdam based Junkiebund, a drug users' union run by and for drug users, was directly involved in the development of the first ever official needle exchange programme (Marlatt 1996).

At the same time, a similar picture was emerging in the UK, although here the impetus came more from the "radical and pioneering" (O'Hare 2007: 141) approach of service providers in Merseyside, rather than from drug users themselves. A drop in centre that also provided substitution treatment was able to provide the first UK needle exchange programme in 1986. Evaluated as resulting in a reduction of needle sharing and use of street drugs, the attraction of new people into service provision, and overall increases in the health of dependent drug users, these initiatives gained the support of the local police and the right wing government of the day (headed by Margaret Thatcher) which authorised the provision of funding to implement needle exchange programmes throughout the country. This prominence of the harm reduction movement was consolidated by the hosting of the first international harm reduction conference in Liverpool in 1990. From here, substitution treatment and needle exchange programmes, the hall marks of harm reduction, spread quickly throughout Europe and to Australia, North America and New Zealand.

These origins of the harm reduction movement thus began out of a concern about the health of drug users during the HIV/AIDS crisis of the 1980s and were championed by the efforts of drug users and those service providers working closely with them. At this stage, the movement clearly prioritised interaction with and help for drug users over efforts to ensure they abstained from drug use entirely. Indeed, it was marked by a tendency to regard abstinence as an idealistic and unachievable aim that had provided an obstacle to the service engagement of many drug users (Marlatt 1996). Further, many of the drug users and service providers involved in the early stages of the movement, acknowledged that there could be rational reasons for people to choose to use illegal substances (Erickson 1997), a position not commonly acknowledged within official drug policy discourse even today. Harm reduction could thus provide a model distinct from the traditional public health arena, that perceived drugs users as neither criminals nor patients, but rather as rational beings capable of practising responsible drug use if given the opportunity to do so. In the eyes of some, the movement thus became inextricably linked with the desire for radical drug policy reform or the development of alternative, and much more liberal, strategies of drug control.

Marlatt (1996) describes the early harm reduction movement as based around four central aims: to provide a public health alternative to a predominantly law enforcement focused approach; to provide low threshold access to service provision; to recognise that abstinence as an ideal end goal is, in many cases, unrealistic, at least in the short term; and to tend towards a bottom up, grassroots organisational structure. As harm reduction has matured and entered the mainstream, however, the focus has fundamentally shifted to the first two of these four aims. The need to provide robust general public health intervention as part of a drug control strategy, and to implement specific strategies, such as needle exchange and substitution treatment, designed to reduce the harm caused by law enforcement initiatives, have gained acceptance. They have, however, been tempered by a lingering association with the drug policy reform movement, leading many national governments and international bodies to connect harm reduction with legalisation, to view it as encouraging drug use in general, and as keeping people stuck in patterns of drug use rather than focusing on helping them to break free. More radical facets of the movement—such as the deprioritisation of abstinence from drugs, acknowledgement of the benefits drug use could bring, association with calls for a more liberal attitude towards the use of drugs, and its grassroots nature—have, to some extent, been edited out of the official harm reduction discourse in an effort to make the concept more palatable to drug policy makers.

Roe (2006) contends that as harm reduction practices have become more widespread and, as they have attracted support from some national governments and international organisations, so they have become top-down policies rather than bottom-up movements. One result of this move towards the top-down nature of the implementation of harm reduction, has been the re-evaluation of abstinence as an important eventual outcome of all harm reduction initiatives (Kellogg 2003). For example, the stabilisation of the drug user via substitution treatment should no longer be seen as an end goal in itself, but rather as a step along the road to total abstinence. Another has been the shift, documented by Hunt and Stevens (2004), from concentrating on the harm done *to* drug users, so important in capturing the early support during the HIV/AIDS crisis, towards the harm done *by* drug users to wider society such as the nuisance caused by drug related litter and the use of drugs in public places. "The harms to be reduced can be suffered by drug-users and non drug-users, by individuals and groups, either directly or indirectly. Initiatives can be called harm reduction, even if they have no intention to reduce harm to drug-users themselves" (Hunt and Stevens 2004: 337). This evolution of the harm reduction movement has brought some benefits: the acceptance of the need to reduce drug related harm as well as drug use is more widespread. It has, however, also exposed certain limitations to a mainstream version of harm reduction as an alternative strategy of drug control.

These limitations are explored in Bourgois and Schonberg's (2009) ethnography of homeless heroin users in New York. They brand harm reduction as a "middle-class public health discourse" (Bourgois and Schonberg 2009: 231), suggesting that for many dependent and vulnerable people who use drugs, the primary aim of harm reduction—to use drugs in a less risky fashion—clashes with "the realities of practical survival on the street". For example, although vulnerable and marginalised people who use drugs may have received messages about reducing risk around drug use by not sharing needles or by moving from street drugs to a substitution treatment programme, the chaotic and unpredictable nature of their lifestyles and their lack of general opportunities may prevent them from being able to act on these messages. This leads to a situation where people who use drugs in a risky manner are encouraged to see themselves as at fault for their own situations and allows wider society to view them as dysfunctional and irrational because they don't follow procedures to reduce risk (Rhodes 2002). Ultimately, as Ruane (2015: 71) suggests, it means that harm reduction has accepted and/or facilitated "culturally predominant portrayals of users as criminal, irresponsible and dangerous".

Moore and Fraser (2006) document a general shift in responsibility for individual health from the government to the individual themselves in neoliberal societies. Scholars in the drugs field such as Miller (2001) and Keane (2002) have linked Foucault's (1979, 1991) ideas about encroaching social dominance over the body (biopower), and shifts in power or responsibility from the government to the individual (governmentality), to limitations in the development of harm reduction as a viable alternative system of drug control. Miller (2001) argues that harm reduction actually increases surveillance of drug users as they become regulated in their efforts to stay healthy and adhere to methods of drug use that minimise their own personal risk. While public health discourses were once used to afford the most vulnerable people who use drugs the status of victim or patient, they are now used to brand the most chaotic and dependent drug users as doubly deviant—for using drugs in the first place, and for failing to do so in a less risky manner. Under a conceptualisation of drug users as rational citizens, capable of self-regulation (Keane 2002), or as "informed choice makers" (O'Malley 2009: 11), the responsibility for controlling and developing responsible drug use lies firmly with the individual and government cedes accountability. This is a problematic development as it ignores the "inequalities in risk negotiation" (Rhodes 2002: 86) (for example, gender, ethnicity, material factors) that constrain people's ability to act on messages about risk reduction. It also lets governments off the hook in the sense that it ignores social and environmental factors, such as poverty and inequality (Miller 2001), that impinge on people's ability to adopt less risky practices, and allows the blame instead to be solely placed on the 'risky' drug users themselves.

Based on the discussion thus far, this chapter has argued that, once the failure of the war on drugs approach has been acknowledged and its unintended consequences have been appreciated, an important step in producing more effective global drug policies is to shift the primary aim of drug control policies from a reduction of drug use to a reduction of drug related harm. It has documented considerable existing progress in this area, but has noted that as harm reduction has achieved greater acceptance, so it has had to tone down its more radical elements and take its place as part of a range of potential public health oriented drug policy options. Finally, it has argued that a neoliberal interpretation of harm reduction can lead to an under appreciation of the role that societal factors, such as inequality and poverty, can play in stimulating drug use. The next section will explore the need to develop harm reduction strategies that are also able to address issues such as these.

Addressing the Harm That Arises from Social and Material Inequality

As outlined in the previous sections, harm reduction developed as part of the 'new public health' agenda of the 1980s and 1990s which sought to balance individual and collective action in efforts to increase health awareness. Both movements aimed to inspire "inter-sectoral and multi-level activity encouraging individual, community, policy, and environmental change" (Rhodes 2002: 85). The critiques of harm reduction explored above, however, suggest that, under neo-liberal influences, and as it has become increasingly part of mainstream drug policy discussions, harm reduction has tended to focus on *individual* rather than wider societal change. Recent attempts to address these critiques have been made by returning to and emphasising the wider role of social, political and environmental factors in the use of drugs.

Rhodes's body of work on risk environments (2009, 2002) draws attention to the importance of understanding the wider context within which drug use takes place. At the micro level, this will include factors such as social networks and relationships, peer group influence, settings where drug use typically occurs, and neighbourhood in which the drug user lives. At the macro level, it includes factors such as gender of the drug user and policy context of the region in which the drugs are used.

Importantly for the discussion here, macro level factors also include material and social inequality. The thrust of Rhodes' (2002) argument is that it is wrong to suggest that all drug users are equal, that all will experience drug related harm equally, and that all are equally capable of employing strategies to minimise the harm they encounter. The most vulnerable and dependent drug users will often be suffering from issues such as poverty, homelessness, discrimination, and lack of opportunity. Material and social inequalities such as these make the harm experienced as a result of drug use and drug control policies greater, and also make it harder to access and adhere to harm reduction messages and practices. Rhodes (2009: 199) thus suggests that responsibility for the reduction of harm should be "*shared* between individuals and social-economic structures as a force of resistance to neoliberal versions of risk rationality emphasising individual responsibility (and *blame*)" (Rhodes 2009: 199).

Taking this argument further, Rhodes (2002: 91) suggests that if the "primary determinants of harm are economic and social, then the remedies must also be economic and social". Strategies that seek to reduce the harm caused by drugs and drug policies are an important step towards an alternative style of drug control, but may be less effective at preventing the use of drugs in the first place or dealing with inequalities in experience of harm. Stevens (2011: 1), in his work on the political economy of drug policy, finds that, while white middle class people are generally more likely to use drugs, "the most damaging patterns of drug use and their worst consequences are concentrated in deprived neighbourhoods and groups". He therefore proposes that an effective drug policy should seek to address issues such as social, racial and economic inequality: in fact, the primary aim of drug policy should not be to reduce the number of overall drug users, or even to reduce the overall amount of drug related harm, but to reduce the various forms of inequality within society. If such an endeavour were to be successful, levels of drug related harm, and of drug use itself eventually, could be expected to decrease.

The Global Commission (2014) report on 'Pathways to Drug Policies that Work', also emphasises the need to reduce economic inequality and social marginalisation to provide people with exit routes out of drug use and to help prevent them from starting to develop dependent use in the first place. Interestingly, while much of the discussion on harm reduction in general, and on the relationship between inequality and drug use more specifically, tends to originate from and be concerned with the global North and consumer drug countries, this report also seeks to apply recommendations to drug producing countries and the global South more generally. For example, in terms of improving social and economic conditions, the report contends that many of those involved in the production, harvesting, processing, transporting and trading of illegal drug crops are simply "taking refuge in this illicit economy for reasons of survival of their families" (The Global Commission 2014: 24). Following this argument, drug policies that make addressing issues such as poverty and deprivation the priority, instead of reducing the production and supply of crops, could be expected to enjoy some success.

Calls to refocus drug policy aims towards combatting inequality in all its forms have not enjoyed the prominence or acceptance of harm reduction messages related more specifically to the way in which drugs are used and controlled. There have, however, been some recent attempts to draw these ideas together under the umbrella term of 'public good'. In an attempt to return to and build on the ideals of the 'new public health' agenda that emerged in the 1980s and 1990s, Strang et al. (2012: 71) outline the notion of public good as shifting the focus from the individual drug user to communities in general by seeking to engender social benefits such as: "better public health, reduced crime and greater stability and equality of life for families and neighbourhoods". In relation to the control of drugs, a public good approach specifies the need to include laws, regulations and enforcement, but only in conjunction with measures designed to help drug users to reduce the riskiness of their drug use practices, and to address the wider social, economic, political and environmental contexts within which drug use occurs. In sum, a drug policy based on the underlying aim to reduce the harm caused by drug use and drug control, should also seek to reduce the harm that is related to, and which may predate, drug use, such as social and material inequality.

Addressing the Harm That Is Experienced by Drug Producing Countries and That Arises as a Result of Human Rights Abuses

Another related area that is often absent from dominant harm reduction discourse is the need to address the harms that occur in drug producing countries. As we have seen in Chapter 2, many of the unintended consequences of a war on drugs approach to illicit drug control, focused on controlling and curbing the supply side of drug markets, have disproportionately impacted on drug producing countries. Yet, in relation to this kind of harm, the harm reduction movement has very little to say. The development of harm reduction as an alternative to a war on drugs approach has been characterised by a tendency to focus on the demand side of the drugs issue rather than the supply side. Indeed, its tendency to shift focus from restricting the supply of drugs to reducing the demand for drugs and improving the lives of those who do use drugs, has often been celebrated. The problem with this interpretation, however, is that some of the greatest harms related to the unintended consequences of drug policy lie on the supply side of the issue and are encountered by those producing and/or supplying drugs.

Greenfield and Paoli (2012) analysed the suitability of harm reduction when dealing with drug production and supply and concluded that, while it has not thus far shown much development in this direction, it would be an appropriate tool to reduce the harms associated with the supply of drugs. Examples of supply side harm reduction interventions do exist, but are few and far between. Farthing and Kohl (2012) draw attention to Bolivia's recent and modestly successful attempt to reduce the violence in coca growing communities by employing harm reduction strategies. Bolivia is known for its long standing cultural use of the coca leaf, but production of coca leaf for traditional markets had become entwined with the wider and more profitable market for processed cocaine destined for global markets and, as a result, those involved had experienced increasing levels of violence. The harm reduction programme allowed a limited number of farmers to register to cultivate coca for supply to traditional users only and subject to allowing surveillance to ensure limits weren't contravened, and saw significant reductions in drug market associated violence and some reductions in the amount of coca diverted to the illegal drug market. Another example is provided by efforts to move away from the harmful policy of indiscriminately spraying crops with harmful chemicals in an effort towards curbing drug production. Indiscriminate crop spraying causes unintended harm by creating widespread environmental damage, contaminated food and water supplies and destroying the livelihoods of already impoverished communities. Instead harm reduction strategies are employed by encouraging farmers (for example by paying them over the odds) to produce alternative and legal crops.

Finally, if harm reduction is interpreted broadly in line with the previous section on the need to address inequality as part of a harm reduction strategy, there have been some recent relevant developments around sustainable development. In 2015 United Nations member states developed a sustainable development agenda designed to take "bold and transformative" (United Nations Devleopment Programme 2015: 1) to eradicate global poverty. Specific goals include ending hunger, promoting good health and well being, providing quality education, achieving gender equality, ensuring access for all to clean water and affordable energy, stimulating economic growth, implementing secure societal infrastructure, and reducing inequality generally. The UNGASS 2016 Outcome Document makes many references to the importance of promoting sustainable development as part of our international drug control system, evidencing increasing global recognition of the links between poverty, inequality and drug related harm, and indicating that a reduction in poverty and inequality can also be expected to have an impact on the prevalence of global drug use.

As well as disproportionately experiencing the unintended harmful consequences of drug control strategies, producer countries have also experienced significant human rights abuses as a result of the war on drugs approach to drug policy. These abuses have been outlined in Chapter 2 and concern issues such as the routine extra-judicial killings of those involved in the drugs trade and use of the death penalty for those convicted of drug related crimes. Human rights abuses are also present in those countries which are predominantly known for their consumption of drugs. For example, a report produced for the Beckley Foundation Drug Policy Programme (Barrett et al. 2008) highlights: the arrest and ill treatment of drug users to meet drug reduction targets in Russia, Ukraine, Kazakhstan and the UK; detention and coercive treatment, sometimes including forced labour and moral education as in China; the denial of treatment and low threshold services to those who are imprisoned or to other vulnerable populations as in the UK and Europe; and the discriminatory application of drug control as seen in the US where African-American men are sent to prison on drug charges at 13.4 times the rate of white men. Harm reduction, as an alternative approach to drug control, seeks to reduce the harms caused by the unintended consequences of drug policy, and ought therefore to address human rights contraventions as a matter of priority.

In relation to these human rights issues, however, harm reduction has also remained relatively silent, tending instead to maintain a narrow focus on the individual drug user, usually in Western consumer countries, and on a set number of provisions outlined earlier in this chapter such as needle exchange programmes, substitution treatment, drug consumption rooms, street level nursing etc. Indeed, harm reduction and human rights have an uneasy relationship. Arising out of the drug policy reform movement, some divisions of the harm reduction movement have seen the human rights issue as being fundamental, especially in relation to the basic right of individuals to exercise control over their own bodies and minds and use drugs if they wish to do so (Hathaway 2001). Keane (2002: 229) suggests that under this framework prohibition is viewed as "not only irrational but immoral because it violates the autonomy of the individual that is at the core of what it is to be human". Such an approach to addressing the harms arising from human rights abuses, however, maintains a rigid Western focus on the rights of the individual to use drugs without being subjected to harm such as criminalisation.

Others (e.g. Ezard 2001) have suggested that human rights are an important part of harm reduction because state actions such as criminalisation, stigmatisation and discrimination increase and exacerbate the existing vulnerabilities of those who use drugs. The need for an increased focus on human rights in developing alternative drug policy approaches is becoming more acknowledged (Harm Reduction International 2016), by the United Nations and its associated bodies, for example. In these alternative drug policy approaches, human rights are often linked to harm reduction as by Navi Pillay (cited in, Freeman and Sierra 2005: 92) the UN commissioner for human rights: "drug users suffer discrimination, are forced to accept treatment, marginalised and often harmed by approaches which over-emphasise criminalisation and punishment while under-emphasising harm reduction and human rights". A desire to address human rights issues, in both consumer and producer countries, is not, however, yet viewed as an intrinsic part of harm reduction by many of those involved in the movement.

Thus far, this chapter reports an increasing interest in drug control strategies that aim to reduce the harm caused by drugs rather than the use of drugs themselves, and advocates that this represents a step towards creating more effective global drug policies. It cautions, however, that harm reduction in its current form is limited by a tendency to focus on the demand for drugs, the individual drug user and the global North. To provide a truly effective alternative drug policy approach, it must also seek to address wider societal harms that are related to drug use, such as poverty and inequality, and to address supply side harms that are experienced in producer countries and the harms that arise as a result of human rights abuses. The final section of this chapter aims to establish the extent to which harm reduction has been accepted and implemented as an alternative strategy for drug control.

How Prevalent Is the Concept of Harm Reduction in Existing Systems of Drug Control?

The extended discussion above allows us to observe that alternatives to law enforcement dominated systems of drug control do exist. We can begin to build up a fairly robust picture of what an alternative system of drug control should look like in general terms: it should at least partly focus on the reduction of harm to those who use drugs and to the communities and societies that are affected by drugs, both in terms of the direct consequences of drug use and of the unintended consequences caused by policies implemented to control the use of drugs; it should consider the importance of upholding principles of human rights towards drug users and those involved in the drug trade; and it should also seek to address wider societal problems such as inequality and poverty and to reduce the harm that occurs in producer countries and on the supply side of the drugs issue in general. The evidence evaluated above indicates that interest in these approaches is both longstanding and increasing.

This section uses three case studies to critically explore the extent to which harm reduction rhetoric has actually penetrated and impacted on official drug discourse. The first further documents the very narrow global reach of harm reduction; the second explores Portuguese efforts to build a drug policy that is rooted in the principle of harm reduction; and the third considers the extent to which the language of harm reduction has been adopted in official documentation. The chapter concludes that, despite the rising disillusionment with war on drugs approaches and an increasing appetite for alternatives, much work remains to be done in terms of shifting the focus on drug control.

Harm Reduction's Narrow Global Reach

Europe has a long established tradition of harm reduction and, as such, provides a good starting point for a discussion of the extent to which it has been accepted as an alternative strategy of drug control. Within Europe, Rhodes and Hedrich (2010: 9) suggest that "controversy has to a large extent, been replaced by consensus". For example, the principle of therapy over punishment has been adopted in the general guidelines of drug policies in a growing number of countries and some form of needle exchange programme and substitution treatment programme is offered in every European Union Member State. Even Sweden, a country which has traditionally only allowed harm reduction measures on an experimental basis (Chatwin 2003) has relatively recently recommended that needle exchange programmes be made permanent and a greater number and variety of substitution treatment programmes be made available (Goldberg 2005; Johnson 2006). The European Monitoring Centre for Drugs and Drug Addiction (EMCDDA 2010) itself reports that the principle of harm reduction is widely valued throughout Europe. Despite this seemingly exemplary record, however, a slightly more in-depth exploration of the evidence suggests that, even at the centre of harm reduction, there is much work still to do. The EMCDDA 2010 annual report (EMCDDA 2010) reported that the 12 countries that have joined the EU since 2004 account for only 2% of substitution treatment in Europe as a whole, indicating that a strong disparity between East and West remains. While commending the work the EU has done in this area so far, MacGregor (2011) suggests that more work is also needed in relation to the prevention of hepatitis and the reduction of drug-related harm for vulnerable groups such as sex workers, migrant populations and people who are imprisoned.

As already raised in the previous section, this uneven geographical spread of harm reduction is even more pronounced when considered on a global scale. The 2016 Global Report on the state of harm reduction (Harm Reduction International 2016) indicates that 158 of the world's countries and territories document injecting drug use and that, in 2016, only 90 of those countries offered needle exchange programmes and only 80 offered opioid substitution treatment programmes. In terms of global coverage: Europe, Oceania and North America remain the most dedicated supporters of harm reduction; followed by Asia and Latin America where it has made moderate inroads; and at the bottom of the scale, the Middle East, North Africa and sub Saharan Africa where its coverage is considerably less comprehensive. This evidence further emphasises the point made previously that harm reduction is currently relatively limited in its scope, and predominantly focused on Western countries which are net consumers of drugs. As noted in the discussion above, possibilities for the application of harm reduction principles to the producers and suppliers of drugs are very much under-explored: these principles remain firmly rooted in the demand reduction side of drug control.

The global report on the state of harm reduction (Harm Reduction International 2016) further notes that, despite the increasing profile of harm reduction as an alternative strategy of drug control, there has been no increase in the overall number of countries and territories implementing harm reduction measures since 2014. Furthermore, in terms of specific vulnerable populations, only 8 countries implement needle exchange programmes in prison—Armenia, Germany, Kyrgyzstan, Luxembourg, Moldova, Spain, Switzerland and Tajikistan. So, while, as documented, the harm reduction response to the control of illicit drugs is growing in terms of profile and influence, we can relatively easily determine that this growth is limited in terms of geography with harm reduction predominantly being applied to demand reduction in Western countries that present as net consumers of illicit substances.

Portugal as an Isolated Example of National Drug Policy Grounded in Harm Reduction

Where alternative systems of drug control that predominantly focus on the reduction of harm, rather than the elimination of drugs per se, have been incorporated, they have tended to be add ons to existing law enforcement focused drug strategies. For example, as discussed above, crises such as those posed by HIV/AIDS from the 1980s onwards have precipitated the initiation of harm reduction measures such as needle exchange and/or substitution treatment programmes or, more recently, a rise in the number of drug-related overdoses has contributed to the limited implementation of pill and powder testing programmes and to the development of naloxone treatment strategies. Individual nation states have been able to commit to providing these measures to reduce the overall harm caused by drugs themselves and, importantly, by the policies designed to control them, but they have not tended to precipitate a fundamental change in overall policy development away from a law enforcement process and towards a harm reduction dominated discourse. As Hathaway (2001: 133) suggests: "While harm reduction has arisen out of sheer desperation in many places, it is seldom adopted in principle".

One example of a country which has undergone a fundamental shift from a law enforcement based policy to one which is rooted in public health and harm reduction is provided by Portugal (Chatwin 2011). Modern Portuguese drug policy stems from a 1983 law incorporating elements of UN drug policy conventions. This change in law coincided with a relatively rapid increase in the use of drugs in Portugal as well as a move from cannabis as the most popular drug towards cocaine and heroin (Mendes 2000). In practice, penalties for drug use began to increase at this time (Almeida, cited in Hughes 2006). In general, however, the issue was ascribed relatively low importance and the implementation of increasingly severe laws were prioritised over the development of public health measures and initiatives designed to reduce the harm caused by drugs.

As the 1990s progressed, the number of drug users and, perhaps more importantly, the number of dependent drug users, increased significantly, forcing the Portuguese government to place more emphasis on the illicit drug problem and to develop appropriate strategies. Mendes (2000) reported that in the mid-1990s there were an estimated 25,000–100,000 drug users out of a population of ten million. Portugal developed a significant population of heroin users with six to ten cases per 1000 adults being reported in the 1990s (Allen et al. 2004). Rates of drug-related infectious diseases such as HIV, AIDS and hepatitis B and C increased dramatically from 47 in 1990 to 590 in 1997 (Hughes and Stevens 2010), while arrests for drug related offences increased from 4667 in 1991 to 6380 in 1995 and 11,395 in 1998 (van het Loo et al. 2002). A significant proportion of heroin users were intravenous drug users which Allen et al. (2004) have attributed as contributing to the rise in infectious diseases and arrests reported above as well as a threefold increase in drug-related deaths during this decade. As a result, Portugal compared unfavourably with other European countries in terms of drug-related deaths, drug-related infectious diseases and drug-related arrests (Allen et al. 2004; Hughes 2006), although overall rates of drug use remained significantly below the European average.

In 1995, a Socialist government was elected in Portugal and an increased emphasis was placed on solving the drug problem. In response to highly visible rising levels of dependent drug use, as well as increasing recognition of the consequences for wider society, public health measures rooted in harm reduction principles began to be implemented in Portugal at an increased rate, and the need for drug policy reform was recognised. Hughes (2006) documents the provision of mobile needle exchange programmes from 1996, outreach work from 1997 and methadone treatment programmes from 1998. At the same time, an influential group of health professionals and politicians, including the President of Portugal, Jorge Sampaio, began to campaign strongly for a change in the national drug policy strategy (Hughes 2006). It is important to note here that the over-arching impetus behind the appeal for reform was not that illegal drugs were an insignificant problem that should therefore avoid criminal sanction, but that they were a "highly significant problem [and] that criminalisation was *exacerbating* the problem" (Greenwald 2009: 6).

In the late 1990s, steps towards drug policy reform in Portugal gathered pace. In January 1997, drug abuse was declared public enemy number one and in 1998 a Commission for a National Drug Strategy (CNDS) was appointed. The overwhelming conclusion reached by this commission was that the last 20 years of drug policy in Portugal had been a failure (Hughes 2006) and detailed recommendations for the development of future strategy were provided. By far the most publicly debated of these was to decriminalise the personal use of all drugs so that drug users would not be criminalised or stigmatised because of their drug use, but would instead be drawn to the attention of the authorities and, where appropriate, offered treatment. The recommendations, however, encompassed far more than a call for decriminalisation and, in fact, amounted to a comprehensive move towards a national drug strategy based firmly on public health strategies and harm reduction principles. In further recommendations, treatment was to be ensured for all who sought it, harm reduction programmes such as needle exchanges and substitution treatment were to be extended, effort was to be expended to ensure the reintegration of dependent drug users into wider society, harm reduction measures were to be extended to prisoners and, where possible, dependent drug users were to be given treatment rather than imprisonment (van het Loo et al. 2002). Altogether a much more humanistic and pragmatic policy (Council of Ministers 1999) was proposed.

While the appointment of a commission to examine the national drug problem and make recommendations about future strategy is by no means unusual in terms of European experience, it is extremely rare for recommendations, especially where they are radical, as in the case of Portugal, to be adopted wholeheartedly. Nevertheless, this is what happened in Portugal. The commission's report was completed by October 1998 and debates on its findings were opened in November of the same year. The future of national drug policy became a cross-party issue with both left- and right-wing parties entering fully into discussions. From 2001, the use and possession of up to ten days' supply of all drugs (Vastag 2009) was formally decriminalised while harm reduction measures and public health treatment opportunities continued to be upscaled. The users of drugs and their individual circumstances were placed at the centre of policy with the ultimate goal being to facilitate their reintegration into society (Portuguese Institute for Drugs and Drug Addiction 2005). Vitalino Canas, the then Portuguese drug strategy coordinator, summarised the changes to Portuguese national drug policy: 'the new framework, born of humanist principles, rests on the cornerstone of treatment, prevention and the attempt to dissuade new consumers rather than on punishment' (Canas 2002: 18).

Given the very limited number of national drug policies founded on principles of harm reduction rather than drug reduction, evaluation of Portuguese drug policy efforts has taken on some importance. Since the fundamental shift in the nature of drug policy which took place in Portugal in 2001, there have been many evaluations of its effectiveness (for example, Pinto Coelho 2010; Greenwald 2009; Hughes and Stevens 2010; Transform 2014; Vastag 2009). The majority of these have been cautiously positive with Greenwald (2009) providing a particularly positive and Pinto Coelho (2010) a particularly negative appraisal. Vastag (2009: 1), for example, reports that: "the number of deaths from street drug over-doses dropped from around 400 to 290 annually, and the number of new HIV cases caused by using dirty needles to inject heroin, cocaine and other illegal substances plummeted from nearly 1,400 in 2000 to about 400 in 2006". Hughes and Stevens (2010) document an increase in the number of drug users in treatment from 23,564 in 1998 to 38,532 in 2008. Portuguese national drug reports also show a continued decrease in the number of individuals imprisoned for drug law offences and a decrease in the number of offenders arrested for contraventions of the drug law (Portuguese Institute for Drugs and Drug Addiction 2008). The main area of contention remains in regard to the overall number of drug users in Portugal—"Key stakeholders in Portugal were in general agreement that there has been small to moderate increase in overall reported drug use among adults" (Hughes and Stevens 2010: 9). It is important to keep in mind here that, despite these increases, the prevalence of drug use in Portugal continues to be deemed well below the European (and American) average (Szalavitz 2009).

Media attention and international commentary tend to focus on Portugal's controversial decriminalisation strategy above all else, but several of the academic evaluations draw out the important role that public health, harm reduction and the impetus for wider societal change (e.g. the expansion of the Portuguese welfare state) have played in ensuring successes (Stevens and Hughes 2016; Transform 2014). The removal of criminal sanctions for minor drug infractions has played a part in the changing nature of Portugal's experience of the illegal drugs issue, but the importance of an increase in treatment services, an increase in harm reduction provision, and an increase in measures intended to address inequality in general [for example, the introduction of a minimum income (Transform 2014)] should not be overlooked. Hughes and Stevens (2010) caution that it is very difficult to causally link any of these policy related and societal changes to specific facets of the Portuguese drug experience, but suggest that, in comparison with Spain over the same time period, change in the Portuguese drug situation has been positive.

Given the fairly significant amount of time that has passed since the Portuguese change in law, the cautiously positive evaluations, and the supposed increase in global interest in harm reduction in general, it is somewhat surprising that other countries haven't been inspired by this example to change their policies in similar ways: that is, in adopting a fundamental shift from law enforcement based policies towards those that centre on the principles of harm reduction, public health and public good. Several countries have shown interest in learning from the Portuguese experience—for example, Norway (Ferreira 2010) and the UK (Beaumont et al. 2010) have both sent representatives to Portugal to investigate their drug policy more closely—but as yet this interest has not resulted in policy emulation elsewhere.

Collectively, the evaluations of Portuguese drug policy since the 2001 change in legislation, suggest that while drug related harms, such as death, disease and crime, have decreased, the number of people using drugs has remained stable or slightly increased. If the underlying principle of harm reduction is accepted—that reducing drug related harm is more important than reducing the number of people who are using drugs—this result should not be surprising and should not present an obstacle to the wider adoption of an alternative system of drug control rooted in the reduction of harm. The fact that Portugal's success has not resulted in policy emulation elsewhere strongly suggests a lack of commitment to the wider principles of harm reduction, and a perception that harm reduction strategies are only suited to the addressing to specific harms such as an outbreak of HIV/AIDS or a sharp rise in heroin related overdoses.

Reference to Harm Reduction in Official International Drug Policy Documentation

Further evidence of the secondary status of harm reduction approaches to drug control is provided by a perusal of official international UN and EU drug policy documents, which tend to avoid the controversial term 'harm reduction'. For example, the UNGASS 2016 Outcome Document (UNODC 2016), discussed in the previous chapter, which summarises the latest global position on drug policy provides a case in point. Despite significant focus on harm reduction in the run up to UNGASS 2016, the term itself does not feature once in the document which summarises the outcome of discussions. This is particularly surprising because, in the official discussions preceding UNGASS 2016 46 member states mentioned harm reduction in a positive light, the European Union advocated harm reduction as part of its common position and 11 member states (Brazil, Costa Rica, Colombia, Czech Republic, Estonia, Latvia, Lithuania, Poland, Romania, Slovenia and Uruguay) made explicit statements of support for harm reduction. Of course, support was far from unanimous with several Asian countries failing to support harm reduction and, notably, Australia, a former champion of harm reduction, failing to mention the issue at all.

Given this fairly widespread support, however, and considering evidence for the effectiveness of needle exchange programmes and substitution treatment, and from the national Portuguese policy, it is somewhat surprising that the term 'harm reduction' does not feature in the Outcome Document, which otherwise takes care to promote the importance of public health strategies as part of a balanced approach to drug control. Avoidance of the term harm reduction on the international stage can be traced back to its lingering association with radical drug policy reform, outlined earlier in this chapter. Although harm reduction is not mentioned as a guiding principle, some reference is made to specific harm reduction interventions such as the use of naloxone in reducing opioid overdose and general harm reduction principles such as trying to avoid the stigmatisation of people who use drugs. It is notable, however, that the language used in regard to these recommendations is considerably weaker than elsewhere in the document. Language used around treatment and demand reduction interventions in general tends to ask countries to 'consider', 'promote' or 'encourage', rather than to 'implement', 'respond' or 'strengthen' as are used in reference to law enforcement strategies.

The Outcome Document does make reference to the harm reduction related concepts of: public health ["we reiterate our commitment to promoting the health, welfare and well-being of all individuals, families, communities and society as a whole" (UNODC 2016: 4)]; human rights ["we reaffirm the need to … promote protection of and respect for human rights and the dignity of all individuals in the context of drug programmes, policies and strategies" (UNODC 2016: 4)]; and sustainable development ("we note that efforts to achieve the Sustainable Development Goals and to effectively address the world drug problem are complementary and mutually reinforcing") (UNODC 2016: 3). This provides important evidence that alternative strategies to a war on drugs approach are entering the global drug policy debate, but at the same time confirms a failure to officially endorse policies that are entirely based around the reduction of harm, rather than the reduction of use. A brief exploration of EU drug policy related documents confirms this finding.

As already established, many European countries were early adopters of harm reduction policies and initiatives, but the EU has resisted attempts to redesign drug policy so that is more fundamentally aimed at reducing drug related harm. An evaluation of the 2000–2004 European Action Plan on Drugs suggested that implementation of the plan had failed to result in any progress towards either of its key aims—to reduce the number of people using drugs and the availability of drugs (Commission of the European Communities 2004). MEP Giusto Catania further claimed that none of the six over-arching objectives of the Action Plan had been met and therefore produced a report proposing "a radical change in EU drug policy [towards] harm reduction and a scientific and balanced approach" (ENCOD 2007: 1). In December 2005, to considerable surprise, the report was approved by the European Parliament, however, despite this seemingly official support, in the same year a new European Anti-Drugs Strategy and Action Plan were also implemented, neither of which made any significant reference to harm reduction or any other kind of radical change in overall aims and objectives.

More recently, harm reduction has achieved a stronger foothold in EU drug policy documents—for example, there are many references to harm reduction in the detailed objectives of the Action Plan (Rhodes and Hedrich 2010). The latest strategy lists its first objective as to contribute to a measurable reduction of the demand for drugs *and of drug related health and social risks and harms* (Council of the European Union 2012). In the run up to UNAGSS, the EU also produced a common statement, representing the collective views of member states, which states that a measurable reduction in drug use and drug related harm would be "welcomed and promoted" (European Union 2016) by Europe. These developments suggest significant European progress in official support for harm reduction. It is important to note, however, that the aim of reducing harm is still portrayed as secondary to a reduction in drug demand. It is also interesting that neither the EU common position for UNGASS 2016 or their recent proposal on how to control the proliferation of New Psychoactive substances do not acknowledge the failure of the war on drugs approach or recognise that the implementation of stringent control measures may bring adverse consequences for users.

Conclusion

The evidence presented in this chapter has demonstrated that an alternative approach to drug control—one that recognises the importance of reducing drug related harm as the main priority of drug control—has long existed and is achieving a higher profile. This strategy has shifted the focus to the demand side of the drugs issue and is most prevalent in Western countries which present as net-consumers of drugs. Originally, it arose from a desire to reduce and alleviate the harms experienced by people who use drugs, and was particularly inspired by the AIDS/HIV crisis that arose in the 1980s and 1990s. Over time, and as it has achieved a more mainstream profile, it has developed to focus on the harm done by drug users as well as to them, has come to place significant responsibility on the drug user as a rational actor in their own drug use, and has sometimes been somewhat watered down to fit a more palatable general public health message. More recently, attempts have been made to extend the notion of harm to also encompass societal and material inequalities, and human rights abuses. These strands, however, remain severely under-developed.

Evidence of its effectiveness is modestly positive and primarily comes from evaluations of needle exchange programmes, substitution treatment programmes, and the controversial changes Portugal made to its drug policy in 2001. The strength of this evidence should not be over-estimated—it is not to be supposed that a harm reduction approach to drug control will provide a 'silver bullet' solution that sees the elimination of drug use, or even of drug related harm. It should also be remembered that attempts to causally relate changes in drug policy with trends in drug use and harms should be treated with caution. It is noteworthy, however, that, as Chapter 2 demonstrated, the effectiveness of a war on drugs approach to drug control is seriously undermined. It is therefore reasonable to assume that alternative approaches are *at least as effective* as law enforcement ones, and have the additional benefit of reducing some of the harms that arise from both drug use and drug control.

Yet an in-depth perusal of harm reduction reveals that it is by no means universally accepted. It is mainly rooted in Western consumer countries and the demand side of the drug issue—its potential for application in producer countries and on the supply side in general remains under-explored. Most countries that have expressed interest in these approaches have viewed them as add ons to existing law enforcement policies designed to alleviate the harm caused to users and communities, rather than as founding principles of drug control in their own right, as in Portugal. Finally, due to lingering associations with the drug policy reform movement, explicit reference to harm reduction, has been lacking in United Nations international drug policy documentation and slow to develop in similar EU documentation. To date, harm reduction has thus failed to win the official endorsement a zero tolerance approach has enjoyed.

In order, then, to move towards a more effective global drug policy, the central point arising from this chapter is that we need to move away from an exclusive emphasis on the reduction of drug use, towards an equal or greater emphasis on the reduction of drug-related harm, in all its forms. Efforts to reduce drug-related harm should also include the harm that comes from inequality and from human rights abuses, and should be extended to producer as well as consumer countries and to those who are involved in the supply of drugs as well as drug users. It is not enough to include these strategies as an adjunct to law enforcement measures, enacted perhaps to address harms arising from particular policies, such as denying access to clean needles in the AIDS/HIV crisis. Instead they should be given equal footing, or even placed at the centre as we have seen in is the case in Portugal. Drug policy needs to evolve to a position where public health, public good, harm reduction and human rights are seen as the building blocks for overall strategy. A vital part of increasing confidence in alternatives forms of drug control and stimulating a wider range of interventions from which to choose, is concerned with encouraging the development of innovative strategies of drug policy control, an issue which will be explored in the next chapter.

References

Allen, L., Trace, M., & Klein, A. (2004). *Decriminalisation of drugs in Portugal: A current overview*. London: DrugScope and the Beckley Foundation.

Anderson, D., & Jarvinen, M. (2007). Harm reduction—Ideals and paradoxes. *Nordic Studies on Alcohol and Drugs, 24*, 235–252.

Barrett, D., Lines, R., Schleifer, R., Elliott, R., & Bewley-Taylor, D. (2008). *Recalibrating the regime. The need for a human-rights based approach to international drug policy*. The Beckley Foundation Drug Policy Programme. https://www.internationaldrugpolicy.net.

Beaumont, P., Townsend, M., & Helm, T. (2010, September 5, Sunday). Britain looks at Portugal's success story over decriminalising personal drug use. *Observer*.

Bourgois, P., & Schonberg, J. (2009). *Righteous Dopefiend*. London: University of California Press.

Canas, V. (2002). *The policy for the fight against drugs and drug addiction in Portugal: Recent developments*. London: Speech Given to DrugScope.

Chatwin, C. (2003). Drug policy developments within the European Union; the destabilizing effects of Dutch and Swedish drug policies. *British Journal of Criminology, 43*, 567–582.

Chatwin, C. (2010). User involvement in the illegal drugs field: What can Britain learn from European experiences? *Safer Communities, 9*, 51–60.

Chatwin, C. (2011). *Drug policy harmonization and the European Union*. Basingstoke: Palgrave Macmillan.

Commission of the European Communities. (2004). *Communication from the commission to the council and the European Parliament on the results of the final EU drugs strategy and action plan on drugs (2000–2004)*. http://www.emcdda.europa.eu.

Cook, C., Bridge, J., & Stimson, G. (2010). The diffusion of harm reduction in Europe and beyond. In European Monitoring Centre for Drugs and Drug Addiction's (Ed.), *Harm reduction: Evidence, impacts and challenges*. https://www.emcdda.europa.eu.

Council of Ministers. (1999). *National drug strategy* (Resolution of the Council of Ministers No. 46/99). http://www.drugtext.org.

Council of the European Union. (2012, December 29). EU drugs strategy (2013–2020). *Official Journal of the European Union*.

de Jarlais, D. C. (1995). Editorial: Harm reduction—A framework for incorporating science into drug policy. *American Journal of Public Health, 85*(1), 10–12.

EMCDDA. (2010). *Annual report 2010: The state of the drugs problem in Europe*. http://www.emcdda.europa.eu.
ENCOD. (2007). *Common press release of Giusto Catania MP and ENCOD*. http://www.encod.org.
Erickson, P. G. (1997). Reducing the harm of adolescent substance use. *Canadian Medical Association Journal, 156*(10), 1397–1399.
European Union. (2016). *European Union Common Position on UNGASS 2016*. www.unodc.org.
Ezard, N. (2001). Public health, human rights and the harm reduction paradigm: From risk reduction to vulnerability reduction. *International Journal of Drug Policy, 12*, 207–219.
Farthing, L., & Kohl, B. (2012). Supply-side harm reduction strategies: Bolivia's experiment with social control. *International Journal of Drug Policy, 23*, 488–494.
Ferreira, S. (2010). Portugal's drug laws draw new scrutiny. *Wall Street Journal*. European Coalition for Just and Effective Drug Policies. http://www.encod.org.
Foucault, M. (1979). *The birth of biopolitics: Lectures at the college de France 1978–1979*. New York: Palgrave Macmillan.
Foucault, M. (1991). Governmentality. In G. Burchell, C. Gordon, & P. Miller (Eds.), *The Foucault effect: Studies in governmentality*. Chicago: The University of Chicago Press.
Freeman, L., & Sierra, J. L. (2005). Mexico: The militarization trap. In C. A. Youngers & E. Rosin's (Eds.), *Drugs and democracy in Latin America: The impact of U.S. policy*. Boulder, CO: Lynne Rienner Publishers Inc.
Global Commission on Drug Policy. (2014). *Taking control: Pathways to drug policies that work*. http://www.globalcommissionondrugs.org.
Goldberg, T. (2005). Will Swedish and Dutch drug policy converge? The role of theory. *International Journal of Social Welfare, 14*, 44–54.
Greenwald, G. (2009). *Drug decriminalization in Portugal: Lessons for creating fair and successful drug policies*. The Cato Institute. http://www.cato.org.
Greenfield, V. A., & Paoli, L. (2012). If supply-oriented drug policy is broken, can harm reduction help fix it? Melding disciplines and methods to advance international drug-control policy. *International Journal of Drug Policy, 23*(1), 6–15.
Harm Reduction International. (2016). *The global state of harm reduction 2016*. https://www.hri.global.
Hathaway, A. (2001). Shortcomings of harm reduction: Toward a morally invested drug reform strategy. *International Journal of Drug Policy, 12*, 125–137.

Hughes, C. (2006). *Overcoming obstacles to reform?: Making and shaping drug policy in contemporary Portugal and Australia.* PhD thesis, Department of Criminology, University of Melbourne.

Hughes, C., & Stevens, A. (2010). What can we learn from the Portuguese decriminalisation of illicit drugs? *British Journal of Criminology, 50*, 999–1022.

Hunt, N. (2003). *A review of the evidence-base for harm reduction approaches to drug use.* Release, http://www.forward-thinking-on-drugs.org/review2.

Hunt, N., & Stevens, A. (2004). Whose harm? Harm reduction and the shift to coercion in UK drug policy. *Social Policy and Society, 3*(4), 333–342.

Inciardi, J. (Ed.). (1999). *The drug legalisation debate* (2nd ed.). Thousand Oaks: Sage Publications.

Johnson, B. (2006). The development of user influence on Swedish drug policy, 1965–2004. In J. Anker, V. Asmussen, P. Kouvonen, & D. Tops (Eds.), *Drug users and spaces for legitimate action* (NAD Monograph No. 49). Helsinki: Nordic Alcohol and Drug Council.

Keane, H. (2002). Critiques of harm reduction, morality and the promise of human rights. *International Journal of Drug Policy, 14*, 227–232.

Kellogg, S. H. (2003). On "gradualism" and the building of the harm reduction—Abstinence continuum. *Journal of Substance Abuse Treatment* 25, 241–247.

Lenton, S., & Single, E. (1998). The definition of harm reduction. *Drug and Alcohol Review, 17*, 213–220.

MacGregor, S. (2011). Written evidence to the House of Lords' enquiry into the European drug strategy. In House of Lords. *The EU drugs strategy: Oral and Written evidence Home Affairs Subcommittee of the European Select Committee.* http://www.parliament.co.uk.

Marlatt, G. A. (1996). Harm reduction: Come as you are. *Addictive Behaviours, 21*(6), 779–788.

Mendes, S. (2000). Property crime and drug enforcement in Portugal. *Criminal Justice Policy Review, 11*, 195–216.

Miller, P. (2001). A critical review of the harm minimization ideology in Australia. *Critical Public Health, 11*(2), 167–178.

Moore, D., & Fraser, S. (2006). Putting at risk what we know: Reflecting on the drug-using subject in harm reduction and its political implications. *Social Sciences and Medicine, 62*, 3035–3067.

Nadelmann E. (1993). Progressive legalizers, progressive prohibitionists and the reduction of drug-related harm. In N. Heather, A. Wodak, & E. Nadelmann (Eds.), *Psychoactive drugs and harm reduction: From faith to science.* London: Whurr Publishers.

Newcombe, R. (1992). The reduction of drug related harm: A conceptual framework for theory, practice and research. In O'Hare et al. (Eds.), *The reduction of drug related harm*. London: Routledge.
O'Hare, P. (2007). Merseyside, the first harm reduction conferences, and the early history of harm reduction. *International Journal of Drug Policy, 18*, 141–144.
O'Malley, P. (2009). *Drugs, risks and freedoms: Illicit drug "use" and "misuse" under neo-liberal governance* (Legal Studies Research Paper No. 09/120). Sydney Law School.
Pinto Coelho, M. (2010). *Decriminalization of drugs in Portugal—The real facts!* World Federation Against Drugs, 2 February. http://www.wfad.se/latest-news/1articles/123-decriminalization-of-drugs-in-portugal–the-real-facts.
Portuguese Institute for Drugs and Drug Addiction. (2005). *National plan against drugs and drug addiction 2005–2012: Executive Summary.* http://www.idt.pt.
Portuguese Institute for Drugs and Drug Addiction. (2008). *'Portugal': New development, trends and in-depth information on selected issues*. 2008 National Report (2007 data) to the EMCDDA by the Reitox Focal Point. https://idt.pt.
Race, K. (2008). The use of pleasure in harm reduction: Perspectives from the history of sexuality. *International Journal of Drug Policy, 19*, 417–423.
Rhodes, T. (2002). The risk environment: A framework for understanding and reducing drug related harm. *International Journal of Drug Policy, 13*, 85–94.
Rhodes, T. (2009). Risk environments and drug harms: A social sciences for harm reduction. *International Journal of Drug Policy, 20*, 193–201.
Rhodes, T., & Hedrich, D. (2010). Harm reduction and the mainstream. In European Monitoring Centre for Drugs and Drug Addiction's (Eds.), *Harm reduction: Evidence, impacts and challenges*. https://www.emcdda.europa.eu.
Roe, G. (2006). Harm reduction as paradigm: Is better than bad good enough? The origins of harm reduction. *Critical Public Health, 15*(3), 243–250.
Rolleston Report. (1926). *Departmental committee on Morphine and Heroin addiction*. London: HMSO.
Ruane, D. (2015). Harm reduction of psychedelic support? Caring for drug-related crises at transformational festivals. *Journal of Electronic Dancemusic Culture, 7*(1), 55–75.
Souleymanov, R., & Allman, D. (2016). Articulating connections between the harm reduction paradigm and the marginalisation of people who use illicit drugs. *British Journal of Social Work, 46*, 1429–1445.

Stevens, A. (2011). *Drugs, crime and public health: The political economy of drug policy*. London: Routledge-Cavendish.

Stevens, A., & Hughes, C. (2016). Decriminalisation and public health: The Portuguese approach to drug policy (translation). *Mouvement, 86*, 22–33.

Stimson, G. V. (1995). AIDS and injecting drug use in the United Kingdom, 1987–1993: The policy response and the prevention of the epidemic. *Social Science Medicine, 41*(5), 699–716.

Strang, J., Babor, T., Caulkins, J., Fischer, B., Foxcroft, D., & Humphreys, K. (2012). Drug policy and the public good: Evidence for effective interventions. *The Lancet, 379*, 71–83.

Szalavitz, M. (2009). Drugs in Portugal: Did decriminalisation work? *Time*. http://www.time.com.

Transform. (2014). *Drug decriminalisation in Portugal: Setting the record straight*. https://www.tdpf.org.uk.

United Nations Development Programme. (2015). *Perspectives on the development dimensions of drug control policy*. https://www.undp.org.

UNODC. (2016). *Outcome document of the 2016 United Nations General Assembly special session on the world drug problem. Our joint commitment to effectively addressing and countering the world drug problem*. New York: United Nations. http://www.unodc.org/documents.

van het Loo, M., van Beusekom, I., & Kahan, J. (2002). Decriminalisation of drug use in Portugal: The development of a policy. *Annals of the American Academy of Political and Social Science, 582*, 49–63.

Vastag, B. (2009, April 7). 5 year's after: Portugal's decriminalization policy shows positive results. *Scientific American*. http://www.scientificamerican.com.

4

Step Three: Encourage the Development of Innovative Strategies of Drug Control

Most countries around the world collect data on drug prevalence and related issues within their national borders. This information is fed up to international bodies, for example the European Monitoring Centre for Drugs and Drug Addiction (EMCDDA) and the Organization of the American States (OAS) Inter-American Drug Abuse Control Commission (CICAD). In turn, the United Nations Office on Drugs and Crime (UNODC) produces an annual 'world drug report' based on collated regional evidence. Yet this plethora of data, collected in some cases over several decades, has not enabled national and international policy makers to identify individual drug control strategies and suggest, with any degree of certainty, that they have been successful. Whatever kind of drug strategy has been employed—whether repressive or liberal, demand or supply focused, law enforcement or harm reduction orientated—no country has eliminated, or significantly reduced, the prevalence of drugs. The vast majority of countries around the world contain active drug users who continue to experience drug-related problems such as ill-health and criminalisation, indicating that drug-related harm has not been eliminated either.

One of the difficulties in ascertaining success is that there is no common global understanding of success in the drug policy arena and,

C. Chatwin, *Towards More Effective Global Drug Policies*,
https://doi.org/10.1007/978-3-319-92072-6_4

hence, common indicators of success are under-developed (Flynn 2001). Taking Europe as an example, in Sweden, the generally low levels of prevalence of drug use (EMCDDA 2015) have been attributed to the uniformity and totality of their zero-tolerance approach to illicit drugs, and have been deemed to be a strong indication of the 'success' of their policy in global terms (UNODC 2007). In the Netherlands meanwhile, where levels of prevalence are generally higher, the decreasing number of dependent drug users and their general health and longevity (EMCDDA 2015), have been similarly drawn upon to indicate the 'success' of the Dutch approach (Grund and Breeksema 2013). In this case, whether you think Swedish or Dutch drug policy more successful will depend on whether you think the primary goal of drug policy should be to reduce the overall number of drug users, or to reduce the harm experienced by those who use drugs. On the global stage, these problems of interpretation are exacerbated.

Another issue concerns the differential experience of illicit drugs in global terms. Some countries primarily experience the consumption of drugs, others the production of drugs, and yet others the trafficking or movement of drugs through their borders. According to Strang et al. (2012): some countries are in the midst of a specific drug epidemic, while others are dealing with the after effects of an epidemic that peaked 10 years ago; for some heroin is the main drug of choice for dependent drug users, while in others, for example much of South and Central America, it is cocaine and/or amphetamines; and needle exchange programmes and substitution treatment options may be highly relevant in countries where injecting is the primary route of use, whereas they are of much lesser importance in a country where smoking or inhaling is the norm.

Furthermore, evidence suggests that large cities, no matter where in the world they are located, are likely to have more in common with each other in terms of drug-related issues, than are a city and a rural area in the same country (Chatwin 2011; Kaplan and Leuw 1996). These factors have also contributed to the difficulty in determining the success of individual policy strategies as what works in one place may well be useless in another: "the specific problems and the most appropriate type of interventions will vary over time and between societies and geographical locations" (Strang et al. 2012: 80). Finally, as many scholars have commented (for example, Chatwin 2011; Stevens 2011; Reinarman et al. 2004) there is little evidence to suggest much relationship between drug control strategies and drug prevalence/harm trends in general.

With these points in mind, this chapter argues that encouraging diversity and innovation in drug policy strategies is something that should be aimed for in the global response to illicit drugs. While nothing has proved to be particularly successful, nobody agrees on what success looks like, and different strategies are likely to be successful in different global locations, it simply does not make sense to limit the number of options on the table. This chapter begins with an exploration of the 'room for manoeuvre' in terms of innovation and diversity in international drug policy. It offers a detailed account of some of the different strategies related to decriminalisation and regulation of illicit substances—particularly cannabis—currently in operation around the globe, and the benefits this range of options can bring. Finally, it suggests that international drug conventions do limit the potential for variety in global drug policy and explores avenues of reform here.

Room for Manoeuvre: Flexibility Within the International Drug Conventions

The first area to explore is how much variety and innovation are allowed under the international drug conventions. While the vast majority of countries around the world are signatories of the international drug conventions, that there is some degree of flexibility contained within them is evidenced by the wide range of drug control strategies implemented around the globe. Some countries operate very strict drug control policies that may even include the death penalty for drug-related offences and which coerce drug users into treatment programmes that may include forced labour and inhumane practices. Others have implemented much more tolerant systems where the use and possession of small amounts of illegal substances have been removed from the criminal justice system altogether and instead are dealt with via civil or administrative penalties.

Several evaluations of the international drug control conventions (Bewley-Taylor and Jelsma 2011; Bewley-Taylor and Jelsma 2012; Bewley-Taylor et al. 2014; Dorn and Jamieson 2000) have provided clear evidence that flexibility surrounds, in particular, the penalties instituted against the use and possession of illicit drugs for personal use. Bewley-Taylor and Jelsma (2012: 3) suggest that the international conventions are "the result of political compromise [and their] interpretation…should be seen as an art not a science". For example, despite their strongly prohibitive stance, the treaties do not actually require the use of drugs and the possession of small amounts of drugs for personal use to be treated as 'serious' offences (Bewley-Taylor and Jelsma 2011). Even greater flexibility is allowed by the provision of an "escape clause" (Bewley-Taylor and Jelsma 2012: 6) stating that whether or not these behaviours are criminalised is dependent on the constitutional principles and basic concepts of an individual country. It can thus be inferred that if a country can argue that criminalising the use and possession of illicit substances for personal use is unconstitutional, then they can proceed with alternative strategies. As Bewley-Taylor and Jelsma (2012) document, this escape clause has been invoked in several instances—for example, Argentina, the Netherlands, Alaska and Germany.

Further flexibility enters the treaties via the relatively vague interpretations of medical use—if an illegal drug can be found to have medical benefits, then that can also be used as a reason to seek alternatives to criminalisation, for medical users of the substance at least (Bewley-Taylor and Jelsma 2011). Harm reduction strategies outlined in the previous chapter, even the more controversial ones such as the provision of drug consumption rooms, can also be argued for under the terms of the treaties as they are related to the use of illicit substances, rather than their production, supply or trafficking (Bewley-Taylor and Jelsma 2012). Finally, there is scope for the provision of social care rather than punishment for the users of drugs and, according to Dorn and Jamieson's (2000) review of national drug policy flexibility in the UK, for the separation of 'social supply' (very low-level supply activities that take place among friends and not for profit) (Potter 2009) from the more serious supply side offences.

Flexibility around the treatment of drug use and drug users is responsible for many of the significant differences in national strategies around the globe. It is the reason some signatories to the international conventions imprison (or even kill) their drug users, others coerce them into inhumane treatment systems, while still others protect them from criminalisation and facilitate their use of drugs in less risky or harmful ways. It is important, however, to note that these flexibilities do have limits and would be severely stretched by the creation of fully regulated legal markets, as recently seen in Uruguay and some American states for cannabis. Flexibility is further confined to the realms of use and possession of illegal substances for personal use. In terms of supply and trafficking offences, there is a lot less room for manoeuvre. These behaviours must be criminalised, penalised, and generally treated as the more serious types of offences.

A brief perusal of the international conventions has demonstrated that the scope for variety and innovation in drug policy *does* exist, at least in relation to the use and users of drugs. Cannabis is a substance which has long attracted the greatest degree of variety and innovation in relation to its governance, as many countries have come to view it as less harmful than other substances. Examples of innovative drug policy strategies in relation to cannabis abound, and include several recent and controversial developments. It is this area of policy—the use and possession of cannabis for personal use—to which we now turn to further document the variety of policy options developed in this area and to explore the boundaries of flexibility in the international conventions.

Variety and Innovation in Cannabis Control Around the Globe

As already established, the variety of policy options for cannabis have developed as a result of flexibility within the international conventions regarding the treatment of drug use and drug users which has led to the depenalisation, decriminalisation or regulation of certain drugs in certain situations. Terms such as these are often used interchangeably, but actually represent distinct points on a drug policy continuum from criminalisation to legalisation. Depenalisation denotes a policy where a particular behaviour (e.g. use of cannabis) remains criminal but the punishment of imprisonment has been removed, decriminalisation denotes a policy where a behaviour is no longer criminalised but punishments (e.g. fines, warnings) can still be applied, and regulation denotes a policy where a behaviour is not criminalised and cannot be punished, but where certain restrictions apply (e.g. as is the case for use of alcohol and tobacco). Depenalisation and decriminalisation are relatively well established policy options with various UN bodies (such as UNAIDS and the World Health Organisation) endorsing their success and historical experience demonstrating that they do not result in catastrophic drug epidemics (Eastwood et al. 2012).

Eastwood et al. (2012) describe how some countries (for example, Uruguay and Spain) never criminalised cannabis use and possession in the first place and others have had decriminalisation policies in place since the early 1970s (for example, the Netherlands and the American state of California. The Transnational Institute (TNI) (2016: 6) also highlights how some countries (for example, Morocco, India and Cambodia) criminalised cannabis, but effectively "turned a blind eye" to their own laws and tolerated cannabis use and users for all practical intents and purposes. In terms of those that have overtly depenalised or decriminalised cannabis, it is important to recognise that this has been done in a variety of ways sometimes relying on, for example, arguments of medical or religious need, and at other times on arguments about lack of public interest in prosecutions in this area.

In the past fifteen years, however, many more countries have moved towards the decriminalisation model, mainly in relation to cannabis, but sometimes in relation to the possession of all drugs for personal use. Within Europe, with its propensity for harm reduction and tendency to be at the forefront of liberal drug policy, examples of depenalisation (Austria, Germany and Poland) and decriminalisation (Luxembourg, Croatia, and Slovenia) abound (EMCDDA 2017a). Portugal represents the most developed European decriminalisation model—as outlined in the previous chapter, the possession of all drugs for personal use was decriminalised in 2001 as part of the overhaul of national drug laws to align them with public health principles. Elsewhere, Argentina,

Armenia, Australia, Chile, Colombia, Costa Rica, Ecuador, Jamaica, Mexico, Paraguay and Peru have all adopted some form of decriminalisation policy as part of a new wave (Eastwood et al. 2012).

Even more recently, some countries/regions (for example, Uruguay and various American States) have taken further steps in relation to their *cannabis* policies, surpassing the decriminalisation of this drug by implementing fully regulated markets that also encompass the production and/or supply of cannabis. These regulated markets, often operating on a fully commercialised basis, present a significant challenge to the existing international drug conventions which stipulate that all signatories must prohibit illegal drugs. Sticking to cannabis, this chapter will now provide some examples of innovations in policy that go beyond the depenalisation or decriminalisation of cannabis *use* and move towards the decriminalisation or regulation of the *supply* of cannabis.

The Not-for-Profit Collective Cultivation Model: Cannabis Clubs in Spain

A recent cannabis policy innovation is provided by the development of cannabis social clubs, first in Spain and then elsewhere. Spain has long been a country with a relatively liberal approach towards the control of drug use and drug possession. Never formally criminalised, since the 1970s, the possession of small amounts of any drug has been consistently diverted from the criminal justice system, or decriminalised. Subsequent legal decisions established that shared consumption, joint purchase and the gifting of drugs for compassionate (e.g. medical) reasons were also decriminalised (Barriuso Alonso 2011). In relation to cannabis particularly, cultivation, provided it was on a scale for personal use, became somewhat established as a matter outside the auspices of the criminal justice system. In the 1990s, cannabis activists built on the combination of legal practices described above, to argue for the right to cultivate cannabis collectively.

In 2001, the first 'cannabis social club' was realised. Members of these clubs must already be established as cannabis users and invited to join by existing members. They pay a small fee to cover the running of the operation to the club, which uses that money to grow a cannabis crop based on the combined demand of the existing membership. All members are entitled to share in the harvest. It is important to note here that this was not a top-down measure driven by the Spanish government or an attempt to regulate the supply of cannabis officially, but was rather an informal model that arose through the "persistent testing of Spain's legal boundaries by civil society" (Marks 2015: 4). Since its inception, this model has grown exponentially, and most recent estimates suggest there are now between 800 and 1000 cannabis social clubs operating throughout Spain (Decorte et al. 2017), although it must be remembered that estimates are difficult due to the transitive and sometimes clandestine nature of these clubs.

As Spanish cannabis social clubs have never been officially regulated by the government, they remain largely self-regulating, but a number of common principles have been laid out and largely, at least originally, adhered to by social clubs themselves. These have been summarised as: registering as a regional and official association; seeking to reduce the harms associated with the supply and use of cannabis (e.g. by promoting responsible consumption); being closed to the general public who have not become members; imposing limits on the quantities of cannabis consumed by individuals (e.g. 3 grams per person per day); supplying cannabis only for immediate use (e.g. by only allowing small amounts of cannabis to be taken away); and, crucially, operating on a not-for-profit basis (Murkin 2015).

Since the development of cannabis social clubs in Spain, other countries have seen the benefits and several have attempted to institute their own cannabis social clubs. For example: cannabis social clubs have been tolerated in Belgium, Slovenia and the Netherlands; are being considered in Switzerland and Germany; operate in secret in France, Italy and the UK; and have been established, but are not yet cultivating in Austria (Marks 2015). Bewley-Taylor et al. (2014) also document their presence in Argentina, Colombia and Chile, and they have become adopted by Uruguay as a part of their regulation of the entire cannabis market (explored further later in this chapter). This popularity has led the European Coalition for Just and Effective Drug Policies to establish a set of cross-country principles authenticating the model which include: that supply must be dictated by demand (i.e. the amount of cannabis grown depends on how many members a club has); non-profitability; transparency (of organisation, cultivation methods, major decisions) for members; a public health orientation; and a willingness to enter into dialogue with authorities (ENCOD 2014).

One of the main reasons behind the popularity of cannabis social clubs is encapsulated by Barriuso Alonso (2011: 6) as lying largely in the decision to create a not for profit system in stark contrast to the existing black market: "The constant quest for profit has brought about underhand practices, increases in health risks…, and reduced consumers to a passive role where their only possible decision is to buy or not to buy. In a CSC [cannabis social club] on the other hand, members have greater rights and decision-making capacity about their consumption than they would have in a commercial relationship". Marks (2015: 10) has further documented that, since the introduction of social cannabis clubs to Spain, "there has been an increase in the amount of cannabis cultivated, a decrease in the amount of cannabis imported and a decrease in the amount of cannabis consumed". The decrease in the amount of cannabis consumed is of particular importance as critics of any relaxation in cannabis policy often suggest that any relaxation will inevitably lead to an increase in the amount of cannabis consumed. Here, the opposite has been shown to be the case. Finally, the introduction of cannabis social clubs is thought to be a relatively 'soft' change to cannabis laws, at least in countries where the possession of cannabis for social use is already decriminalised, and, as such, would not represent a contravention of international treaties (Bewley Taylor et al. 2014).

There are, of course, also important weaknesses in the cannabis social clubs model. Bewley Taylor et al. (2014) note that commercialisation is creeping into the Spanish system with entrepreneurs attracted to the market and creating ever larger clubs that cannot hope to satisfy their needs by small-scale cultivation, and which must presumably look elsewhere to supplement their supply. Decorte (2015), in his work which is primarily centred on Belgian cannabis social clubs, further suggests that the different rules applied by different organisations, and the transient nature of those organisations, are also weaknesses, and adds that social clubs remain vulnerable to criminalisation, the involvement of profit driven actors, and violence from rival criminal entrepreneurs involved in the black market. Many of these problems could, of course, be solved by official recognition of cannabis social clubs and legal overview of their guidelines and regulations.

One final point to draw out here is that the precise details of the operation of cannabis social clubs can and should differ across different legal jurisdictions. Just as the cannabis social club model won't be right for every country, in countries where the model is adopted, its implementation will differ according to local laws. "The CSC cannot be patented—it is an idea, a theoretical concept. In each country, region, perhaps even in every city, both activists and authorities will have to find their own interpretation" (ENCOD 2014: 1). This lends further weight to the argument laid out at the beginning of this chapter that there are no universal solutions to different facets of the illegal drugs issue and that to attempt to reduce the number of available options for controlling the use of drugs is a dubious strategy.

Cannabis Use for Medical and Religious Purposes: The Jamaican Drug Law Amendment

Another model of recent innovative cannabis provision concerns the decriminalisation or regulation of cannabis for medical use. Many countries have recently legalised non-psychoactive forms of cannabis such as CBD extracts for medicinal purposes, but that is not the main focus of the discussion here. Instead, this section discusses the decriminalisation or regulation of cannabis itself, with all its psychoactive effects, when it is used, possessed, cultivated or exchanged for medical purposes. Even this is a fairly widespread model with several countries in Europe (including Croatia, the Czech Republic, Finland, Germany, Italy and the Netherlands) and elsewhere (Argentina, Australia, Canada, Chile, Colombia and Israel) operating medical cannabis systems.

Perhaps the most well known systems of medical cannabis come from the, now more than 20, American states that have adopted the system. California, for example, became the first state to create a regulated market for use of cannabis for medical purposes in 1996. At first, change happened slowly with dispensaries reluctant to get involved and fearful that they would face sanctions but, over the years, the model accelerated rapidly into the commercialised and popular system that exists today. Klein (2016) reports that in 2005 there were only four medical cannabis dispensaries in Los Angeles, but by 2009 the figure had jumped to 800 and documents the changing nature of the market during that time period: "In less than half a decade the cannabis marketing system in California underwent a dramatic transformation, moving from an illegal underground market to a large semi-legal market operating visibly and in the open" (Klein 2016: 85). Part of this acceleration in provision of medical cannabis was facilitated by a 2003 change in law which allowed individuals to register voluntarily as medical cannabis patients, making their access to dispensaries easier. It is important to note that this amendment did not create any specific guidelines for officially regulating dispensaries, meaning that regulation is devolved to local administrations and varies widely (Freisthler and Gruenewald 2014).

What sets the more recent Jamaican medical cannabis model apart from previous systems is its attempt to regulate fully the provision of medical cannabis and its inclusion of the decriminalisation of the use of cannabis for religious or sacramental purposes in addition to medical purposes. Jamaica has long been a country where cannabis is readily available with a significant amount being grown on Jamaican soil for export to other countries, yet it has also employed relatively strict laws against cannabis possession and has experienced a high volume of arrests and criminal justice system interactions with respect to this substance (Davenport and Pardo 2016). In 2015, the Jamaican government passed an act that decriminalised the possession of up to 2 oz of cannabis, allowed the cultivation of up to 5 plants by individuals, and aimed to create a licensing authority to oversee the regulation of cannabis production and sale for scientific, medical, therapeutic and religious purposes. The full details of the system are still under development, but it is expected that retail licenses will be granted to pharmacies that can sell for medical/therapeutic purposes, herb houses that can sell for immediate consumption, and spas that use cannabis based products as part of the range of treatments that they offer (Jones et al. 2017). Unusually in the world of cannabis policy innovation, tourists and visitors to Jamaica will be allowed to purchase permits to use cannabis for medical, therapeutic or religious reasons.

Davenport and Pardo (2016: 60) highlight that the aims behind the Jamaican amendment are to "deliver economic impact and reduce criminal justice costs". They suggest that the Jamaican authorities are seeking to capitalise on their position as already established producers of cannabis and hoping to draw this source of revenue into the official economy, surmising that, as the rest of the world becomes more liberal in their cannabis policy, Jamaica might be well placed to supply them officially with the substance. There is some evidence to suggest that these aims may be realised, with Canada reportedly exploring Jamaican supply options for their medical cannabis market (TNI 2015), and Snap (2016) reporting 14,000 fewer arrests since the amendment was passed. Snap (2016: 20) also designates the amendment as part of a "paradigm shift" amongst Latin American countries that have experienced particularly negative effects of the war on drugs and are seeking to implement progressive policy innovations.

The Jamaican innovations demonstrate a new way of addressing cannabis control without providing a direct challenge to the international conventions: "The Amendments were everywhere lauded for the creativity and deftness with which they achieved a balance between observing Jamaica's international obligations to control the use of narcotics, while creating sufficient space within the existing domestic legal regime to allow the emergence of a legal, medical and therapeutic industry" (Hylton 2016). Bewley-Taylor et al. (2014), however, caution that cannabis is included in the strictest schedules of the international treaties, meaning that their medical and therapeutic benefits are not officially recognised, and that similar innovations, for example in US states, have previously attracted the disapproval of the International Narcotics Control Board.

In addition to these concerns about whether the innovations do honour the terms of the international conventions, other critiques have been levelled against the Jamaican proposals. Davenport and Pardo (2016) call into question the ability for the official system to replace the existing well established illegal market via which cannabis can currently be obtained very cheaply and without recourse to the application for permits or the use of licensed premises. Jones (2016), in his work with small scale farmers in Jamaica growing cannabis illegally, casts doubt on whether the cannabis currently grown would be of high enough quality to satisfy international markets such as those operating in Canada. Finally, Jones et al. (2017) raise the important issue highlighted earlier in this chapter of whether the amendments will work in Jamaica. They argue that the regulations draw heavily on existing schemes already implemented in North America with little regard to local customs and practices, and may not work as intended within the Jamaican environment. It remains to be seen whether this will be the case, but the example does chime with the idea that there are no universal drug policy solutions, and that what works well in one environment may well not work in others. It will be interesting to watch further developments in this area.

A Partially Regulated Market: Coffeeshop Policy in the Netherlands

Perhaps one of the most well-known and longest standing drug policy innovations with regard to cannabis comes from the Netherlands. In the 1970s, alarmed by rising numbers of young people criminalised for their use of cannabis under existing policy, the Dutch government implemented a change which recognised a difference between cannabis as a 'soft' drug and other, more dangerous, 'hard' drugs such as heroin, cocaine and amphetamines (Boekhaut van Solinge 1999). Keeping in line with the international conventions, the use and sale of small amounts of cannabis was to be tolerated under the principle of expediency, which designates that while the sale and possession of cannabis remains illegal, it is never in the public interest to prosecute where relatively small amounts are concerned. The key aim here was to effect a 'separation of the markets' between hard and soft drugs, so that young users of cannabis would be protected from coming into contact with the suppliers of more dangerous drugs. Originally, the government envisioned a system of 'house dealers' being permitted to sell cannabis products to young people attending youth clubs under protection from prosecution. By the 1980s, in response to a wider age demographic seeking to benefit from this policy, a small network of commercial premises where the small-scale sale and open use of cannabis were tolerated (coffeeshops) had emerged and, in the 1980s, were officially recognised by Dutch authorities (Tops 2001).

Over the intervening years, the coffeeshop policy has attracted external criticism and the system has been subjected to increasing regulation. In the 1980s they were not permitted to advertise themselves, to cause undue public nuisance, to sell to people under 18 years of age, to sell more than 30 grams to any one customer or to sell or permit the use of hard drugs on the premises (de Kort and Cramer 1999). In the 1990s, they were further restricted from operating near a school, selling more than 5 grams to any one customer and keeping more than 500 grams on the premises at a time. Local authorities were granted more extensive powers to ban or close coffeeshops contravening any of the regulations and municipal governments were granted the autonomy to decide whether to allow coffeeshops within their boundaries at all (Boekhout van Solinge 1999). Intraval (2007) figures show that there has been a decrease in the overall numbers of coffee shops as well as in the numbers of municipalities with any coffeeshops at all. More recently, a raft of restrictive measures has been proposed which some have seen as resulting from a paradigmatic shift in Dutch drug policy in general (Lemmens 2003; Uitermark 2004). These, however, have met with limited success.

In 2012, in an effort to further curb the use of cannabis and the nuisance arising from drug tourism, the government attempted to introduce a 'weedpass' system whereby Dutch cannabis users had to register to use coffeeshops and being granted access required citizenship (Grund and Breeksema 2013). The initiative was extremely unpopular with Dutch cannabis users and early evaluations in Maastricht, where a trial had been initiated prior to 2012, swiftly demonstrated that implementation resulted in low numbers of registrations and a significant increase in use of illegal markets (Wouters et al. 2012). The mayor of Amsterdam refused to implement the measure and there are now only a few Southern municipalities which still operate it. Similarly, the Dutch government has stated its intention to disallow sales of cannabis that have a 15% or higher tetrahydrocannabinol (THC) content (Grund and Breeksema 2013), but have struggled to implement this restriction.

Historical data demonstrates that, although overall levels of cannabis use have increased in the Netherlands since the introduction of the separation of the markets policy, these increases have been in line with European trends and current prevalence levels are just above the European average (Chatwin 2015). Supporters of Dutch cannabis policy (Rolles 2014; Grund and Breeksema 2013) point out that, regardless of whether it has reduced *cannabis* use, an effective separation of the markets for cannabis and other drugs has contributed to a relatively low number of dependent drug users, drug-related deaths and levels of HIV/AIDS and other infectious diseases found amongst the drug using population. Furthermore, statistics (EMCDDA 2017b) demonstrate an ageing of the population of dependent drug users, indicating that fewer young people are becoming dependent on drug use and indicating further success of the separation of the markets policy.

One final important point to note in relation to the Dutch coffeeshop policy is that it represents a significant inconsistency as there is no provision within the Dutch law for the supply of cannabis to coffeeshops. While 'front door' sales have been legitimised, the 'backdoor' cultivation or supply of cannabis remains wholly a part of the illegal market, meaning that it is only a partially regulated market. In contrast with recent government policy, public opinion polls suggest that a majority favour extending the current system so the entire cannabis market is regulated. In 2013, 65% of those surveyed reported that they would be in favour of introducing to the Netherlands a more comprehensive system whereby the production, sale and consumption of cannabis were all legalised (Rolles 2014). Furthermore, 41 municipalities within the Netherlands have endorsed a manifesto proposing the regulation of cannabis production, and 25 of the 38 largest municipalities have applied to the Ministry of Justice for permission to experiment with various forms of authorised cannabis production and wholesale supply (Rolles 2014).

Fully Regulated Markets: US States and Uruguay

Fully regulated cannabis markets, often described as operating from 'seed' (production of cannabis) through to sale, go one step further than any of the models previously discussed. They are not confined to the decriminalisation of possession for personal use, the home cultivation of a few plants for personal use, or the possession/sale of cannabis for specific (usually medical) purposes. Instead, they offer a system whereby cannabis can be officially obtained for recreational purposes via a licit and regulated market. It is the decriminalisation of cannabis sales, specifically, that represents innovation in these cases (Kilmer and Pacula 2016). While decriminalisation of possession and small scale home cultivation can be justified within the 'wriggle room' of the international treaties, Room (2013: 345) declares that "without question" fully regulated markets are operating outside the confines of the treaties. The "limits of latitude are … clearly established and finite" (Bewley Taylor et al. 2014: 52), meaning that international rules and agreements are being broken.

Yet, since 2012, there have been several geographical locations which have created fully regulated, commercial cannabis markets. The majority of these have been in the United States: Alaska, California, Colorado, Oregon, Massachusetts, Maine, Nevada and Washington. (The District of Colombia has also regulated personal use and home cultivation, but does not allow commercial sales so is not discussed here). The first US states to apply this model were Colorado and Washington where members of the general public voted, in respective referenda, to create fully regulated cannabis markets. As the states with the most long-standing experiences in this area, as well as having been subject to the most extensive academic scrutiny, Colorado and Washington will remain the focus of the discussion here.

The American efforts to create fully regulated cannabis markets should be viewed as "part of a long running process of 'softening' the official zero-tolerance approach" (Crick et al. 2013: 1), and as an extension of the prevalent medical marijuana laws already existent. It is significant to note that, in all American States, the innovations were dependent on voter approval. Key motivations from the respective campaigns included reduction of the impact of the black market, fewer cannabis related arrests and criminal justice interventions, limited access to cannabis for young people, greater assurance of product quality, a reduction in criminal justice system overall costs, and a source of revenue generation via taxes (Bewley Taylor et al. 2014).

There are many similarities between the systems in operation in Colorado and Washington (and elsewhere in the US excluding the reforms in the District of Colombia). They are based on regulation of production, processing and sale of cannabis, and aim to regulate each of these stages via licensing systems. Additionally, they both place age limits on sales (over 21), the amount that can be purchased/possessed at any one time and limit the provision of retail outlets so that they are not, for example, in the vicinity of schools. Finally, they have both implemented taxation systems on the market, rigid security conditions, third party laboratory testing, and complex tracking systems that aim to monitor individual plants from production right through to sale (Bewley Taylor et al. 2014).

Within these broadly similar systems, there are of course important differences regarding the detail of the regulations: for example, home cultivation of up to six plants, access to the system by tourists and visitors and the provision of medical cannabis are all allowed in Colorado, but not in Washington. In Colorado entrepreneurs are allowed to produce *and* sell cannabis products, whereas in Washington each stage of the process is separated out, so those who produce the drug cannot also sell it. In Colorado, different regions of the state can opt out of the need to have cannabis dispensaries, whereas this is not possible in Washington. Licensing fees are generally lower in Washington, while in Colorado a large proportion of the revenue generated is pledged to go directly into funding the State's education system.

A key feature of systems in both Washington and Colorado, worthy of particular note here, is their commercialisation, meaning that it is an aim of the respective systems to create a profit driven market for cannabis. This aspect of the American states' (apart from the District of Colombia) regulated cannabis markets has attracted criticism. Pardo (2014) details how American laws around free speech have made it difficult to place restrictions on the advertisements of cannabis products and Caulkins and Kilmer (2015) caution that once many individual entrepreneurs and businesses become invested in the market, it can be difficult to make significant changes and maintain flexibility within the system. These are important points: previous experience suggests that fully commercial markets (as we have for alcohol and tobacco) may not be the best models for protecting health and minimising problematic use, and have led 2013: 347) to accuse the American systems of "losing sight of a coherent public health perspective".

Finally, in relation to the experience in these American states, it is important to remember that these individual systems are in direct contravention of Federal United States laws. Obama issued a statement explaining that he would not seek to interfere in the voter led Colorado and Washington innovations, but this commitment is somewhat questionable under the new Trump presidency which seems, at this stage, much less favourable towards any relaxations of cannabis policy. There is still a question mark over the entire enterprise because Federal laws, which continue to prohibit cannabis, officially take precedence over state laws. Furthermore, the International Narcotics Control Board (INCB), charged with guarding the interests of the international conventions, has voiced "grave concerns" (Bewley Taylor et al. 2014: 55) over the American developments indicating some degree of international disapproval and placing the US, as traditional aggressive champion of the treaties, in a very awkward position.

Recent innovations in Uruguay have gone even further than the American states, instituting a nationwide seed to sale regulated cannabis market. Uruguay has always operated a liberal drug policy, never criminalising the personal possession of cannabis (or any other drug). In 2012, however, as part of an overall strategy to improve public safety, the then President Mujica, aimed to alleviate perceived violence levels and separate the markets for cannabis from other more dangerous substances such as 'Pasta Base' (similar to free base cocaine) (Musto 2017), by introducing a regulated cannabis market. The system, still not fully operational in all aspects, allows access to cannabis by one of three methods: home cultivation of up to 6 plants, membership of an officially regulated network of cannabis social clubs, or via a licensed pharmacies system.

Over and above the nationwide nature of the innovations, there are other noteworthy key differences between the models operated in Uruguay and the American states. Cerda and Kilmer (2017) describe the Uruguayan system as operating a 'middle ground' between prohibition and full commercialisation as operated in the US. Rather than a market free for all, retail sales will only be tolerated as part of a heavily regulated (Walsh and Ramsey 2016), paternalistic system where users will be required to register as such and will be subjected to strict limits on the overall amount they can purchase or produce. The Uruguayan authorities have also committed to keeping the overall price of cannabis at very low levels in order to reduce the black market more effectively. Also noteworthy is the top-down nature of the implementation. In many other jurisdictions (for example, the US, the Netherlands and Spain), innovations have arisen due to public opinion pressure or because of grassroots led initiatives that have gradually become officially tolerated. While grassroots organisations did have some influence on the Uruguayan initiative, particularly in the development of the home cultivation and cannabis social club branches of the proposals (Musto 2017), the Uruguayan cannabis regulation was largely pushed through by the President himself and other members of the political elite. The general public was consistently and significantly against the implementation of the proposals (Cerda and Kilmer 2017).

Uruguay has experienced some difficulties with the implementation of their system. For example, cannabis social clubs have been relatively difficult to get off the ground and remain a less popular route for obtaining cannabis, in part due to the strict regulations governing their size and making it difficult for them to be financially viable (Queirolo et al. 2016). Another example is provided by the system of cannabis retail via licensed pharmacies which only started operations in 2017 and is still working on a very limited basis. Cerdo and Kilmer (2017) posit that this could be due to the extremely complex nature of implementing a fully regulated cannabis distribution system. Indeed, the actual implementation of regulated cannabis markets can be more difficult than passing legislation in the first place, and similar implementation problems have been experienced in other areas, such as Oregon. The need for users to register in order to gain access to their cannabis has also caused concern amongst the grassroots supporters of the legislation.

Broadly speaking, however, the advantages of the Uruguayan system are thought to outweigh the disadvantages. In direct comparison with American systems, Pardo (2014: 733) outlines the main advantages as "the ability to prohibit advertising and branding, the potential for state monopoly distribution, and the ability to set prices and organise the production market". Unsurprisingly, the Uruguayan innovations have attracted the censure of the International Narcotics Control Board and Bewley Taylor et al. (2014: 58) describe the relationship as "troubled [as] Uruguayan officials have struggled to find the right legal justification for their model of cannabis regulation under the UN treaty regime, or to provide proper argumentation justifying the need to breach it." Based on the examples provided by the US states and Uruguay, other countries, such as Canada, are now seeking to implement their own versions of a fully regulated cannabis market.

The Benefits of Diversity and Innovation in Drug Policy

The previous section largely focused on the discussion of *one* broadly connected subset of drug policy innovations (around the creation of decriminalised and regulated markets for illegal substances) in relation to *one* substance (cannabis). Of course, this is not to suggest that important and interesting drug policy innovations are not taking place in other areas of the drug policy debate or in relation to other substances. The main point, however, of this extended example has been to emphasise the variety of innovative drug control. In relation to this example, a system which allows first the creation of decriminalised or regulated markets for cannabis, and then further allows the development of many variations on the theme, is more desirable than one which doesn't allow the creation of drug policy innovations, or which restricts the forms which those innovations can take. This section explores the benefits inherent in a system which allows this kind of innovation in drug policy.

With policy making in general, what has worked in one place, will not necessarily work in another. With reference to the example explored above, different approaches to innovation in cannabis policy will be acceptable and/or effective dependent on geographical location, specific experience of the drug problem, existing legislation, size of the area or region (e.g. city or rural area), different political and cultural contexts, and many other factors. ENCOD (2014) and Quierolo et al. (2016) make this point in relation to cannabis clubs which work differently in different places dependent on existing cannabis legislation and whether they are envisioned as part of a more fully regulated market or not. Jones (2016) discusses the point in relation to Jamaica where he suggests, innovations may have been made without due attention to different cultural and political contexts, and without due consideration of the existing illegal drug market.

Furthermore, Pardo (2014) reminds us that "no reform of such breadth and depth will be perfect in its initial design. Leaders will have to promote a flexible approach when adjusting any aspects of these systems". The very nature of innovation is the creation of something new, something that is not an already established method. Before the method becomes part of the established arsenal for dealing with a particular problem, a multitude of adjustments will be necessary. The more systems that are in operation, the more future jurisdictions wishing to implement these kinds of changes will be able to learn from the successes and failures of their predecessors. Early adopters such as those discussed above must also be able to easily make changes to their own systems, at least in the early days, as more information and evidence comes to light about more effective ways of doing things. It is entirely possible that those systems which are developed at a later stage will be superior because they are able to build on the experience and evidence of other systems—a point which can be seen when comparing the ad hoc Dutch coffeeshop system operating in a very grey area with later systems which have been more fully imagined from the outset.

In fact, interesting and valuable conclusions have already been drawn from research on new systems of cannabis innovation. For example, Pardo (2014) in a relatively early comparison of regulated cannabis markets, notes that Washington and Colorado remain vulnerable to the trappings of commercialisation, while the Uruguayan system may fail to completely eliminate the black market because of the relatively restrictive nature of the regulations. He urges policy makers to watch developments closely and emulate the strengths of existing experiments while avoiding the weaknesses. More recently, Caulkins and Kilmer (2015) use a detailed exploration of existing systems of cannabis regulation to outline four key dimensions that policy makers should consider when attempting to implement their own arrangements: who is allowed to produce and supply cannabis (pharmacies, state licensed premises, cannabis clubs); what are the regulations for control (age, amount of substances, hours of sale); what kind of products can be distributed (edibles, plants, harvested cannabis); and what price and taxation levels should be set (profit, not for profit).

Kilmer and Pacula (2016) urge us to view the more recent changes described above, not as new and unexpected phenomena, but as part of a gradual shift in approach to cannabis policy that has taken place over the last 40 years or more: a series of constant incremental innovations, some of which have served an individual country well for many years but not held wider appeal, some of which have captured global attention, and others which have driven major adjustment in the search for the right approach. As Caulkins and Kilmer (2015) suggest, regulation of cannabis, or indeed regulation in general, "is not a binary-choice between commercial legalization and continuing prohibition" and to view it as such is to miss an opportunity to explore and experiment with different policies in order to find those that are most effective, while bearing in mind that effectiveness may not be constant across different cultures and political and geographical contexts. Given the recent increase in pace and degree of cannabis innovation, it would seem sensible to redirect the energy spent debating the morality and viability of a relaxation in cannabis laws towards debating how best to implement new ideas in different settings.

Any diversity of strategy within the illegal drugs field in general, or the issue of the regulation of cannabis in particular, should be seen as a strength. In relation to the different developments in cannabis policy, Uchtenhagen (2014: 357) suggests that a "policy allowing for experimentation alongside credible documentation and evaluation of effects not only improves the chances for evidence-based decisions, but also the chances for public acceptance". In other words, it is only through experimentation with innovative policy options that we will discover effective and appropriate drug policy interventions. It is thus clear that the development of innovative strategies of drug control should be encouraged: the discussion above may even suggest to the casual reader that they are in fact being encouraged. It is not clear, however, that this is the case. The next section of this chapter will examine the limitations imposed on these developments by International systems of drug control, and will argue that they should "somehow show more flexibility in order to allow this irreversible dynamic of reform to influence, adapt and modernise the system" (Vasconi 2013: 23).

Limitations to Drug Policy Innovation

The varied range of cannabis policy in operation on a global scale—the zero tolerance approach still in operation in the majority of jurisdictions; the decriminalisation of possession for personal use seen most notably in Portugal, but also in many other countries; the emergence of cannabis clubs in Spain and elsewhere; the state provision of cannabis for medical and religious purposes; the coffeeshop policy long operated in the Netherlands; and the introduction of regulated markets in some US states and Uruguay—could all be interpreted as further confirmation that considerable drug policy innovation is possible under the existing international conventions. As outlined at the beginning of this chapter, Bewley-Taylor and Jelsma (2011: 9) conclude that there is "considerable room for manoeuvre", particularly in national responses to the use and possession of illegal substances. It is the aim of this section to establish that, while this remains the case, there are significant limitations to the degree of flexibility achievable.

One example of the limitations imposed on a country seeking to innovate in its cannabis policy while remaining within the terms of the international conventions is provided by the coffeeshop system in the Netherlands. In their effort to separate the markets for cannabis and other more harmful drugs, the use, purchase and small scale sale of cannabis is generally tolerated, and is primarily facilitated through the coffeeshop system. The crime of possession of cannabis, however, has never been formally repealed in an attempt to maintain compliance with the international conventions. Furthermore, a significant grey area inherent in this policy is what Korf (2008) has termed the 'back door' issue. While use, purchase and small scale sale of cannabis may be tolerated, there exists no legal way for coffeeshops themselves to attain larger amounts of cannabis, because the production and commercial supply of cannabis is not tolerated. Newer regulations also mandate that coffeeshops cannot keep more than 500 g in total on the premises at any one time which, if adhered to, places severe restrictions on the economic viability of any individual business. This places coffeeshops in a precarious semi-legal position whereby the front door sales of cannabis are regulated, but their backdoor supply remains in the hands of criminals. As such, it cannot aim to eliminate the black market for cannabis.

A recent review of the Netherlands' separation of the markets policy concludes that: "If there is one lesson to take away from the Dutch experiences, it is that when taking steps towards regulating cannabis… these should include the entire chain of supply, from production to consumption" (Grund and Breeksema 2013: 12). As outlined above, evidence suggests that the general public and local governing authorities would support an extension of cannabis regulation to encompass the entire market. Until very recently, however, such a course of action has been perceived as impossible to implement under the current international conventions. Room and Mackay (2012: 7) thus conclude that inconsistencies and limitations in Dutch cannabis policy have been created *because* policy has developed in accordance with norms of international drug control: "The international treaties, then, have blocked experimentation with regulated domestic drug markets, and have constrained efforts by governments to decriminalise possession of controlled drugs for personal use".

Further limitations of policies developed within the framework of the international conventions can be observed by a more general examination of decriminalisation. Many countries now operate some form of decriminalisation (removal of or reduction in criminal penalties) of the possession of drugs for personal use. However, in an effort to stay within the parameters of the UN conventions, they often retain some form of civil or minor criminal penalties against those behaviours (Room 2012): while removal of all penalties would remain difficult under the treaties, a softening of existing penalties, from criminal to civil, is more palatable. Room and Reuter (2012) however, report that, despite widespread decriminalisation efforts towards cannabis, the number of cannabis users coming into contact with the criminal justice system has actually increased, and attributes that finding to the fact that civil or more minor criminal penalties are actually easier to enforce. As penalties are reduced they become more likely to be operationalised and, counter-intuitively, the result is a widening of the net (Room et al. 2010) of those caught up in efforts to control the use of drugs—crucially, *because countries are trying to work within UN conventions* (Room 2013; Room and Reuter 2012). If they were not, they would be able to remove penalties entirely. Bewley-Taylor (2013: 61) therefore suggests that "working inside the confines of the UN treaty system and generating changes *in* rather than changes *of* regime actually sustains larger structures of harm": If we want to reduce harm, then we need to entirely change the regime rather than seek to amend it.

A final example is provided by the fact that the most radical cannabis policy innovations—those taking place in some US states and in Uruguay—are largely considered to be operating outside the parameters of the international conventions and have been subject to intense and ongoing criticism from the International Narcotics Control Board which, as already noted, operates as a 'watchdog' to ensure the spirit of the conventions are being upheld (Bewley-Taylor and Trace 2006). This 'outsider' status places limitations on the transparency of information available around the innovations, which can make it more difficult for policy emulation to take place, and which compromises the integrity of evaluations. Collectively, these examples suggest that international conventions are limiting valuable experimentation with and innovation in drug policy. The next section, therefore, briefly explores options for reform of the international conventions.

Reform of the International Drug Policy Conventions

Several options for reform of the international conventions have been put forward by scholars who feel that the continuing situation of countries either seeking to work within these limitations, or operating in the grey area outside the conventions, are untenable. Bewley-Taylor et al.

(2014) outline these in a recent report for the Transnational Institute, specifically in relation to the reforms described above that have centred around cannabis. The first option would be to reschedule cannabis so it no longer comes under schedule I and schedule IV of the international drug control system. These schedules are reserved for the most dangerous substances that are not generally perceived to have any medical or scientific benefits. A move away from these schedules would undoubtedly create greater flexibility in cannabis policy innovation. With specific relevance to cannabis innovation are modifications inter se which would allow two (or more) countries to modify the terms of the treaties between themselves in a manner that might allow, for example, Jamaica to supply Canada with cannabis as part of its proposed regulated market.

Bewley-Taylor et al. (2014) also highlight the possibility of individual countries denouncing the treaties as they currently stand, and then re-accessing to them with new reservations (for example, to exclude cannabis or some other substance from the terms of the treaty). Under this model, the terms of the treaties themselves would stay the same, but the country that had denounced them and re-accessed would no longer be bound by all the terms. Other, more radical, avenues include: collectively seeking to amend specific areas of the treaties as they currently stand (e.g. around the creation of regulated cannabis markets); collectively seeking to renegotiate the current treaties entirely so they offer a better representation of modern drug control around the world; or for individual countries to denounce the treaties altogether and completely withdraw from them as they currently stand. As Bewley-Taylor et al (2014: 60) suggest, however: "Implementing any of these options would entail procedural complications and political obstacles. None of them provide an easy opt-out from the current treaty requirements proscribing the shift to legal regulation."

Bolivia's attempts to revise the treaties in relation to cultural and indigenous chewing of the coca leaf, outlined in Chapter 2, provide a case in point (also notable for being the only example to draw upon). As previously described, in 2009 Bolivia proposed an amendment to the 1961 Single Convention on Narcotic Drugs to exempt the practice of chewing the coca leaf for *traditional* or *cultural* purposes. Supporters of a continued strict interpretation of the conventions, including North America, much of Europe and all the most economically powerful nations (Room and Mackay 2012), however, were easily able to block the amendment which can be rejected if a significant number of objections are raised. In this case, objections concerned the risk of creating a political precedent by agreeing to Bolivia's amendment and thus jeopardising the integrity of the international drug conventions (Bewley-Taylor et al. 2014). Instead, the Bolivian government took the decision to denounce the international conventions, before re-accessing with a reservation around the use of coca leaf for traditional purposes. While an application to re-accede with reservations can be challenged, it requires a third of all signatories to block the proposal and in 2012 Bolivia was able to implement this strategy successfully. It has not, however, escaped criticism for these actions. In the 2012 Report of the International Control Board (INCB 2012: 13), for example, the decision was branded as "contrary to the fundamental object and spirit of the 1961 Convention ... that could jeopardize the very fundament of the international drug control regime in the long run".

These difficulties surrounding achieving a treaty amendment and being criticised for taking individual action have led Bewley-Taylor (2013) to suggest that some of the obstacles might be overcome by encouraging groups of 'likeminded' countries to come together to form an alliance and apply joint pressure in the search for reform. The main problem with this line of strategy of course is, as Bewley-Taylor himself rightly points out, that "there is seldom a unanimously accepted vision of exactly what a recalibrated regime should look like ...it is currently difficult to identify a single point of reform, or set of goals, around which states might coalesce" (Bewley-Taylor 2013). This lack of agreement remains the central barrier to treaty reform: if at the micro level a small group of countries cannot agree a likeminded approach, what hope is there for change at the macro level necessitating global agreement on future terms of drug control.

Based on the experiences outlined above, Jelsma (2011) has suggested that agents of international drug control may prefer continued violation of the treaties rather than lengthy, but ultimately fruitless, attempts to change them, which can also draw attention to their continuing validity.

Other scholars have therefore rejected the need for reform of the international treaties and have instead suggested that we should seek to capitalise on the flexibilities already inherent within the system. Collins (2017), for example, argues that the international conventions do not create an inflexible international system of drug control that cannot be changed, but rather represent the desires and agreements of the signatories about the ways in which it is thought best to approach the problem. He suggests that a common misinterpretation that is made by analysts in this area is that, because the treaties preceded the war on drugs, they must therefore have caused it. These lines of argument echo comments from William Brownfield, US Assistant Secretary of State for the Bureau of International Narcotics and Law Enforcement Affairs in 2014 outlining a framework for allowing increased variation in national and regional policies by allowing flexible interpretation of the treaties while defending the integrity of the core of the conventions (Brownfield, cited in Collins 2017). It is worth pointing out that the previously discussed UNGASS 2016 Outcome Document (UNODC 2016) does also refer to greater flexibility in interpretation of the treaties which has been seen by some as further support for this viewpoint. Any significant success with this strategy, however, would depend on the INCB relaxing its current stance as vociferous defender of the status quo with regard to the treaties (Room 2012).

It seems clear then that something must be done to ensure that limitations are not placed on the development of new innovations in drug policy. There are great difficulties in getting large numbers of countries to agree on matters such as these: for example, at the recent UNGASS meeting, broadly speaking, Asia supported a continuation of the pursuit of a drug free world, Russia defended the war on drugs, and Europe and the US downplayed the differences in global drug policy and pursued a flexibility agenda (Collins 2017). With this level of disagreement, none of the options for treaty reform looks to be particularly viable on a world stage. Equally, however, there are disadvantages to the proposals to seek to continue to work within the confines of the conventions based on arguments of ever greater flexibility. Jelsma (2015), for example, cautions that international agreements in other areas (for example, human rights) will ultimately be weakened if there are no consequences to contravening international conventions in the area of illegal drugs. Furthermore, Bewley-Taylor and Jelsma (2016) note that countries such as the Russian Federation and China, which practise strict national drug policies and which have faced accusations of drug-related human rights abuses, will also be able to exploit flexibilities to retain practices such as forced treatment or the death penalty. This chapter has thus established that drug policy innovation is happening and that it has the potential to bring many benefits, but that the international drug conventions provide an obstacle to continued efforts in this area.

Conclusion

This chapter has argued that there are no universal solutions to drug policy. Drug policy control options that have successfully eradicated the use of drugs and/or the harm caused by the use of drugs, have not thus far been developed. Furthermore, different countries have different experiences of the drug problem along many different parameters: whether they are primarily consumer, producer or transit countries; their political and cultural contexts; and their specific experiences of the problem in terms of substance, route of ingestion etc. These differences can, of course, also make themselves apparent within different regions of the same country. The next step towards improving global drug policy thus concerns itself with acknowledging this lack of success and encouraging both diversification and innovation in drug policy in the search for more effective strategies.

A certain degree of drug policy innovation does currently exist as is highlighted by the extended example of the breadth of cannabis policy innovations explored in this chapter. Despite the existence of several international treaties governing the control of drugs, many different ways of dealing with this particular substance have been engendered around the globe. As outlined in the discussion above, many scholars have already seized upon this area of flourishing innovation to make important policy contrasts and comparisons that further the development of our knowledge in controlling this area. As Kleinman et al. (2014) summarise: "The places that legalise cannabis first will provide—at some risk to their own populations—an external benefit to the rest of the world in the form of knowledge, however the experiments turn out". It is difficult to imagine how we could move forward in terms of drug policy and move towards more effective, context appropriate strategies, if we do not or cannot innovate.

The cannabis example, however, also illuminates some of the limitations to innovation that currently exist. Both the international conventions themselves and the International Narcotics Control Board (INCB) have, to date, placed limits on the degree of flexibility with which innovations can be implemented. For example, some countries have implemented systems operating in legal grey areas or unregulated areas in their political contortions to keep within the terms of the treaties as they perceive them; others have come under increasing pressure from bodies such as the INCB or have been blocked in their efforts by those opposed to their innovations, and still others are generally regarded to be operating entirely outside the confines of the treaties calling the whole system into question. In order to ensure that future drug policy innovation and diversity are encouraged, we therefore need to solve the problem of interpreting and/or reforming the international drug conventions.

References

Alonso, B. (2011, January). *Cannabis social clubs in Spain: A normalising alternative underway* (Series on legislative reform of drug policies Nr 9). Spain: Transnational Institute. http://www.tni.org.

Bewley-Taylor, D. (2013). Towards revision of the UN drug conventions: Harnessing like-mindedness. *International Journal of Drug Policy, 24*(1), 60–68.

Bewley-Taylor, D., & Jelsma, M. (2011). *Fifty years of the 1961 single convention on narcotic Drugs: A reinterpretation*. Series on legislative reform of drug policies. Transnational Institute: http://www.tni.org.

Bewley-Taylor, D., & Jelsma, M. (2012). *The UN drug control conventions: Limits of latitude*. Transnational Institute: https://www.tni.org.

Bewley-Taylor, D., & Jelsma, M. (2016, June). *UNGASS 2016: A Broken or B-r-o-a-d Consensus? UN summit cannot hide growing divergence in the global drug policy landscap* (Drug Policy Briefing 45). Amsterdam: Transnational Institute. http://www.tni.org.

Bewley-Taylor, D., & Trace, M. (2006). *The INCB: Watchdog or guardian of the UN drug control conventions?* The Beckley Foundation Drug Policy Programme.
Bewley-Taylor, D., Jelsma, M., & Blickman, T. (2014). *The rise and decline of cannabis prohibition*. Amsterdam: Transnational Institute. http://www.tni.org.
Boekhout van Solinge, T. (1999). Dutch drug policy in a European context. *Journal of Drug Issues, 29*, 511–528.
Caulkins, J., & Kilmer, B. (2015). Considering marijuana legalization carefully: Insight for other jurisdictions from analysis in Vermont. *Addiction, 111*, 2082–2089.
Cerda, M., & Kilmer, B. (2017). Uruguay's middle ground approach to cannabis legalization. *International Journal of Drug Policy, 42*, 118–120.
Chatwin, C. (2011). *Drug policy harmonization and the European Union*. Basingstoke: Palgrave Macmillan.
Chatwin, C. (2015). *Mixed messages from Europe on drug policy reform: The cases of Sweden and the Netherlands*. Brookings. https://www.brookings.edu.
Collins, J. (2017). Rethinking "flexibilities" in the international drug control system—Potential, precedents and models for reform *International Journal of Drug Policy*. https://doi.org/10.1016.12.014.
Crick, E., Haase, H. J., & Bewley Taylor, D. (2013, November). *Legally regulated cannabis markets in the US: Implications and possibilities*. (Policy Report 1). Swansea, UK: Global Drug Policy Observatory. https://www.swansea.ac.uk/gdpo.
Davenport, S., & Pardo, B. (2016). The Dangerous Drugs Act Amendment in Jamaica: Reviewing goals, implementation, and challenges. *International Journal of Drug Policy, 37*, 60–69.
Decorte, T. (2015). Cannabis social clubs in Belgium: Organizational strengths and weaknesses, and threats to the model. *International Journal of Drug Policy, 26*(1), 122–130.
Decorte, T., Pardal, M., Queirolo, R., Boidi, M. F., Sánchez Avilés, C., & Parés, O. (2017). Regulating cannabis social clubs: A comparative analysis of legal and self-regulatory practices in Spain, Belgium and Uruguay. *International Journal of Drug Policy, 43*, 44–56.
de Kort, M., & Cramer, T. (1999). Pragmatism versus ideology: Dutch drug policy continued. *Journal of Drug Issues, 29*, 473–492.
Dorn, N., & Jamieson, A. (2000) *Room for manoeuvre: Overview of comparative legal research into National drug laws of France, Germany, Italy, Spain, the Netherlands and Sweden and their relation to three International drugs conventions*. A study of DrugScope for the independent inquiry on the Misuse of Drugs Act 1971. London.

Eastwood, N., Fox, E., & Rosmarin, A. (2012). *A quiet revolution: Drug decriminalisation policies in practice across the globe* Release: http://www.release.org.uk.
EMCDDA. (2015). *European Drug Report 2015*. http://www.emcdda.europa.eu.
EMCDDA. (2017a). *Statistical Bulletin 2017*. http://www.emcdda.europa.eu.
EMCDDA. (2017b). *European Drug Report 2017*. http://www.emcdda.europa.eu.
ENCOD. (2014). *What is a cannabis social club?* ENCOD. http://www.cannabis-social-clubs.org.
Flynn, P. (2001). *Social consequences of and responses to drug misuse in member states social, health and family affairs committee, parliamentary assembly*. Luxembourg: Office for Official Publications of the European Communities.
Freisthler, B., & Gruenewald, P. J. (2014). Examining the relationship between the physical availability of medical marijuana and marijuana use across fifty Californian cities. *Drug and Alcohol Dependence, 143*, 244–250.
Grund, J. P., & Breeksema, J. (2013). *Coffeeshops and compromise: Separated illicit drug markets in the Netherlands*. Open Society Foundations. http://www.opensocietyfoundations.org.
Hylton, A. (2016, April 23, Saturday). Setting the record straight on the ganja law. *Jamaica Observer*. http://www.jamaicaobserver.com.
INCB. (2012). *International Narcotics Control Board 2012 report*. www.incb.org.
Intraval. (2007). *Coffeeshops in Nederland* (English summary). http://www.wodc.nl.
Jelsma, M. (2011, January). *The development of international drug control: Lessons learned and strategic challenges for the future* (Working Paper). Geneva: Global Commission on Drug Policies.
Jelsma, M. (2015). *UNGASS 2016: Prospects for treaty reform and UN system-wide coherence on drug policy*. Brookings. http://www.brookings.edu.
Jones, S. (2016). Farming medical ganja in Jamaica. *International Journal of Drug Policy, 36*, 151–155.
Jones, S., Porter, R., & Bishop, C. (2017). The implementation of medical ganja in Jamaica. *International Journal of Drug Policy, 42*, 115–117.
Kaplan, C., & Leuw, E. (1996). A tale of two cities: Drug policy instruments and city networks in the European Union. *European Journal on Criminal Policy and Research, 4*, 74–89.
Kilmer, B., & Pacula, R. L. (2016). Understanding and learning from the diversification of cannabis supply laws. *Addiction, 12*, 1128–1135.
Klein, K. (2016). Entrepreneurship, identity and the transformation of marketing systems: Medical cannabis in California. *Journal of Macromarketing, 57*(1), 85–101.

Kleinman, M. A. R., Ziskind, J. A., & Collins, J. (2014). *Lawful access to cannabis: Gains, losses and design criteria. Ending the drug wars: Report of the LSE expert group on the economics of drug policy.* London, UK: London School of Economics and Political Science. https://www.lse.ac.uk.

Korf, D. J. (2008). An open front door: The coffeeshop phenomenon in the Netherlands. In S. Rodner, B. Sznitman, B. Olsson & R. Room (Eds.), *A cannabis reader: Global issues and local experiences—Perspectives on cannabis controversies, treatment and regulation in Europe.* Luxembourg: Office for Official Publications of the European Communities, EMCDDA monograph no. 8.

Lemmens, P. H. (2003). Dutch government backs down on heroin prescription, despite successful trial. *Addiction, 98*, 247–249.

Marks, A. (2015, February) *The legal Landscape for cannabis social clubs in Spain*. Observatorio Civil de Drogos and Transnational Institute.

Murkin, G. (2015). *Cannabis social clubs in Spain: Legalisation without commercialisation*. Transform: https://www.tdpf.org.uk.

Musto, C. (2017). *Regulating cannabis markets: The construction of an innovative drug policy in Uruguay* (Unpublished thesis). Canterbury, UK: University of Kent. https://www.kent.ac.uk.

Pardo, B. (2014). Cannabis policy reforms in the Americas: A comparison of Colorado. *Washington and Uruguay' International Journal of Drug Policy, 25*, 727–735.

Potter, G. R. (2009). Exploring retail-level drug distribution: Social supply, "real" dealers and the user/dealer interface. In Z. Demetrovics, J. Fountain, & L. Kraus (Eds.), *Old and new policies, theories, research methods and drug users across Europe*. Lengerich, Germany: Pabst Science Publishers.

Queirolo, R., Boidi, M. F., & Cruz, J. (2016). Cannabis clubs in Uruguay: The challenges of regulation. *International Journal of Drug Policy, 34*, 41–48.

Reinarman, C., Cohen, P., & Kaal, H. (2004). The limited relevance of drug policy: Cannabis in Amsterdam and San Francisco. *American Journal of Public Health, 94*, 836–842.

Rolles, S. (2014). *Cannabis policy in The Netherlands: Moving forwards not backwards*. https://www.tdpf.org.uk.

Room, R. (2012). Reform by subtraction: The path of denunciation of international drug treaties and reaccession with reservations. *International Journal of Drug Policy, 23*, 401–406.

Room, R. (2013). Legalizing a market for cannabis for pleasure: Colorado, Washington, Uruguay and beyond. *Addiction, 109*, 345–351.

Room, R., & MacKay, S. (2012). *Roadmaps to reforming the UN drug convention* (A Beckley Foundation Report). http://www.beckleyfoundation.org.

Room, R., & Reuter, P. (2012). How well do international drug conventions protect public health? *The Lancet, 379*, 84–91.

Room, R., Fischer, B., Hall, W., Lenton, S., & Reuter, P. (2010). *Cannabis policy: Moving beyond stalemate*. Oxford: Oxford University Press and The Beckley Foundation.

Snap, Z. (2016). Drug policy innovations in Latin America. *Latin America Policy Journal*. Harvard Kennedy School Student Publication. www.hkslapj.com.

Stevens, A. (2011). *Drugs, crime and public health: The political economy of drug policy*. London: Routledge-Cavendish.

Strang, J., Babor, T., Caulkins, J., Fischer, B., Foxcroft, D., & Humphreys, K. (2012). Drug policy and the public good: Evidence for effective interventions. *The Lancet, 379*, 71–83.

TNI. (2015). *Canadian company to tap into Jamaica for medicinal cannabis supply*. https://www.tni.org.

TNI. (2016). *UNGASS 2016: Watershed event or wasted opportunity?* https://www.tni.org.

Tops, D. (2001). *A society with or without drugs? Continuity and change in drug policies in Sweden and The Netherlands*. Lunds dissertations in social work 5, Lund University, Lund.

Uchtenhagen, A. (2014). Some critical issues in cannabis policy reform. *Addiction, 109*(3), 356–358.

Uitermark, J. (2004). The origins and future of the Dutch approach towards drugs. *Journal of Drug Issues, 34*, 511–532.

UNODC. (2007). *Sweden's successful drug policy: A review of the evidence*. http://www.unodc.org.

UNODC. (2016). *Outcome document of the 2016 United Nations General Assembly Special Session on the world drug problem. Our joint commitment to effectively addressing and countering the world drug problem*. New York: United Nations. http://www.unodc.org/documents.

Vasconi, C. (2013, June 20–21). *Where next for Europe on drug policy reform?* Lisbon, Portugal: Expert seminar. Transnational Institute.

Walsh, J., & Ramsey, G. (2016). *Uruguay's drug policy: Major innovations, major challenges*. Brookings. https://www.brookings.edu.

Wouters, M., Benschop, A., van Laar, M., & Korf, D. J. (2012). Cannabis use and proximity to coffeeshops in the Netherlands. *European Journal of Criminology, 9*(4), 337–353.

5

Step Four: Ensure That Drug Policy Innovations are Evaluated, and Evidence on Their Effectiveness is Shared Widely

Drug policy innovations are only useful in a system that also allows for evaluation of novel strategies and which has sufficient resources to disseminate the results widely (Uchtenhagen 2014). Traditionally, the gap between evidence and policy has been particularly marked in the field of drug policy, with war on drugs policies continuing to operate in stark contrast to the significant evidence about their ineffectiveness (Wood et al. 2010). Recent years have seen much discussion of the importance of 'evidence-based policy' in building effective drug control strategies (Boaz and Pawson 2005), alongside a counter debate about the low value that is usually placed on evidence in drug policy making (Stevens 2011b). Most research in this area now suggests that "good policy is presumed to be based on a solid evidence base" (Ritter 2009: 70), with the caveat that evidence must also compete with political and public opinion in the actual implementation of policy.

More specifically, Wood et al. (2010: 311–312) suggest that: "reorienting drug policies towards evidence-based approaches that respect, protect, and fulfil human rights has the potential to reduce harms deriving from current policies and would allow for the redirection of the vast financial resources to where they are needed most: the implementation

C. Chatwin, *Towards More Effective Global Drug Policies*,
https://doi.org/10.1007/978-3-319-92072-6_5

and evaluation of evidence-based prevention, regulatory, treatment, and harm-reduction interventions". This chapter charts the rise of evidence based policy in general, and its application to the field of illicit drugs in particular. It critically explores existing metrics for the effectiveness of drug policy. Finally, it proposes the encouragement of policy transfer and lesson drawing strategies as methods to spread information about available responses to illicit drugs, to facilitate the exchange of ideas and, where appropriate, to stimulate policy emulation.

Evidence Based Policy

Calls for an evidence based drug policy have their roots in the development of Evidence Based Policy (EBP) more generally. In the 1980s and 1990s a long-standing trend towards Evidence Based Medicine (EBM) accelerated. The aim was to close the gap between research and practice, ensuring that medical decisions and practices were firmly rooted in robust research evidence and variation between different health care providers was reduced. This drive for knowledge and information favoured certain types of evidence—such as meta-analyses, systematic reviews and randomised controlled trials—as these methods were perceived to be the most reliable in the field. Quickly the increasing emphasis on the need for evidence to underpin decision making spread to other fields—particularly health and social policy (Naughton 2005)—and was seized upon by many governments around the world, but particularly in the UK and Australia whence much of the relevant literature comes. These governments were keen to buy into a culture of linking policy in a variety of areas to proof, thus securing wider public support. EBP as the movement more widely became known after its dissemination from the medical field, has become very firmly established in many regions around the globe as it is hard to oppose the idea that policy should be grounded in our best information about what works (Pearce et al. 2014).

Weiss (1977) describes how this trend has forced researchers, particularly in the field of social sciences, to think much more carefully about the usefulness of their research and how best to make it easily accessible to policy makers, as well as easily translatable into policy practice. This "utilitarian turn" (Monaghan 2008: 209) means that it is no longer enough for research to be conducted purely to enhance academic understanding—to be truly useful it must also aspire to promote real world change. The appetite for EBP has spread beyond governments and policy makers to encompass the general public, who now expect, as a matter of course, to see rational and scientific policies that are rooted in evidence, as well as to research funders who now demand to see extensive consideration of outputs, impact and dissemination before granting money to any research proposal (Mulgan 2004).

The most straightforward interpretation of EBM or EBP has often been conceptualised as a rational, problem based or linear model whereby a problem is defined, research is conducted to fill a gap in knowledge and the resulting evidence is utilised to provide policy options (Naughton 2005; Weiss 1986). Research can also follow policy, with a problem being defined, a policy implemented, and then research conducted to evaluate the effectiveness of policy (Young et al. 2002). Within these models of EBP a strict hierarchy of evidence (Mullen 2016) is often maintained with a strong preference for systematic reviews and randomised control trials over more qualitative methods such as case studies or knowledge generated from either service providers or users (Backstrand 2004). Linear or rational models of EBP are strongly influenced by the medical and scientific fields where hierarchies of evidence are well-established.

In terms of social and wider health related policy arenas, Mulgan (2004) describes three types of field: stable policy fields, policy fields in flux, and new and emerging policy fields. He suggests that evidence has a critical role to play in all fields, but it is only in stable policy fields where there is fairly widespread consensus that we can talk about policy being truly evidence based. In unstable or emerging fields where there is a lack of consensus about effective strategies, the rational, linear model of evidence based policy has been widely criticised for providing an over-simplistic view: "Policy-making rarely, if ever follows such a rational line of progression" (Berridge and Thom 1996: 34).

In complex and unstable policy fields, it has to be acknowledged that scientific research based evidence is only one among many competing factors influencing the policy making process. The "single-minded pursuit of truth and adherence to scientific methods" enshrined in the rational, linear models does not bear much resemblance to arenas where decisions rest on "searching for compromise, admitting uncertainty and finding flexibility" (MacGregor 2011: 49). So, in these policy areas where there are different ways of conceptualising the problem and often wildly different opinions about how to approach it, as well as a conflicting picture of research evidence, little of which adheres to the medical hierarchical model of best evidence, the interpretation of the evidence base remains ambiguous and can vary widely. For example, the existing vested interests of different kinds of 'actors'—policy makers, the general public, media representatives, members of various lobbying groups, international institutions and so on—will have an important impact on the way that evidence is interpreted. In fact, "evidence is only given meaning and purpose when it is taken up by particular actors for specific strategic purposes within the policy process" (Lancaster 2016: 147).

In addition to the lack of consensus in research findings and resulting ambiguity of interpretation of evidence, many researchers (e.g. Mulgan 2004; Ritter and Bammer 2010) have documented other barriers to the reproduction of linear, rational models of evidence based policy in complex social and health policy fields. For example, the mismatch between the need for rapid implementation of policy so policy makers can be seen to be doing something about a problem, and the relatively slow pace with which researchers must apply for funding to conduct an, often lengthy, research project, with more time required for analysis and dissemination of results. Another example is the mismatch between the lengthy formats in which academic knowledge is produced and limited time which policy makers have to to evaluate the evidence. These problems with the rational, linear model for complex policy areas that are in flux or are newly emerging have led to the development of many other models of EBP more suited to these areas.

Models that aim to represent the complexities of EBP in relation to unstable policy areas describe a process whereby policy is *informed by*, rather than *based on* evidence: "disparate bodies of knowledge become multiple sets of evidence that inform and influence policy rather than determinate it" (Head 2008: 4). In these fields "our questions are changing as well as our answers" (Mulgan 2004: 222) and evidence thus only exists in relation to theories and concepts, or ways of making sense of the issue in hand.. Perhaps the most well known alternative EBP model to the linear, rational model is provided by Weiss's (1977) enlightenment model which views EBP not as an extension of EBM, but as something "qualitatively different" (Black 2001: 277). Through the enlightenment model, Weiss (1977) portrays a subtle and indirect role for evidence in many social science arenas—research, rather than being conducted and applied in relation to a specific problem, is viewed as an ongoing process which helps to shape social discourse and public and political opinion over time.

There have been many other attempts to model more complex forms of EBP. Valentine (2009) highlights the importance of power relations in the utilisation of evidence in unstable policy fields and the need to chart evidence using the compass of policy makers in these areas. Lancaster (2016) cautions that we cannot seek to understand the application of evidence without exploring the motivations of the actors who encounter it and who evaluate it according to different criteria depending on their status as drug user, politician, medical professional etc. Stevens (2007) has advocated the evolutionary or 'survival of the fittest' model which suggests that where a wide variety of conflicting evidence exists, the evidence that already fits with dominant discourses will be perceived as the best and most useful evidence: "research comes to influence policy when it is consistent with the ideas of those in positions of power (Monaghan 2008: 210)." Finally, Baachi (2009) draws these points together by arguing that, in social science and other related fields, problems are often not stable and well defined or agreed upon by all. Instead the perception of problems fluctuates constantly in relation to factors such as public opinion, media emphasis and political acumen. Baachi's argument suggests that these factors, as well as the policy process itself, can provide an overall framing of a problem which influences the kind of evidence which is accepted as reliable and the kind of research which is commissioned.

Evidence-Based Drug Policy

Turning now to the issue of illegal drugs and the impact which evidence can hope to have on policy in this field, Valentine (2009: 444) suggests that it is an area in which arguments for evidence based policy have been "especially strong" given its relation to the medical field from which evidence based ideas originally stemmed. This has resulted in a sustained drive for the creation of an evidence base: "the paradox has been however that with more information, there may be even less understanding" (MacGregor 2011: 43). As Roumeliotis (2015) notes, there are some senses in which illegal drugs can be viewed as a science problem, for example in some of the work around addiction, and it can therefore sometimes be appropriate to call on scientific evidence to 'solve' the problem, or to expect evidence based policy making to adhere to a rational or linear model whereby a problem arises, advice is called for, findings are analysed and implementations are made.

For example, the advent of early harm reduction measures such as substitution treatment and needle exchange programmes can be viewed as having been implemented as a result of both research evidence and the promotion of specific findings by expert advisors (Duke and Thom 2014; MacGregor 2011). Ritter and Bammer (2010) provide another example in the development of the new heroin treatment buprenorphine in Australia. In this case the Australian government was interested in developing new heroin treatment options and expert researchers were influential in attracting support for the exploration of the suitability of buprenorphine. Clinical trials were run to provide further evidence of its effectiveness and, given the positive nature of results, experts continued to work with both government and industry to implement the treatment option.

Roumeliotis (2015), however, goes on to suggest that actually drugs are at least as much of a social science problem as a scientific one, and actually represent a complex field which is in flux. In her work with Australian policy makers in the drugs field, Ritter (2009) points out that many of the issues with the evidence based policy model that are outlined above, are highly evident within the drug policy field. For example, it is an area in which quick decisions must often be made, in which policy makers are very time pressured and are often not able to peruse research findings at length, in which debate is polarised, and in which there is a lot of research but a general lack of consensus about the nature of the research findings. Ritter (2009) also highlights that the illegal drugs field is very much bound up with moral values and, therefore, highly susceptible to emotional responses. These factors generally mean that rational, linear models of the way that evidence based policy should work are not particularly appropriate for many localised parts of the illegal drugs field: more complex models which seek to draw on the values and relationships of power groups, the intentions and existing beliefs of specific actors, and the overall way in which the problem is framed may be more useful.

To further illustrate the difficulty in applying evidence to illegal drug related problems in the quest for more effective policy making, Roberts (2014) provides several examples. Take David Nutt, an eminent drug researcher in the UK particularly known for his attempts to create a continuum of drugs based on a scale of how harmful they are. Nutt et al.'s (2007, 2010) scale of harm claims to be rational and based on scientific evidence, and almost certainly does represent a step forward from many of the moralistic ways in which individual governments have categorised illegal substances to date. As the authors themselves acknowledge, however, despite the best of intentions towards scientific rigour, when categorising different types of harm and ranking them against each other in terms of severity, it is virtually impossible to prevent subjectivities from entering the debate. Judgement of the severity of different types of harm will be particularly affected by the values and existing beliefs of those involved. The fact that there is considerable change in the positioning of different drugs along the continuum between the 2007 and 2010 studies serves to further emphasise this point.

Another example is provided by the change of policy effected in Portugal in 2001 and more fully described in Chapter 3 of this book. As many years have now passed since the move towards a national drug policy more fully centred on the principle of harm reduction, there have been a considerable number of evaluations of Portuguese drug policy. The problem is that these evaluations have been interpreted in different ways by different researchers at different times. Greenwald (2009), for example, has lauded the rise in the number of drug dependent users who are in treatment and the fall in the amount of drug related death and disease as evidence of the effectiveness of the change in policy. Conversely, Pinto Coelho (2010) has identified the rise in levels of use of some drugs as evidence of the failure of the same policy. Portugal thus provides a good example of an issue on which there is a growing body of evidence, but on which there is no consensus, and different individuals are therefore able to interpret the available evidence in different ways most suited to their overall purposes.

Mulgan (2004) observes new and emerging policy fields as suffering from similar problems in relation to the creation of evidence based policy as more established fields that are complex and in flux. In the drugs field, we can draw on the example, also noted by Roberts (2014), of newly emergent regulated cannabis markets discussed in more detail in the previous chapter. Or on the many responses to the newly emergent area of new psychoactive substances. At this stage, it is very difficult to imagine how these models could be objectively and scientifically evaluated in a manner that would not remain open to interpretation depending on who was using the evidence and for what purpose. The 'success', for example, of one type of regulated cannabis market over another will depend on many factors, not least of which how you define success in the first place and, as we have already seen, there is a notable lack of agreement about this in the drugs field.

Another way of thinking about these kind of social policy related problems and their relationship with evidence is provided by Rittel and Weber (1973). Their work designates social science and social policy related problems, such as what to do about illicit drugs, as 'wicked' problems (as opposed to 'tame' problems which can expect to be 'solved' by using traditional scientific methods). 'Wicked' problems have no definitive formulation or framework for understanding that is shared by everyone; they are never completely 'solved'—there is always more that could be done, and the effectiveness of implementations designed to address them needs to be evaluated over a long period of time. Ultimately, this means that there are no universal 'solutions' to 'wicked' problems—usually we find a list of possible policy options that may be 'better' or 'worse' than each other and that effectiveness might vary widely over different geographical locations or timepoints. As a complex or 'wicked' problem, illegal drugs constitute therefore an area within which policy can be viewed as evidence *informed* rather than evidence *based* (Duke and Thom 2014).

The previous chapter of this book emphasised the important role of innovation and experimentation in the development of effective drug policy, a factor which further verifies drug policy as a complex policy field in flux described by Mulgan (2004: 221) as giving rise to "fertility and experimentation". Sanderson's (2009) model of intelligent policy making has been proposed as an alternative to evidence based policy making and provides a good fit for conceptualising the way evidence can most appropriately be used in areas such as illicit drug policy. In areas where there is uncertainty about what is the best way to proceed, Sanderson (2009: 700) urges us to "treat our policies as hypotheses to be tested in practice, to be piloted where feasible and appropriate and to be subject to rigorous evaluation". Even where policy areas are more established, we still need to implement rigorous monitoring and evaluation processes "to test the validity of the assumptions upon which the policy is based" (Sanderson 2009: 714).

If we apply Sanderson's model to some of the areas previously discussed in this book we can further see its usefulness for policy making. For example, in terms of the various forms of cannabis regulation which are currently being trialled around the globe, many of these could be considered as efforts to pilot contrasting systems of regulation in an attempt to increase the overall range of options when seeking to control the use of drugs. Uruguay, the American states, Jamaica and Canada can thus be viewed as the "pioneers" (Mulgan 2004: 221) of this area of drug policy development. Their efforts, however, will only be truly useful if their attempts are carefully and comparatively evaluated to see what is and isn't working, always bearing in mind the caveat that different implementations will have greater and lesser effect depending on the localities in which they are implemented. The usefulness of innovation in drug policy development therefore depends on the degree to which it is evaluated and monitored and to which the results are then disseminated to interested parties around the globe. Without such a system of evaluation and dissemination, innovations will not have the desired effect of improving global drug policy.

Cross-National Comparative Research and the Development of Metrics of Drug Policy Effectiveness

The previous section outlined the rise of Evidence Based Policy (EBP) across a variety of fields, particularly those with some link to health and social care. It suggested that, while the need for EBP is often emphasised in the drugs field, its application is not straight forward due to the complex and fluid nature of our understanding in this area. With these difficulties in mind, this section will now turn to an exploration of some of the existing evidence on drug policy performance at the national and regional level. It outlines some of the specific problems inherent in cross-national data comparisons in the drugs field, and further considers the usefulness of existing metrics of drug policy effectiveness in general.

Many countries in different areas of the world collect data on key indicators such as: the prevalence of drug use; the number of drug users whose use has been defined as problematic; the number of drug related deaths; the number of drug users with diseases such as HIV, AIDS and Hepatitis C; the number of drug-related crimes; the amounts of drugs seized by law enforcement agencies, and the quantity of hectares devoted to illegal substance cultivation. This information is often encouraged and/or collated by a regional agency. For example, the European Monitoring Centre for Drugs and Drug Addiction (EMCDDA); the Inter-American Observatory on Drugs (OID); or the ASEAN Narcotics Cooperation Centre (ASEAN-NARCO). Regional agencies such as these are often responsible for emphasising the need for robust data across these key indicators and are able to maintain an oversight of preferred data collection methods, steering member states towards standardised techniques wherever possible. In some cases, they are also responsible for producing regional annual reports on the state of the drug problem.

In a final stage in the evidence gathering process, regional and national data are fed up to the United Nations Office on Drugs and Crime (UNODC) which is responsible for producing an annual World Drug Report comparing data from across the globe. These reports give us global figures for overall drug use, facilitate comparisons between countries and regions, and offer explorations of topical issues. The 2017 World Drug Report (UNODC 2017), for example, tells us that around 5% of the global adult population used drugs at least once in 2015, that North America is the global region which reports the highest drug-related mortality rate (based on number of drug-related deaths per million population) while Latin America and the Caribbean reports the lowest: it also contains a discussion of the impact of various new cannabis policies on the global stage.

While international agencies such as those described above play an important role in encouraging the national collation of data, moving towards standardised methods of data collection and providing a platform for effective dissemination of results, they do not usually offer endorsements of particular policy styles based on their findings. In other words, they do not (very often) use the data they have collected to make specific judgements about which drug policies are the most successful, inviting other regions to emulate them. The final section of the 2017 World Drug Report (UNODC 2017), presents comparative data throughout, but keeps its policy recommendations at the general level, encouraging, for example, member states to continue treating the negative health impacts surrounding opioid use as a priority and the development of alternatives to imprisonment for drug-related offences of the most minor nature. A perusal of the EMCDDA mission statement (EMCDDA 2018: 1) further elaborates this position: "The EMCDDA exists to provide the EU and its Member States with a factual overview of European drug problems and a solid evidence base to support the drugs debate…it offers policy makers the data *they need* for drawing up informed drug laws and strategies". Such a statement clearly designates a scientific role to the institution itself, concerned with the collation, presentation and dissemination of data, leaving individual governments and policymakers to draw their own conclusions. The reasons for this are explored below.

Given that the data collected by agencies such as the EMCDDA, OID, ASEAN-NARCO and the UNODC represents evidence on a range of national, regional and global drug policy trends, it is interesting to reflect on why this has not very often resulted in judgements about the relative effectiveness of national policies. There are several reasons for this. As outlined in Chapter 3, the first reason is based in the fact that drug policy interventions robustly evaluated as being effective, are few and far between. The vast majority of countries that report on the state of the drug problem within their borders do find that people use drugs, that some of those users become problematic in their use, that death and disease are sometimes associated with use, and that drug-related crimes and seizures of illegal drugs are reported. None have shown a sustained and consistent trend towards the significant reduction or eradication of all these problems. Some mainstream harm reduction measures such as needle exchange and substitution treatment have stood up to robust evaluation (Hunt 2003) as able to reduce drug-related harm (although not necessarily use), but this is not generally the case for other interventions or policy styles.

Furthermore, several researchers and experts have suggested that overall policy direction and/or the introduction of specific new policy interventions seem to have little impact on the state of the drug problem within a jurisdiction. Reinarman et al. (2004), for example, studied cannabis users in San Francisco and Amsterdam. Despite being cities with very different methods of cannabis control, their findings suggested strong similarities in demographics of cannabis users, age of onset and patterns of use, and in motivations for use. Stevens (2011a), in his book on drugs, crime and public health, documents the failure to find evidence for the impact of UK drug policy on patterns and trends in drug use in the UK, and suggests that a better strategy might be to move to a more general focus, with policy interventions aiming to reduce drug use and the problems associated with it indirectly by improving societal factors such as inequality. Finally, an in-depth exploration of EU data on the drug problem (Chatwin 2011), fails to find any consistent correlation across countries between broad drug policy style and extent of the drug problem across key indicator areas.

It is also important to highlight the problematic nature of cross-national comparative research to provide reliable data, particularly where it is conducted on a global scale. Galtung (1990: 107) notes the problematic nature of trying to create a universal social science which transcends "geography and history with all that implies of structural and cultural diversity". These kind of structural and cultural diversities can lead to fundamental differences in style of work and/or research methods which are particularly enhanced when scholars from different countries also come from different disciplinary perspectives (Hakim 2000). Furthermore, the different institutions undertaking and funding research in various geographical locations, may have different agendas and these will not always be easily identifiable. These factors make it difficult to draw reliable conclusions from cross-national comparative research in general.

In the drugs field, these underlying factors result in differences in methods and styles of data collection that can have important impacts on the data itself (Chatwin 2011). Consider the fact that not all countries or regions provide data on every key indicator and many provide data sets for only some substances or some age ranges: the UN for example acknowledges its own paucity of data in relation to Africa and Asia (Bewley-Taylor 2016). To further complicate matters, methods of collecting data vary widely from country to country or region to region: data may have been collected in different time sets (every year, every other year, every 5 years), via different media (telephone, face to face interview or internet survey), and from significantly different sample sizes. Finally, it is important to recognise that national or regional policy style can also have an impact on the quality of the data collected. In a country where harm reduction principles are generously employed and tolerant policies generally practised, then people who use drugs may be more willing to come forward and report themselves as such. On the other hand, in a country where the eradication of drugs from society is an acknowledged aim and people who use drugs are subject to strict penalties, they may be significantly less willing to do so.

The factors outlined above can impact on all statistical comparisons at the international level on the prevalence of drug use, but when it comes to other key indicators, there can be even more substantial issues. Take, for example, the area of 'problem drug use' (as it is often termed), under which countries and regions present data on the number of people who have become dependent on their use of drugs. A real difficulty here is that there is no common understanding of what defines a 'problem drug user' The UNODC and other institutions recognise this, and try to steer data collectors towards standard practices, but this is not always successful. The UNODC, for example, suggests that "While there is no established definition of problem drug users, they are usually defined by countries as those that regularly use illicit substances and can be considered dependent, and those who inject drugs" (UNODC 2011: 13). In more recent reports, however, reference is also made to signs of drug use that has become problematic such as being enrolled in a treatment programme and suffering from a drug-related disease (UNODC 2017).

The EMCDDA has attempted to impose a definition of 'problem drug use' on its member states: "injecting drug use or long duration / regular use of opioids, cocaine and/or amphetamines" (EMCDDA 2017: 1). It recognises, however, that there are limitations to this definition as it does not include the use of other drugs such as cannabis or ecstasy, or the more irregular use of opioids, cocaine and/or amphetamines, both of which can sometimes result in problems. In terms of data collection, a perusal of available evidence (EMCDDA 2017; UNODC 2017) suggests that there remain a variety of methods for estimating drug use that has become problematic in nature. These include collecting information on the number of drug users seeking treatment for serious drug use, the number of drug users arrested for serious drug use (or discovered to have serious drug use on arrest), the number of drug users who die for reasons related to their habit, and the number of people that have AIDS or are HIV positive and are also drug users. Furthermore, while some countries include all drugs (even cannabis) in their estimations of 'problem drug use', others only include regular heroin use.

Another example of this lack of agreement of around international definitions essential to evaluating the drugs field is provided by the key indicator of drug-related mortality rates. The UNODC acknowledges that "The definition and reporting of drug-related deaths may vary from country to country" (UNODC 2017: 26) and goes on to suggest that it could include some or all of the following conditions: "deaths from HIV/AIDS and hepatitis C acquired through injecting drug use; behavioural disorders caused by use of psychoactive substances; intentional self-harm and self-poisoning (suicide) by exposure to psychotropic substances; and unintentional deaths and trauma resulting from drug use (motor vehicle accidents and other forms of accidental deaths" (UNODC 2017: 26-6). Some reporting countries and regions include all these factors in their estimates, whereas others do not. The point to take from the examples of both defining 'problem drug use' and 'drug-related mortality' is that if different countries and regions are defining these key concepts in different ways and including different data in their overall analysis, then it becomes very difficult to compare the relative effectiveness of different national policy styles in any meaningful way.

Thus far, the discussion has established that part of the difficulty in making judgements about which kind of drug policy is most effective lies in the fact that, to date, efforts to eradicate or significantly reduce drug use have seen little success. Judgements are further impaired by the fact that, where comparative data exists across key indicators, the quality of the data, from a comparative perspective, leaves a lot to be desired. A final reason for the difficulty in making judgements about effective drug policy based on available evidence lies in the 'wicked' (Rittel and Weber 1973) nature of the drugs issue, meaning that there is no universal or common understanding (on a global basis) of what 'success' looks like. The problems of defining success and attempting to implement a 'solution' to the drug problem will now be explored.

Defining success in the field of illicit drugs remains difficult precisely because it is a complex problem which can be framed in different ways depending on the existing perspectives, beliefs, morals and values of those involved. Consider, for example, the somewhat divergent drug policies operated in Sweden (where there is zero tolerance of drug use, the ultimate aim is a drug free society, there is no separation between different drugs in terms of penalties, treatment can be coercive and users are actively pursued by law enforcement agencies) and the Netherlands (where cannabis is separated from other drugs, the use and small scale sale of cannabis are tolerated via the coffeeshop system, the main goal is to reduce the harm experienced by the users of drugs rather than to reduce drug use itself, and treatment services aim to draw in users even if they aren't ready to give up using drugs).

Proponents of Swedish drug policy have been quick to point to the low prevalence of drug use in the country as evidence of its successful nature in general. The UNODC report, *Sweden's Successful Drug Policy:*

A Review of the Evidence (2007) (in itself a rare endorsement of specific policy style), praises the country for its uniformly negative attitudes toward drug use and attributes these low levels to a cross political party restrictive drug policy. Others (Cohen 2010), have been more critical about Swedish policy and point to dangerously high levels of drug-related death and disease, which are particularly concerning given the generally low levels of drug use in general. In the Netherlands meanwhile, latest figures (EMCDDA 2017) confirm that the prevalence of drug use is higher than in Sweden, particularly for drugs like ecstasy, and that there is some evidence to suggest a significant role in the production and export of substances such as ecstasy and cannabis. Supporters of Dutch drug policy acknowledge these facts, but point to its success in effectively separating the market for cannabis from other illegal drugs and keeping the numbers of dependent users, drug-related deaths and disease to much lower levels (Chatwin 2015; Grund and Breeksama 2013). The point here is that both countries can legitimately claim success because they have different ways of framing the problem, different policy goals, and this leads not just to different kinds of 'solutions', but also, crucially, to different methods for evaluation of effectiveness in general.

To date, efforts to define success have largely been framed by the indicators outlined above: prevalence of drug use, numbers of drug-related deaths, numbers of drug related crimes, seizures of drugs, quantity of hectares devoted to the cultivation of drugs and so on. One part of the debate about the need to consider alternative approaches to controlling the use of drugs (that takes into account issues such as the reduction of harm to users and working within human rights frameworks) has led to a growing critique of the continuing usefulness of indicators and metrics such as these. For example, Bewley-Taylor (2016) notes that many of these indicators are dominated by law enforcement factors while global debates about drug policy effectiveness now focus on a much wider set of concerns, and Werb et al. (2016a) lament the narrow focus of current indicators based solely around reducing the demand and supply of illegal drugs. The main concern is whether these metrics are really determining evidence about how effective policy initiatives are, or whether they tell us more about how tough we are being (Muggah et al. 2015).

This has led to increasing calls, from a variety of countries and regions (Bewley-Taylor 2016) and from NGOs (Global Commission on Drug Policy 2011), for the development of new metrics to improve evaluation of policy effectiveness. Muggah and de Carvalho (2015: 1) suggest that "new metrics can re-frame the global drug policy narrative": by changing the way that effectiveness is measured and moving away from the expectation of being able to 'solve' the problem, we can also change the kind of interventions that are proposed. Bewley-Taylor (2016: 7), for example, suggests that we should move away "from the measurement of interventions, flows and scale, towards metrics that measure outcomes that really matter to individuals and communities", but cautions that deciding on the specifics of what to measure and how to measure will always involve some element of subjectivity drawing on existing beliefs and values, and effort will need to be made to ensure that indicators are not biased towards the priorities of the global North. Ahead of UNGASS 2016 there were calls to redesign metrics as part of that process, perhaps overseen by an expert advisory group (Transnational Institute 2015; Werb et al. 2016b). Although these calls did not come to fruition in the UNGASS 2016 Outcome Document (UNODC 2016), ongoing work in this area suggests they may be returned to at the next high level UN meeting in this area scheduled for 2019.

In an open letter to the United Nations, Werb et al. (2016b) call on national and international stakeholders to commit to revising the existing metrics used to evaluate drug control policies and outline a detailed set of alternative indicators (drawing on the work of the World Health Organisation, the Joint United Nations Programme on HIV/AIDS, UNICEF, and others). These indicators include specific metrics and are based around key areas such as: health (metrics include access to sterile injection equipment, drug-related emergency room presentations, and access to substitution treatment); peace and security (metrics include incidence of drug-market related homicide and violence, drug use-related injuries, and drug use-related traffic accidents); development (metrics include poverty in drug cultivation regions, illicit drug use production and trafficking as proportion of national GDP, and proportion of people with drug dependence that have access to stable housing); and human rights (metrics include proportion of prisoners incarcerated for non-violent drug crimes; level of gender-sensitive service provision, and number of individuals sentenced to death for drug offences) (Werb et al. 2016b).

A recent collaboration between the Global Commission on Drug Policy and the Igarape Institute (Muggah et al. 2015) has resulted in another detailed outline for developing new measures of drug policy effectiveness based around alternative indicators of success aimed at: ending the criminalisation and stigmatisation of drug users; curbing drug use through public health measures; diminishing incarceration of non-violent drug-related offenders; targeting violent organised crime groups and drug traffickers; providing viable alternatives for illicit crop producers; and encouraging experimentation with different models of drug regulation. Finally, even those with more invested in the existing metrics, such as the European Union, have acknowledged that there are a lot of missing indicators in the current data used for assessing the drug situation (European Parliament 2016).

At this point, it is important to understand that while better metrics will have many positive impacts on our ability to understand the drugs issue and design effective responses to it, as well as on our ability to redefine the way that drug policy effectiveness is framed, their development will never result in universal or concrete 'solutions' to the problem. As Rittel and Weber (1973: 160) attest: "there are no 'solutions' in the sense of definitive and objective answers…Social problems are never solved. At best they are only re-solved – over and over again". Further, we should expect a "differential resonance of metrics" in different countries (Bewley-Taylor 2016: 7) meaning that evaluations of drug policy, as we have seen with Sweden and the Netherlands, will always be partly determined by the wider social, cultural, geographic and historic context.

Thus far, this section has outlined the key indicators currently used to determine the effectiveness of drug policy and the problems with using them to make assessments of the success or otherwise of drug-policy interventions. In sum, there is little evidence to indicate success, there are significant problems with the validity of multi=national data comparisons, and there is no agreement about what success looks like or how to define it. The evidence presented here suggests that work is underway to improve the way that we measure the effectiveness of drug policy, but that even if these improvements are implemented, they will not lead to universal solutions to the drugs problem. Bewley-Taylor's (2016: 5) analysis of UN level consensus statements suggests that they "still implicitly frame the multinational approach in terms of solving the world drug problem". This is problematic: it is therefore not just the metrics themselves that need reframing and updating, but also the notion that this is a problem that can be solved if we only try hard enough.

While this presents a rather negative picture of the usefulness of drug policy evaluation in general, it is not the intention to suggest there is no point in attempting to evaluate drug policy implementations and use those findings as the cornerstone of evidence based or evidence *informed* policies. Indeed, the very purpose of this chapter is to suggest that evaluation of drug-policy initiatives is of vital importance if we are to capitalise on the results of increasingly innovative strategies in areas such as the regulation of cannabis markets or the control of new psychoactive substances. The next section of this chapter will present alternative strategies of evaluation, information sharing and evidence building that can provide useful alternatives or companions to the kind of metrics outlined above.

Policy Transfer and Lesson Drawing: Another Kind of Evidence

As outlined in the previous chapter, drug policy diversity and innovation are strengths in an area where existing policies have not generally been noted for their successes. In order, however, to capitalise on these strengths, it is necessary to be able to provide 'evidence' on the nature of different policy implementations and their effectiveness across a variety of contexts and settings. This chapter has already explored the role of 'evidence based policy' in the field of illicit drugs, firstly suggesting that traditional 'scientific' methods of evidence gathering might not be best suited to the drugs field, which presents a complex or 'wicked' social policy problem. It also argues that a perusal of the existing cross-national comparative data suggests a number of deficiencies which can only be partially solved by improving our methods of data collection and the metrics by which we measure drug policy effectiveness. Ultimately, we need to move away from attempting to collect the kind of 'evidence' which aims to resolve the problem and towards building a different kind of evidence that can 'inform', rather than provide the basis for, policies. The final section of this chapter will explore the relevance of policy transfer and lesson drawing literature to the drugs field, and evaluate the extent to which we are already engaged in this kind of evidence building in the territory of illicit drugs.

Hulme (2005: 424) suggests that "policy transfer represents one of the primary instruments of international and global social policy". Policy transfer has its roots in literature about diffusion (Walker 1969) which emerged in the US as a way to conceptualise the dissemination of ideas or practices within and between different states in the federal system. In general, policy transfer has come to represent "the process by which knowledge about policies, administrative arrangements, institutions and ideas in one political system (past or present) is used in the development of policies, administrative arrangements, institutions and ideas in another political system" (Dolowitz and Marsh 2000: 5). A sub-division of policy transfer literature, especially relevant to the discussion here, is Rose's (1991) work on lesson drawing. "Lessons can be sought by searching across time and/or across space…the process of lesson-drawing starts with scanning programmes in effect elsewhere, and ends with the prospective evaluation of what would happen if a programme already in effect elsewhere were transferred here in the future" (Rose 1991: 3).

While hard, top-down policy transfer often results in concrete outcomes, for example the development of strategies and action plans, or the implementation of specific interventions, lesson drawing is more concerned with the spread of ideas (Stone 2001a) and the use of the breadth of existing cross-national experience to inform policy (Page 2000). As globalisation increases, Stone (2001b: 6) describes "a shared experience of learning about problems and the development of a common perspective or international policy culture". This 'soft transfer' of ideas and information generally emphasises the process of 'learning' from each other in the international context, and becomes central to understanding the way that policy ideas and innovations diffuse across the globe in complex social policy areas. Dolowitz and Marsh (2000: 13) further elaborate that this kind of policy transfer does not have to be an "all-or-nothing process", but can rather be used as an inspiration for policy change, which may end up as rather different from the original as it is applied to a new context.

Indeed, policy transfer is often discussed within literature about the harmonisation or convergence of global policy in a particular field, but if applied in the way described above, drawing in particular on lesson learning aspects, then it should *not* lead to policy convergence, but rather to different countries and regions being able to pick and adapt policies form a global smorgasbord of potential options. Under this model, what is being shared is not necessarily practice or policy, but more a body of knowledge or ongoing discourse about an issue which could just as likely lead to policy innovation as policy emulation (Stone 2001b). Dolowitz and Marsh (2000) caution that policy transfer is likely to fail if sufficient attention is not paid to the intricate details of a policy in its original setting, the institutional infrastructure on which it depends, and the social, political and cultural contexts within which it exists. In many cases, there will be significant differences across these dimensions and those who are seeking to transfer policies will therefore have to make significant adaptations to ensure success. Stone (2001b) contends that failure to adapt original policies can occur if dominant global policies are transferred, not because they are expected to be effective, but because there are significant consequences of failing to do so. She also draws attention to the uneven nature of current global lesson drawing practice which tends to prioritise the experiences of the West in global dialogues and ignore the experiences and lessons which can be drawn from elsewhere (explored more fully in Chapter 6).

Dolowitz and Marsh (1996) identify many types of actor engaged in the transfer process: elected officials, political parties, bureaucrats/civil servants; pressure groups; policy entrepreneurs/experts, and supranational institutions. Crucially, in successful policy transfer, these actors will operate across multiple levels of governance (Benson and Jordan 2011), encompassing the global, the national and the local. Many researchers concerned with theorising the way that policy transfer happens, emphasise the pivotal role played by international networks comprised of different types of actor, for example expert groups, academic societies, NGOs and international movements, and networks created as part of the activity of supranational organisations. Knoepfel and Kissling-Naf (1998), for example, argue that networks provide the structural framework within which policy-oriented learning and the exchange of ideas can take place and Stone (2001a: 356) views the creation of global networks as "increasingly important arrangements through which social policies are constructed and implemented".

Successful global networks include a variety of actors drawn together from different countries and regions to perform a range of functions such as the pooling of information, the exchange of ideas, raising awareness about specific strategies, identifying areas of best practice and encouraging ongoing research and analysis in key areas of interest. They are thus ideally situated to facilitate the "soft, informal and gradual ....international diffusion and dissemination of ideas and policy paradigms" (Stone 2001b: 15) and "can work to shape the terms of debate, networking with members of a policy making community, crafting arguments and "brokering" their ideas to potential political supporters and patrons" (Stone 2001b: 15). Benson and Jordan (2011: 371), in a recent review of the literature, conclude that multi-level policy networks operating along these lines are increasingly facilitating the lesson drawing and policy transfer across "many different venues, spanning multiple spatial and temporal scales."

Dolowitz and Marsh (1996) draw particular attention to the role of international governing agencies in driving the spread of ideas around the globe, for example by helping to establish networks, by bringing them together at key events, and by producing reports of their findings. Bulmer and Padgett (2004) report that stronger forms of policy transfer—policy emulation for example—are more likely to occur when backed by supranational institutional support. It is important to remember, however, that supranational involvement can also be accompanied by limiting factors, for example by coercing countries and regions into dominant global practices, and by prioritising the experience and wisdom of the global North. Stone (2001b: 23) thus advocates the important role of nonstate actors, such as NGOs, in the "soft transfer of broad policy ideas … influencing public opinion and policy agendas". Less bound by official discourses and existing practices, non-state actors can generally operate more freely, increasing the potential for lesson drawing and innovation.

Turning once more to the field of illicit drugs, we can see the relevance of many of these ideas. As outlined in the previous chapter, there is a wealth of experience of different policy interventions and strategies from around the globe, yet there is little indication of a one size fits all 'solution' to the problem. There is room, then, for some hard policy transfer in the form of, for example, emulation of specific strategies or implementation of specific interventions. A process of soft policy transfer, on the other hand, underpinned by the creation of networks of international actors coming together to exchange ideas, experience and innovation in the pursuit of ever more effective policies, is also likely to be highly relevant here. The tendency for supranational institutions to coerce individual countries towards global norms and to overlook the experience of the global South also applies in this field. As discussed below, a perusal of both drug-related supranational organisations and NGOs suggests that substantial progress has already been made in relation to both top-down policy emulation and, to a lesser extent, the softer diffusion of ideas.

Perhaps the strongest work in this area has been around 'hard' policy emulation stimulated and encouraged by supranational organisations such as the UNODC, the EMCDDA, OID and ASEAN-NARCO. Policy emulation of this type can occur at many stages—as part of the agenda setting process, development of a policy, implementation of a policy or evaluation of a policy (Bennett 1991). The UNODC, for example aims to "facilitate policy and operational responses on issues related to drug control" (CND 2014: 17), undertakes normative work ensuring national policies remain in line with international drug conventions, and provides national drug strategy and action plan templates for countries seeking to develop or improve their own policy in this area. Similarly, the EMCDDA does this kind of work—for example, it played a substantial role in establishing a drug policy institution in Turkey (Akgul and Gurer 2014) and has helped to shape the national action plans of many of its member states, in particular those from Central and Eastern Europe. It is important to remember here that a question remains over the extent to which this kind of policy emulation is a voluntary process. If countries depend on the UN for funding and support in other areas, or are trying to gain membership of the EU, then they will be motivated to adopt existing policies. Furthermore, the policy templates provided by supranational organisations tend to be open to interpretation: both Portugal and Turkey have based their national strategies on European versions (EMCDDA 2011), yet Portugal has decriminalised the possession of drugs for personal use, while it remains possible to imprison people who use drugs in Turkey.

One area of policy emulation championed by supranational organisations which has brought significant benefits, concerns the creation of standards and practices in relation to data collection. The UNODC has done important work in this area, as has the EMCDDA which is generally recognised as providing the 'gold standard'. OID promotes and supports the creation of national drug observatories within its member states and ASEAN-NARCO encourages and facilitates the collation of data in line with UN standards. An international commitment to improving the quality of data and establishing common points of reference across the field plays an important part in working towards the implementation of evidence based drug policies across the globe. Supranational organisations can also play an important role in this area by creating funded research programmes on specific aspects of the drugs issue. Programmes funded at the European level, for example, have resulted in "an explosion of research in the drug field that is, at least practically, independent of national control and which is collected according to agreed international standards" (Standring 2012: 17).

Supranational organisations also have an important role to play in establishing and bringing together networks of experts to engage in the exchange of ideas and to report on instances of best practice. All organisations discussed in this section hold elite networking events, training programmes and conferences which help to establish and maintain cross-national groups of entrepreneurial actors (Mintrom 1997) or knowledge actors (Stone 2001b). The organisations themselves can play an important role in commissioning, publishing and disseminating reports on particular areas of interest and these are usually made freely available via their websites. In terms of OID and ASEAN NARCO publications, toolkits and guidelines are usually restricted to the area of data standards, but the UNODC also regularly publishes topical reports and field based toolkits. Once again, the EMCDDA proves a frontrunner in this kind of 'soft transfer' of ideas and practices via its comprehensive set of policy briefings, implementation toolboxes, reviews of research evidence, and publications which detail how to respond in particular settings and how to focus on the needs of particular groups of users.

In terms of 'soft policy transfer', NGOs and thinktanks also have an important role to play. Liberated from the need to align with official policies, and without the influence to force agreement, they can provide a more open and honest forum for discussion and exchange. There are an increasing number of NGOs and thinktanks with at least a partial focus on the global governance of drugs and they are particularly well placed to bring policy makers and researchers together to work on global problems. For example, the Transnational Institute (TNI) has a mandate to "strengthen international social movements with rigorous research, reliable information, sound analysis and constructive proposals ...TNI acts as a unique nexus between social movements, engaged scholars and policy makers" (TNI 2018: 1) and conducts all its work from the perspective of the global South. Much of its work is drug related and it was a strong voice seeking to influence debate ahead of UNGASS 2016 discussions.

Another example is provided by Brookings, the American based thinktank active in areas of global development and international affairs, and also seeking to contribute to UNGASS 2016 debates. In 2014 it launched its r *Improving Global Drug Policy Project* which sought to use case studies from across the globe to "evaluate the effectiveness and the problematic side-effects of existing counter-narcotics policies and to emphasise evidence based strategies" (Felbab-Brown and Trinkunas 2015). There are many others doing similar work (for example, the Global Commission on Drugs and the International Drug Policy Consortium) and contributing to the creation of 'global networks' well placed to play a role in the construction and implementation of drug policies. While many of these organisations were initially disappointed about the lack of change in global drug policy (Harm Reduction International 2016; TNI 2016) at UNGASS 2016, the Outcome Document (UNODC 2016: 4) does demonstrate some progress in this area as member states officially recognise that civil society entities "should be enabled to play a participatory role in the formulation, implementation and the providing of relevant scientific evidence".

Conclusion

This chapter has argued that a fourth step to improving global drug policy is to ensure that drug policy innovations are evaluated and evidence on their effectiveness is shared widely. Indeed, that the encouragement of innovative strategies of drug control only becomes worthwhile if the results of such innovations are compared and evaluated for effectiveness across a variety of settings. If drug policy innovations are carefully documented, measured against a variety of metrics, and accurate and comprehensive information about them is freely disseminated to the wider world, then those seeking to make improvements to their own national or regional policies can make an informed choice from a range of options. It is important to remember that drugs are a complex or 'wicked' problem. Evidence tends to be subjective and open to different interpretation depending on the actors involved and their underlying values and beliefs. This means that we are unlikely to find universal solutions or to reach a state where the problem is 'solved'. Instead we can work towards the improvement of data collection and the facilitation of information exchange. The evidence presented here suggests that important work is being done towards both the development of a better set of metrics to assess the overall effectiveness of drug policy and the creation and maintenance of networks of experts that actively engage in policy transfer. If a more effective global drug policy is to be achieved, better evidence is important; it is also critical that supranational institutions acknowledge that better evidence is still unlikely to be applied in a scientific manner to create universally successful policies. Hard policy emulation can play a part, but the soft transfer and exchange of ideas is key to success here.

References

Akgul, A., & Gurer, C. (2014). The European Union and emergence of a drug policy institution in Turkey. *Drugs: Education, Prevention and Policy, 21*(6), 460–469.

Bacchi, C. (2009). *Analysing policy: What's the problem represented to be Sydney.* Australia: Pearson Education.

Backstrand, K. (2004). Civic science for sustainability: Reframing the role of experts, policy-makers and citizens in environmental governance. *Global Environmental Politics, 3*(4), 24–41.

Bennett, C. J. (1991). Review article: What is policy convergence and what causes it? *British Journal of Political Science, 21*, 215–233.

Benson, D., & Jordan, A. (2011). What have we learned from policy transfer research? Dolowitz and Marsh revisited. *Political Studies Review, 9*, 366–378.

Berridge, V., & Thom, B. (1996). Research and policy: What determines the relationship? *Policy Studies, 17*(1), 23–34.

Bewley-Taylor, D. (2016, April). *Towards metrics that measure outcomes that matter* (Policy Brief 10). Swansea, UK: Global Drug Policy Observatory. https://www.swansea.ac.uk/gdpo.

Black, N. (2001). Evidence based policy: Proceed with care. *British Medical Journal, 323*, 275–279.

Boaz, A., & Pawson, R. (2005). The perilous road from evidence to policy: Five journeys compared. *Journal of Social Policy, 34*(2), 175–194.

Bulmer, S., & Padgett, S. (2004). Policy transfer in the European Union: An institutionalist perspective. *British Journal of Political Science, 35*(1), 103–126.

Chatwin, C. (2011). *Drug policy harmonization and the European Union.* Basingstoke: Palgrave Macmillan.

Chatwin, C. (2015). *Mixed messages from Europe on drug policy reform: The cases of Sweden and The Netherlands.* Washington, DC: Brookings. https://www.brookings.edu.

CND. (2014, March 13–21). *Proposed strategic framework on 2016–2017 for the United Nations Office on Drugs and Crime*, Commission on Narcotic Drugs, Fifty-seventh session, Vienna, E/CN.7/2014/CRP.4.

Cohen, P. (2010). Looking at the UN, smelling a rat: A comment on "Sweden's successful drugs policy: A review of the evidence". *Amsterdam Law Forum, 2*(4), 10.

Dolowitz, D. P., & Marsh, D. (1996). Who learns what from whom? A review of the policy transfer literature. *Political Studies, 44*(2), 343–357.

Dolowitz, D. P., & Marsh, D. (2000). Learning from abroad: The role of policy transfer in contemporary policy making. *Governance, 13*(1), 5–24.
Duke, K., & Thom, B. (2014). The role of evidence and the expert in contemporary processes of governance: The case of opioid substitution treatment policy in England. *International Journal of Drug Policy, 25*, 964–971.
EMCDDA. (2011). *European drug report 2011.* http://www.emcdda.europa.eu.
EMCDDA. (2017). *European drug report 2017.* http://www.emcdda.europa.eu.
EMCDDA. (2018). *Mission.* http://www.emcdda.europa.eu/mission-en.
European Parliament. (2016). *A review and assessment of EU drug policy.* Directorate General for Internal Policies, Policy Department C: Citizens' rights and constitutional affairs, Civil liberties, justice and home affairs, PE 571.400.
Felbab-Brown, V., & Trinkunas, H. (2015). *UNGASS 2016 in comparative perspective: Improving the prospects for success.* https://www.brookings.edu.
Galtung, J. (1990). Theory formation in social research: A plea for pluralism. In E. Oyen (Ed.), *Comparative methodology.* London: Sage.
Global Commission on Drug Policy. (2011). *War on drugs: Report of the global commission on drug policy.* http://www.globalcommissionondrugs.org.
Greenwald, G. (2009). *Drug decriminalization in Portugal: Lessons for creating fair and successful drug policies.* Washington, DC: The Cato Institute. http://www.cato.org.
Grund, J. P., & Breeksema, J. (2013). *Coffeeshops and compromise: Separated illicit drug markets in the Netherlands.* New York: Open Society Foundations. http://www.opensocietyfoundations.org.
Hakim, C. (2000). *Research design: Successful designs for social and economic research* (2nd ed.). London: Routledge.
Harm Reduction International. (2016, January 23). *Harm Reduction International has serious concerns with draft UNGASS outcome document.* https://www.hri.global.
Head, B. W. (2008). Three lenses of evidence-based policy. *The Australian Journal of Public Administration, 67*(1), 1–11.
Hulme, R. (2005). Policy transfer and the internationalisation of social policy. *Social Policy and Sociology, 4*(4), 417–425.
Hunt, N. (2003). *A review of the evidence-base for harm reduction approaches to drug use.* Release. http://www.forward-thinking-on-drugs.org/review2.
Knoepfel, P., & Kissling-Naf, I. (1998). Social learning in policy networks. *Policy and Politics, 26*(3), 343–367.
Lancaster, K. (2016). Performing the evidence-based drug policy. *Contemporary Drug Problems, 43*(2), 142–153.

MacGregor, S. (2011). The impact of research on policy in the drugs field. *Methodological Innovations Online, 6*(1), 41–57.

Mintrom, M. (1997). Policy entrepreneurs and the diffusion of innovations. *American Journal of Political Science, 41*(3), 738–770.

Monaghan, M. (2008). Appreciating cannabis: The paradox of evidence in evidence-based policy making. *Evidence and Policy, 4*(2), 209–231.

Muggah, R., & de Carvalho. S. (2015). How new metrics can reset global drug policy. *World Politics Review.* https://www.worldpoliticsreview.com.

Muggah, R., Aguirre, K., & de Carvalho, S. (2015, January). *Measurement matters: Designing new metrics for a drug policy that works* (Strategic paper 12). Brazil: Instituto Igarape.

Mulgan, G. (2004). Government, knowledge and the business of policy making: The potential and limits of evidence-based policy. *Evidence and Policy, 1*(2), 215–226.

Mullen, E. J. (2016). Reconsidering the "idea" of evidence in evidence-based policy and practice. *European Journal of Social Work, 19*(3–4), 310–335.

Naughton, M. (2005). "Evidence-based policy" and the government of the criminal justice system—Only if the evidence fits! *Critical Social Policy, 25*(1), 47–69.

Nutt, D., King, L. A., & Phillips, C. D. (2010). Drug harms in the UK: A multicriteria decision analysis. *The Lancet, 376*(9752), 6–12.

Nutt, D., King, L. A., Saulsbury, W., & Blakemore, C. (2007). Development of a rational scale to assess the harm of drugs of potential misuse. *The Lancet, 369*(9566), 1047–1053.

Page, E. (2000). *Future governance and the literature on policy transfer and lesson drawing* (Future Governance Papers). Swindon, UK: ESRC.

Pearce, W., Wasselink, A., & Colebatch, H. (2014). Evidence and meaning in policy making. *Evidence and Policy, 10*(2), 161–165.

Pinto Coelho, M. (2010, February 2). *Decriminalization of drugs in Portugal—The real facts!* Stockholm: World Federation Against Drugs. http://www.wfad.se/latest-news/1articles/123-decriminalization-of-drugs-in-portugal–the-real-facts.

Reinarman, C., Cohen, P., & Kaal, H. (2004). The limited relevance of drug policy: Cannabis in Amsterdam and San Francisco. *American Journal of Public Health, 94*, 836–842.

Rittel, H. W. J., & Webber, M. M. (1973). Dilemmas in a general theory of planning. *Policy Sciences, 4*, 155–169.

Ritter, A. (2009). How do drug policy makers access research evidence? *International Journal of Drug Policy, 20*, 70–75.
Ritter, A., & Bammer, G. (2010). Models of policy-making and their relevance for drug research. *Drug and Alcohol Review, 29*, 352–357.
Roberts, M. (2014). Making drug policy together: Reflections on evidence, engagement and participation. *International Journal of Drug Policy, 25*, 952–956.
Rose, R. (1991). What is lesson-drawing? *Journal of Public Policy, 11*(1), 3–30.
Roumeliotis, F. (2015). Politics of prevention: The emergence of prevention science. *International Journal of Drug Policy, 26*, 746–754.
Sanderson, I. (2009). Intelligent policy making for a complex world: Pragmatism, evidence and learning *Political Studies, 57*, 699–719.
Standring, A. (2012). An ever closer union—Towards the "soft" convergence of European drug policies. *Drugs and Alcohol Today, 12*(1), 12–19.
Stevens, A. (2007). Survival of the ideas that fit: An evolutionary analogy for the use of evidence. *Social Policy and Society, 6*(1), 25–35.
Stevens, A. (2011a). *Drugs, crime and public health: The political economy of drug policy.* London: Routledge-Cavendish.
Stevens, A. (2011b). Telling policy stories: An ethnographic study of the use of evidence in policy-making in the UK. *Journal of Social Policy, 40*, 237–255.
Stone, D. (2001a). Think tanks, global lesson-drawing and networking social policy ideas. *Global Social Policy, 1*(3), 338–360.
Stone, D. (2001b, April). *Learning lessons, policy transfer and the international diffusion of policy ideas* (Working Paper No 69.01). Centre for the Study of Globalisation and Regionalisation.
TNI. (2016). *The UNGASS outcome document: Diplomacy or denialism?* https://www.tni.org.
TNI. (2018). *Mission.* https://www.tni.org/en/page/mission.
Transnational Institute. (2015). *UNGASS 2016: Background memo on the proposal to establish an expert advisory group.* https://www.tni.org.
Uchtenhagen, A. (2014). Some critical issues in cannabis policy reform. *Addiction, 109*(3), 356–358.
UNODC. (2007). *Sweden's successful drug policy: A review of the evidence.* http://www.unodc.org.
UNODC. (2011). *World drug report 2011.* http://www.unodc.org/documents.
UNODC. (2016). *Outcome document of the 2016 United Nations General Assembly Special Session on the world drug problem. Our joint commitment*

to effectively addressing and countering the world drug problem. New York: United Nations. http://www.unodc.org/documents.

UNODC. (2017). *World drug report 2017*, 26–7. http://www.unodc.org/documents.

Valentine, K. (2009). Evidence, values and drug treatment policy. *Critical Social Policy, 29*(3), 443–464.

Walker, J. (1969). The diffusion of innovations among the American states. *American Political Review, 33*(3), 880–899.

Weiss, C. H. (1977). The enlightenment function of social science research. *Policy Analysis, 3*(4), 531–545.

Weiss, C. H. (1986). The many meanings of research utilisation. In M. Bulmer (Ed.), *Social science and social policy*. London: Allen Unwin.

Werb, D., Kazatchkine, M., Kerr, T., Nutt, D., Strathdee, S., Hankins, C., et al. (2016a). A call to reprioritise metrics to evaluate illicit drugs policy. *The Lancet, 387*, 1371.

Werb, D., Wood, E., Strathdee, S., Kazatchkine, M., des Jarlais, D., Hankins, C., et al. (2016b). *Open letter to the United Nations: A call for a reprioritisation of metrics to evaluate illicit drug policy*. Tornto, Canada: International Centre for Science in Drugs Policy. https://www.icsdp.org.

Wood, E., Werb, D., Kazatchkine, M., Kerr, T., Hankins, C., Gorna, R., et al. (2010). Vienna declaration: A call for evidence-based drug policies. *The Lancet, 376*, 310–312.

Young, K., Ashby, D., Boaz, A., & Grayson, L. (2002). Social science and the evidence-based policy movement. *Social Policy and Society, 1*(3), 215–224.

6

Step Five: Broaden the Horizons of the Drug Policy Debate

The final step towards a more effective global drug policy is recognising the need to broaden our horizons in terms of what is considered a relevant part of the drug policy debate today. This broadening of horizons needs to take place across different dimensions including, but not limited to, those outlined in this chapter. The argument here often draws on themes that have been developed throughout the book, to demonstrate specific areas where the focus of debate has generally been of too narrow a nature. The first section of this chapter thus highlights the fact that the global drug policy debate to date has predominantly been conceptualised from the perspective of Western drug-consuming countries. It argues that, in order to produce a more effective global drug policy, strategies must be implemented within a global framework that gives equal status to contributions from the global South, and which acknowledge the problems faced by both producer and consumer countries in seeking to understand the global drugs issue. The second section explores a multi-level governance approach in response to the control of illicit drugs and emphasises the need to involve local level as well as national and international levels in effective drug policy making. It argues that an increased contribution from civil society, including an

C. Chatwin, *Towards More Effective Global Drug Policies*,
https://doi.org/10.1007/978-3-319-92072-6_6

equal contribution from the global North, will result in a greater understanding of localised strategies and improve opportunities for effective soft policy transfer to occur.

The third section advocates viewing a wider spectrum of potentially harmful substances within drug control policies, regardless of their legal status. For example, it documents recent efforts to include alcohol and tobacco in discussions about substance related harm, and it argues that new drugs, such as New Psychoactive Substances (NPS) and Human Enhancement Drugs (HED), should be considered as part of the same issue. Finally, the fourth section explores the contribution that technological advances have made to understandings of drug markets in particular, and the wider drugs field in general. It argues that widespread technological changes, (rather than the more specific rise of NPS), should be seen as one of the predominant challenges facing global drug policy makers today. Taken collectively, these sections suggest that we need to broaden the horizons of the drug policy debate according to geography, governance, substance and technological advances.

Including the Global South

The concept of globalisation is of increasing importance to the development of social sciences in general (Giddens 1990). "The growing interconnectedness of states and societies" (Held 2000: 42) has allowed greater cross-national understanding of cultural and societal processes, and has led to an attempt to uncover universal truths or a general theory of social science with global applicability (Aas 2013). Bowling (2011: 363) describes different approaches relevant here: research based on *comparisons* between different locations; *transnational* research which explores the intersections between different regions; and *global* research which "aspires to bring together transnational and comparative research from all regions of the world to build a globally inclusive and cosmopolitan discipline".

One important aspect of this work is a desire to understand how other systems of thinking help to expand our bodies of knowledge in general and allow us to examine existing problems, all too familiar at the national level, from new perspectives. Another is that specific local initiatives can become featured on a global basis and used as a stimulus for policy development elsewhere (as discussed in the previous chapter). In this way, it is both the global and the local which are important, as well as the manner in which they interact with each other. Robertson (1995) has applied the term 'glocalization' to emphasise the importance of both contexts in increasing our depth of understanding. As Held (2000) suggests, globalisation is, in essence, a sharing of the local across the global context.

Unsurprisingly, globalisation has become an increasingly important concept for criminology (Bowling 2011; Nelken 2009; Aas 2013). "Criminology's recent history has been marked by a progressive move towards the 'exterior'. Both the scope of criminological knowledge, as well as crime control interventions, are expanding beyond the previously relatively contained world of the nation-state" (Aas 2011: 406). Bowling (2011: 361) suggests that a key focus of criminology has always been to establish "general models of crime, punishment and justice... which claim to be universal". Here, again, the concern is not just with comparing different criminal justice interventions, or the transnational nature of crime, but with the impact of globalisation on the very discipline itself, in terms of both theoretical development and the importation and exportation of criminal justice policies (Chan 2005).

It is clear, then, that the increasingly global nature of society provides the potential for improvement in theories and practices of social science in general, and of criminology in particular. Aas (2011, 2012, 2013), however, in her extensive work in this area, traces an important line of critique in the reading of globalisation and its drive towards universality of theory and practice as outlined above. She delineates an important imbalance in the production of knowledge and the exportation/importation of policy between the global North and the global South, suggesting that 'Americanisation' or 'Westernisation' might be more accurate than globalisation to describe what is occurring. As the world opens up and the exchange of ideas and practices is facilitated, the overwhelming tendency is for theories developed in the global North to be applied to situations in the global South, and practices developed in the global North to be exported to countries in the global South.

Ultimately, the field remains shaped by dominant and powerful states and untouched by greater access to information on the experiences of those at the periphery of global influence.

In line with this analysis, Connell (2007: 368) describes the ability to claim universality in any meaningful context as significantly compromised; instead information is produced and disseminated outwards from the (Americanised, Westernised) centre, meaning that social theory "sees and speaks from the global North". The opportunity presented by globalisation, to interact and learn from each other as equals, can thus be limited by a tendency to impose the dominant and existing world view on those who may not have yet had the good fortune to encounter it. Such an approach also limits the prominence of the local for much of the world: within the global North, the value of the local is emphasised in its ability to influence the rest of the world; but within the global South, the value of the local may actually be diminished as 'global' information is prioritised over local knowledge. Aas (2012) cautions that to feel the full benefits of globalisation, the importance of local context in theoretical and policy development must be acknowledged.

This critique is also pertinent to the discipline of criminology, where American and other Western scholars dominate (van Swaaningen 1999; Morrison 2005). Stan Cohen (1998) was one of the first criminologists to highlight the harm producing aspects of the imposition of Western crime control models on the third world, without seeking to explore their suitability for different societal and cultural contexts, and often with little evidence of their success even in their home setting. Practices such as those described by Cohen reveal an underlying 'ethnocentricity' (Nelken 2009) of criminological thought based on assumptions that what is done in the global North must inherently be right for the rest of the world. Aas (2013: 206) thus suggests: "A vital task for global criminology, if it is to deserve its name, is to disturb the hegemony of Western thought".

The discussion thus far attests to the rising importance of globalisation of thought and practice in social science disciplines, as well as the significant problem that is presented by a failure to interconnect with the global South in any meaningful way. These issues are highly relevant to the field of illicit drugs, as has already been seen throughout this book. Chapter 2 explored the failure of the war on drugs to eradicate or significantly reduce the production, marketing and consumption of illegal substances, and its propensity to cause unintended harm of many varieties as a by-product of its control strategies. The United States has consistently remained one of the most dominant voices since the inception of global drug policy debates and in the 1980s, under the leadership of George Bush Senior, the problem presented by drugs was firmly framed as one that was external to American borders. The focus of the war on drugs became on the production and supply of drugs and, given America's position of power and privilege on the world stage, a large proportion of global drug control efforts were concentrated on drug producing countries. It was thus a war conceptualised by the global North and waged, in the main, on the global South.

As we saw in Chapter 2, this led to many negative unintended consequences for drug producing countries in the global South, for example: the increase of corruption and violence as the power of organised criminal groups grew; environmental harms as crop-spraying programmes contaminated large tracts of land; the erosion of human rights in an effort to achieve global drug-reduction rate targets; and the displacement of the drug trade to new areas as a result of targeted efforts in particular global regions (Pryce 2012). Key to the production of these harms was the framing of the problem as one that could primarily be addressed by reducing the production and supply of drugs: the idea that the best way to stop people consuming drugs is to prevent their very production and movement towards the West. Also relevant to the discussion here was the tendency of global institutions, such as the UNODC, to encourage the export of American drug control strategies to countries with less well-developed policies in this area. For example: the encouragement of imprisonment as a mandatory punishment for drug-related crimes; the establishment of national drug agencies charged with 'solving' the problem; and the introduction of drug-related targets that were often used as an indicator of whether countries should continue to be supported in other areas of development.

Even though the illicit drugs issue increasingly became the focus of global attention, the opportunity was not taken to exchange expert knowledge on an equal footing or consider a variety of strategies for potential transfer. Instead, the existing dominant beliefs about the best way to control drugs were disseminated throughout the world, unaffected by evidence from peripheral areas and without concern about either their effectiveness in the Western context, or their suitability for cross-cultural and cross-societal transfer. In addition to the unintended harms this has caused, Bowling (2011) draws attention to the tendency it has created for developing countries to focus on controlling the drug trade at the expense of potentially more pressing issues such as the reduction of poverty or the creation of strong institutions of governance. Youngers (2005) also reminds us that these strategies have effectively silenced the local in production countries as counterdrug policies are dictated by the US and negotiated with a small group of the political elite, thus denying local experience and devaluing local knowledge production.

As evidence of the failure of the war on drugs approach mounts across the globe, it has become easier to challenge the dominant global drug discourse. In 2013 the Organisation of American States (OAS) published a report on alternative drug policies which gained international influence in a manner not previously seen from those considered to be at the periphery of the drug policy debate. The leaders of three Latin American countries (Colombia, Mexico, and Guatemala) were responsible for requesting the United Nations General Assembly on drugs, originally scheduled for 2018, to be brought forward to 2016 and so provide an opportunity to debate pressing issues of public health, harm reduction and human rights abuses. Perceived by many as being precipitated by the failure of the war on drugs, accompanied by an American relaxation in its own domestic cannabis laws, this development has been described as "a moment of unprecedented Latin American leadership on the global scale" (The Dialogue 2016). The fault lines that have developed in the dominant global discourse, can thus be seen as having provided an opportunity for alternative conceptualisations of the global drug situation and the appropriate range of responses to it.

Allowing the global South to interconnect with (rather than be influenced by) global drug policy debates means that the problem can be re-framed, not just as one caused by the producers and suppliers of drugs and inflicted on countries in the global North, but as an issue to some extent *driven* by the overwhelming desire of the global North to consume drugs. In the fullness of time, such a redressing of the balance will lead to the development of new policies that are aimed at reducing the demand for drugs as well as the supply. Chapter 3 explored the need for the development of viable alternatives to existing models of drug policy and an important way of stimulating new thought is by including new voices in the debate and encouraging new bodies of research evidence. The OAS (2013) report on alternative drug policies provides an important example of this but, despite the rising influence of the global South's contribution to the debate, it is important to recognise that there is still much ground to be covered if we are to challenge the hegemony of Western thought in this area.

In Chapter 4, the importance of encouraging diversity and innovation in drug policy development was emphasised. In this area, the prioritisation of research and knowledge that is produced in the global North remains prevalent. One example is provided by the disproportionate focus on evaluating and sharing information about initiatives developed in the West such as the American States' experiments with cannabis regulation, the coffee shops of the Netherlands, Portuguese decriminalisation and Spanish cannabis clubs, compared with the under-researched areas of Uruguayan cannabis regulation, Argentinian decriminalisation or Jamaican legislative changes. The main thrust of the argument in Chapter 4 rests on the continuing need to innovative in drug policy as we search for more effective strategies that seek to reduce tr harms. It is patently not desirable to limit innovation in drug policy to the global North. For innovation to reach its true potential, it must be a global endeavour.

Another example is provided by the disproportionate sanctions faced by countries from the global South seeking to introduce experimental drug policies. William Brownfield, in his position as US Secretary of State for International Narcotics and Law Enforcement Affairs, consistently presented American regulated cannabis markets as being compatible with a flexible interpretation of the international drug conventions. Yet this position is somewhat undermined when compared with Brownfield's comments on cannabis experiments elsewhere: "Jamaica like all…countries of the world does have to address [their concerns] within their own realities, but at the same time accept that they have ratified and, therefore, have a legal obligation to abide by the terms of the three international drug conventions" (cited in Fox 2015: 1). Countries in the global South are often more dependent on powerful and privileged nation-states, such as the US, for international support and development aid, and are thus considerably more vulnerable to policy critique. It is the very privilege of America's position as central to the global drug policy discourse, that allows it to undertake its own drug policy innovation while at the same time continuing to impose sanctions on other, more peripheral, countries that seek to do the same. To produce a more effective global drug policy, innovations need to be allowed to flourish in all geographical locations. If they are not, then Western knowledge production and framing of the issue will continue to predominate, and the range of control options will remain limited and primarily suited to the global North.

In Chapter 5, the importance of developing better metrics for evaluation of the drug problem were considered and it should be noted here that these metrics must be developed with significant contribution from the global South. If they are not, then the success or otherwise of drug policy endeavours will remain dependent on the priorities of the global North. Youngers (2005: 355) emphasises the irony of "an annual scorecard, on which the largest consumer of illicit drugs in the world grades the progress of other countries in seeking to limit its supply". Similarly, the value of policy transfer via sharing of best practice and networking must not be limited to the imposition of strategies from the global North onto the global South, regardless of suitability. Policy transfer will only succeed if it takes place within an interconnected context where all regions have an equal opportunity to influence each other, and where it is recognised that what works in one geographical or cultural location, will not necessarily work elsewhere without adaptation. As Aas (2013: 15) suggests, it is "precisely because world centres do not, and cannot, provide a template for global change [that] the studies of the periphery offer invaluable insight".

Including the Local Level

Increasingly, in trying to understand the management of complex post-modern societies, the focus has been on governance rather than government: "contemporary history has seen a shift in the overall mode of governance [from] the Westphalian, sovereigntist, statist structure that characterised societal regulation in the modern era" (Scholte 2010: 383). Government is thus conceptualised as just one player in the overall governance of nation states. Since 2000 a tendency has arisen to emphasise the multi-level nature of governance around the globe (Hooghe and Marks 2001). Originating in studies of European integration, the concept has spread outwards into the international arena and generally includes supra-national institutions, national governments and local or subnational contributions. "We can now define multi-level governance as a set of general-purpose or functional jurisdictions that enjoys some degree of autonomy within a common governance arrangement and whose actors claim to engage in an enduring interaction in pursuit of a common good" (Zurn et al. 2010: 4).

Multi-level governance recognises that the policy challenges we currently face are likely to resonate on a global scale, and that our responses therefore ought to encompass the global as well as the national level. The sovereignty of the state becomes less important with the recognition that what we do in our own territories has global implications, as borders become more porous, and as information travels more quickly and easily across time and space. Kaul (2010: 335) describes these developments as resulting in "responsible sovereignty" in which national governments recognise and appreciate the increased interdependence of different nation states in finding solutions to contemporary problems. It is neither realistic nor desirable to seek to deal with many issues in isolation; instead responsible nation states must explore policy strategies that are palatable on the global stage. This leads to the development of supra-national organisations, such as the United Nations, to complement national efforts and to help individual nation states to come together and approach issues in a cohesive manner.

Equally important, however, in multi-level governance theory, is the contribution of the local or subnational level to policy making and problem solving (Scholte 2010). Civil society contributions are often effected via Non Governmental Organisations (NGOs) or social movements more generally, which have coalesced around particular issues. Just as national governments must increasingly recognise that they are part of a wider world and seek to find globally acceptable solutions to their problems, so do individuals feel themselves to be citizens of the world and conceptualise their challenges as global ones. Scholte (2010) suggests that civil society contributions to governance are stronger today than they have ever been, particularly in terms of calling national and supranational organisations to account and providing a regulatory role in respect to them, setting national and global agendas, and increasing a general global focus on human rights or the environment, for example. Such is the global influence of civil society that it has become a recognised player in UN policy processes, for example via the Conference of Non-Governmental Organisations (CONGO).

Local contributions to global governance are particularly important: without them, multi-level governance can seem undemocratic (Garcia 2006). If decisions are increasingly negotiated between national governments and supranational organisations, they become further removed from those they impact most and National governments can act as gatekeepers (Bache 1998; Getimis et al. 2006), limiting the role of actors from sub and supra national levels. Civil society organisations can also give voice to those who are at the margins of society and who would not be heard through more overtly political processes. It is important to also recognise, however, that in terms of the global impact of civil society "so far the promise has outstripped the practice" and that problems such as the dominance of the global North are also prevalent within this sector, meaning that the involvement of "civil society can actually perpetuate and deepen privilege" (Scholte 2010: 394).

Within the field of illicit drugs multi-level governance is clearly evident. National governments retain overall control of their own drug policies, even within supra-national contexts such as the European Union, Organisation of American States or, indeed the United Nations. Nevertheless, there is an important role for supra-national organisations here which often provide a guiding framework—for example via the United Nation's international drug conventions or the European Union's drug strategy and action plan—within which national policy can develop. Finally, specific service interventions for the users of drugs and the communities within which they reside, are often designed and implemented at the local level.

In designing global responses to the issue of illegal drugs, however, the importance of the local level in governance strategies has been undervalued. The main thrust of debate has taken place between supranational organisations such as the UN and the representatives of nation states, often without the direct involvement of civil society. Collins (2017) describes how, since the 1990s, a growing recognition of the failure of the war on drugs has led to increasing attempts from public health activists and libertarian organisations to introduce alternative drug control strategies to global drug policy debates. NGOs in the field of illicit drugs were particularly active in the run up to UNGASS 2016, ensuring that human rights in general, the abolition of the death penalty in particular, sustainable development targets, reform of the international conventions, the need for an expert advisory group on international drug control, and many other issues, were on the agenda and featured in high level debates and UNGASS side events.

While some have been disappointed by the lack of progress achieved towards these goals in the Outcome Document (UNODC 2016), it does represent "a watering down [of] the international consensus and …a shift to national and local policy experimentation" (Collins 2017: 94). In particular the Brownfield proposal (Barrett et al. 2014) which calls for increased flexibility in interpreting the international conventions, helps to secure the freedom for different localities and regions to explore their own diverse responses to the problems presented by illicit drugs. One result of increased flexibility in interpretation of the international conventions would be to increase the proliferation of local level alternative drug policy developments. The more local level examples there are to draw on in the formulation of drug policy, the more opportunity there is to choose interventions most suited to culture, history and public attitude in a particular geographical area. If the aims of global drug policy become focused on abandoning war on drugs strategies in favour of seeking a range of innovative and diverse alternatives, that are framed by the needs of the global South as well as the global North, then broadening the horizons of the drug policy debate—to emphasise and increase contributions from civil society and local levels of government in general—is vital. Taking up the argument from the previous chapter that there are no universal solutions to the global drugs problem, then an increased focus on the local level will stimulate a breadth of responses that are culturally appropriate and context specific.

Evidence suggests that, increasingly, supra-national organisations and national governments are prioritising the contribution from civil society in global drug policy decision making. The EU, for example, identifies civil society participation as one of the five key principles of good governance (Garcia 2006). In 2012 the UN sought to improve the "participatory role of civil society in addressing the world drug problem" (CND 2012: 1) and the Outcome Document (UNODC 2016: 8) contains many references to the greater inclusion of civil society. For example: "We recognize that civil society, as well as the scientific community and academia, plays an important role in addressing and countering the world drug problem, and note that affected populations and representatives of civil society entities, where appropriate, should be enabled to play a participatory role in the formulation, implementation, and the providing of relevant scientific evidence in support of, as appropriate, the evaluation of drug control policies and programmes".

To broaden the horizons of the drug policy debate so that it includes the local level in its fullest sense, it is also important to ensure that local-level contributions are not limited to invitations to submit reports to national and/or supranational committees. Those involved at the local level should also be invited to become parts of more informal networks and in the general exchange of information and occurrence of best practice. Greater involvement of the local level will result in an increase of context specific strategies for dealing with the control of illegal drugs, and will thus aid the process of soft policy transfer that should be seen as a desirable alternative to the top-down imposition of policy from national and supranational levels. Finally, efforts to increase local contributions must be global in their nature. To avoid the problems and power imbalances outlined in the previous section, local strategies originating from the global South must be given as much weight as those from the global North.

Including a Greater Variety of Potentially Harmful Substances

Systems of national and international drug control are generally justified on the presumption that illegal drugs are more harmful than legal substances (Pedersen et al. 2016), and should therefore be subject to stricter controls and, in many cases, criminalisation of the user. Yet, the evidence for harms caused by legal drugs such as alcohol and tobacco is overwhelming. Long-term use of tobacco, for example, has been demonstrated to reduce life expectancy by about 10 years (Doll et al. 2004) and also entails huge health-care costs in terms of chronic illness and fatalities. In 2006, Mackay et al. estimated the yearly health costs of tobacco smoking to be $96 billion in the US and £2.25 billion in the UK. Finally, Nutt et al. (2007) found smoked tobacco to be the most addictive commonly used drug, ahead of both heroin and alcohol.

Similarly, alcohol is highly addictive, relatively easy to fatally overdose on, is associated with depression and mental health issues, and has been found to be a frequent contributing factor in road traffic accidents, assaults and suicide (Babor et al. 2010). Furthermore, it "makes a significant contribution to the global burden of disease" (Hall 2016: 58) being linked to, for example, liver cirrhosis, cancer, cardiovascular disease, stroke and dementia. A recent World Health Organisation (WHO) report on the global alcohol problem finds that alcohol is responsible for 5.9% of global deaths and entails enormous social costs ranging from 1.3–3.3% of the gross domestic product (WHO 2014). Taken collectively, alcohol and tobacco have been found to account for about 90% of drug-related deaths in the UK (Nutt et al. 2007). In Canada the costs of illicit drugs to society were estimated as less than one fifth of the costs for either alcohol or tobacco; while in the global context, the contribution of opioids, cocaine and amphetamines to the global burden of disease was found to account for about one-fifth of the burden from either alcohol or tobacco alone (Room 2006).

As Fischer and Kendall (2011: 1891) thus suggest: "If we assume public health and welfare should be guiding principles for substance control policy, we would not expect to see … alcohol and tobacco … not only legally available, but openly traded". Indeed, there is a relatively long history of research studies which aim to compare the harmfulness of legal drugs such as alcohol and tobacco with the full spectrum of illegal drugs. For example, Hall et al. (1999) compared the severity of health effects for heavy users of different kinds of substances, both legal and illegal, finding that alcohol ranked the highest and Gable (2004) has shown that, in terms of toxic effects, alcohol is more lethal than many of the illicit drugs subject to national and international control.

In 2007 perhaps the most (in)famous study in this area was published in the UK by Professor David Nutt and his colleagues and has sparked a "debate which is long overdue" (Room 2011: 1896). Nutt et al. (2007, 2010) have sought to expose the arbitrary nature of the UK system of drug classification by developing a rational scale of harm that ranks substances based on a comprehensive and scientific appraisal of their relative harms. They have utilised a multi-variate approach to evaluating harm which includes physical harms (damage to organs and bodily systems, toxicity, route of administration, immediate and chronic health problems), dependence harms (addictive qualities including psychological dependence and withdrawal symptoms), and social harms (harm to families and societies, costs to systems of health care, social care and the police). Alongside illegal substances, both alcohol and tobacco are also considered, and in the latest iteration of their research (Nutt et al. 2010) they place alcohol at the top of the list as the most harmful substance, while tobacco is placed sixth out of twenty. Cannabis appears around the middle of the scale, while LSD, ecstasy and magic mushrooms, usually classified as very harmful drugs, are at the bottom. Nutt et al. (2010: 1051) thus conclude: "alcohol and tobacco—the most widely used unclassified substances—would have harm ratings comparable with class A and B illegal drugs, respectively".

Other European research tends to confirm these findings. For example, van Amsterdam et al. (2010) conducted a similar evaluation of relative drug harms in the Dutch context and found that alcohol and tobacco were more harmful than many illegal drugs, with the exception of heroin and crack. Bourgain et al. (2012) explored the comparative damage and benefits of a variety of substances in the French context and identified alcohol, heroin, cocaine and tobacco as the most harmful addictive products. A follow up study, conducted by van Amsterdam et al. (2015) attempted to replicate the findings of these studies in a cross-European context. This study included experts drawn from relevant EU institutions (such as the EMCDDA) and from across different European countries and regions. Again, alcohol, heroin and crack emerged as the overall most harmful substances.

A growing body of research thus suggests that, at the very least, we ought to consider legal drugs such as alcohol and tobacco alongside illegal drugs in our policies and strategies, particularly if they are focused on public health and harm reduction. While most drug researchers do not advocate the full criminalisation of alcohol and tobacco, it does seem counter-productive to exclude them entirely from global or national policies designed to control the use of harmful substances and reduce the overall harm experienced as a result of their use. Of course, most countries do have tobacco and alcohol control policies that focus on the reduction of the harms caused by their use, and the UN and WHO also carry out important work in these areas. It is, however, the artificial separation made between illegal substances and harmful legal substances that proves problematic here. In the pursuit of rational, scientific and objective policies for controlling harmful substances, it makes no sense to exclude two of the most harmful and widely used substances within most societies.

One barrier to including legal drugs such as alcohol and tobacco in national and global drug policy debates is that public perceptions (and often those of politicians too) tend to be much more lenient with respect to legal substances (Rossow 2011). Caulkins et al. (2011) note the complex relationship between harms and benefits in this context. In respect to alcohol, for example, one of the reasons it causes so much societal harm is because it offers so many benefits to its users. These harms are widely acknowledged but are overlooked by the general public and by politicians and policy makers because important weight is also given to the legitimate pleasures that use can bring. Room (2006: 168) further elaborates: "on one hand, alcohol is so deeply enculturated in western societies that even considering it in the same frame as derogated drugs is unacceptable to many. On the other hand, there is an enormous commitment by many involved in the international control system and equivalent national systems to keeping the status quo". Nevertheless, a more effective global drug policy should be focused on objective and scientifically observed harm in all its forms, and should not be limited to a particular set of substances that have been designated as the most harmful and worthy of control in an arbitrary fashion.

In addition to increased calls for alcohol and tobacco to be considered alongside illicit drugs in national and international drug policies, the rise of new drugs in recent years also necessitates a wider interpretation of illegal substances. New drugs, destined to become categorised as illegal, have consistently appeared on the scene throughout the history of global drug control: the primary function, for example, of the 1971 Convention on Psychotropic Substances was to bring a substantial list of psychoactive substances not covered by the 1961 Single Convention on Drugs under the framework of international drug control (Potter and Chatwin 2018). As outlined in Chapter 2, what has changed in recent years is the number of new drugs appearing on the scene as their mass marketisation and distribution has become easier.

Most commonly, new drugs are conceptualised as New Psychoactive Substances (NPS), usually designed to mimic the effects of illegal drugs. NPS have been broadly categorised (UNODC 2013) into nine specific areas: synthetic cannabinoid receptor agonists (e.g. JWH-O18, 'Spice'); aminoindanes (e.g. MDAI); synthetic cathinones (e.g. mephedrone); tryptamines (e.g. 5-MEO-DPT); ketamine and phencyclidine type substances (e.g. 4-MeO-PCP); piperazines (e.g. benzylpiperazine); phenethylamines (e.g. Bromo-DragonFLY); plant based substances (e.g. Khat) and other substances (e.g. DMAA). A broader interpretation of the field of new'drugs, however, also includes substances generally described as Human Enhancement Drugs (HED). Evans-Brown et al. (2012) describe how these are divided into six categories: muscle drugs (e.g. Anabolic-Androgenic Steroids); weight loss drugs (e.g. Xenical); image enhancing drugs (e.g. Melatonin); sexual enhancers (e.g. Viagra); cognitive enhancers (e.g. Ritalin); and mood and behaviour enhancers (e.g. Diazepam). Despite many of these categories containing the potential for psychoactive effect, and despite clear overlap in terms of their marketing and distribution, these substances usually receive a fraction of the attention of those ascribed the label NPS, and are rarely discussed in the same fora (Chatwin et al. 2017).

As discussed in Chapter 2, NPS, and to a much lesser extent HED, are viewed as the primary current challenge facing those working in the drugs field, and have provided the catalyst for significant change in drug policy implementation. The rapid rise of the creation, marketing and dissemination of new drugs led to a realisation, at both national and international levels, that current systems of drug control were not able to adequately control the phenomenon. Traditional systems of drug control generally justify the criminalisation of specific substances based on a scientific assessment of their harms followed by a lengthy and bureaucratic process to bring them under the auspices of existing legislation, and are thus not well suited to dealing with a plethora of new substances emerging in tandem. Around the globe, the overwhelming response has been to implement policies which provide an extension of law enforcement powers without also seeking to address the drug-related harm which often arises as a result of control strategies. The result has been a fundamental shift in many systems of drug control, from criminalisation based on harm towards criminalisation based on the presumption of harm.

Evidence thus suggests that the impact of new drugs on national and international systems of drug control has been significant. In part, this impact has arisen from a tendency to view new drugs as a distinct and separate problem from traditional illegal drugs (heroin, cocaine, ecstasy/MDMA, cannabis etc.) requiring distinct and separate methods of control. The result is three categories of substances which we might seek to control within our societies based on legal status: legal substances (alcohol and tobacco); illegal substances (heroin, cocaine, ecstasy/MDMA, cannabis etc.); and semi-legal substances (NPS and HED). Earlier, the argument was made that if policies are implemented that reduce drug-related harm, rather than focusing only on the reduction of the use of traditional illegal drugs, then legal status becomes less important: alcohol and tobacco should therefore be considered in policies that aim to reduce drug-related harm regardless of the fact that they are legal.

By extension, the concept of harm should also remain central to considerations of how to deal with the emergence of new drugs, and they should also be considered by the same policies and strategies that seek to reduce harm. Such as approach focuses on the similar nature of issues around the use of harmful substances in general, and would result in all harmful substances being governed by the same policies and principles of control.

Continuing with the theme of the value in focusing on the similarities between harmful substances, regardless of legal status, useful evidence can be extracted from comparing the emerging research findings on NPS and HED. As stated earlier, despite emerging at a similar time and sharing many features of production, marketing and dissemination, these two categories of substances are rarely studied in parallel. Exploration of the HED phenomenon, however, reveals overwhelmingly similar issues to NPS: a lack of information about rapidly emerging substances, a tendency of countries to adopt zero tolerance measures on a precautionary basis, and the same online distribution methods (Mulrooney and van de Ven 2015; Chatwin et al. 2017). Social research on the people who use HED chimes with similar work on the users of NPS, and with the concepts we have developed to understand motivations for and cultural contexts of drug use in general. Hanley Santos and Coomber (2017), for example, provide evidence that in an environment where little official information is readily available about HED that are newly available on the market, users tend to seek information from their friends, peers and fellow users within the bodybuilding community, often via online forums. This finding mirrors research (see for example van Hout and Hearne 2017; O'Brien et al. 2015) with NPS users demonstrating one of the primary avenues for information about new substances comes from user based discussion forums on the internet. Hanley Santos and Coomber (2017), for example, draw attention to normalised (Parker et al. 1998) or everyday nature (South 1999) of HED use. Van de Ven and Mulrooney (2017) meanwhile document evidence of 'social supply' (Potter 2009), 'normalisation' (Parker et al. 1998), and 'everyday' nature of drug use (South 1999) within their work on Performance and Image Enhancing Drugs (PIEDS)—a sub-category within HED.

Just as the comparison of HED and NPS research findings reveals overwhelming similarity, so does a comparison of new drug research with traditional drug research. A small but growing body of work explores the problems presented and opportunities missed by studying NPS, HED and traditional illegal drugs in isolation from each other (Barratt et al. 2017; Measham and Newcombe 2016; Potter and Chatwin 2018). Thus, we should "view new drugs as just one part of the ever changing face of contemporary drug use" (Potter and Chatwin 2018: 7) or we will obscure connections and continuities with the wider drugs field (Measham and Newcombe 2016). One consequence of failing to recognise and understand the similar nature of drug-related harm, no matter the legal status of the substance itself, can be that the wider societal problems that often underlie drug use are obscured. An emerging body of literature on NPS use in vulnerable populations (Blackman and Bradley 2017; Ralphs et al. 2017; Quintana et al. 2017; Alexandrescu 2017) has sometimes been used to suggest that these groups are experiencing problems *because* of their NPS use; because of the particular properties of the specific NPS they are using. In fact, as Alexandrescu (2017) points out, drug epidemics of any kind are symptomatic of deeper societal problems and inequalities, rather than inherent to the individual substances themselves: to view them as otherwise is misleading and unhelpful in the development of effective policies.

The thrust of the argument contained in this section is thus that it does not make sense to separate out different categories of drugs, whether it be alcohol and tobacco, or NPS and HED. Instead, the myriad of substances prevalent within modern society should be perceived as being interconnected and studied as part of an over-arching issue. The horizons of the drug policy debate should seek to include all harmful substances, regardless of legal status, and should focus on the *intersections* between different categories of legal, illegal and semi-legal substances, new and old (Chatwin et al. 2018). Doing so will lead us to greater depth of understanding in terms of the social and cultural contexts of drugs use, the motivations for personal use and the theoretical underpinnings that cross-cut these areas.

Including the Full Range of Drug Scene Developments

In their article critiquing the categorisation of NPS, Potter and Chatwin (2018: 6), document a number of technological changes which have played a significant role in the changing nature of drug use in recent years: "chemical and horticultural techniques enable the development of new drugs and the production of old ones; new media technologies facilitate the connections between interested actors, the dissemination of information, and even the distribution of drugs". They draw on Toffler's (1970) ideas about 'future shock' caused by the exponential rate of technological advancement and accompanying social change, and Bauman's (2000) 'liquid modernity' and the challenges posed by the increasingly fluid nature of contemporary life, to argue that these much focused upon NPS are merely part of a "landscape of wider drug-scene developments with connections to more general trends of later modernity and globalisation" (Potter and Chatwin 2018: 6).

Extending here the second of Potter and Chatwin's (2018) examples, provided by the impact of technology on illegal drug markets and other related areas, much recent research has focused on the role of the internet as a facilitator of illicit drug markets. In fact, we can easily trace a history of the long-standing impact of technology in this field by recalling the relatively recent reimagination of many local level illicit drug markets based on the availability of first pagers and then mobile phones. Writing about the late 1990s/early 2000s, May and Hough (2004: 553) describe a UK drug market scene as one radically transformed by the ability of suppliers and customers to communicate easily in a largely anonymous manner: "the pace of change has been so rapid that ethnographic work conducted in Britain before the mid-1990s can now serve only as a very partial guide to the way in which retail drug markets function". May and Hough (2004) further explore the impact of mobile phones on the UK drug market as changing it from one based around 'open markets' where dugs are sold to any buyer, often from a public location, to one based around 'closed markets' where business is only done between those who already know each other or who have been introduced via a mutual friend, and is usually conducted in a private location.

Furthermore, the ease of anonymous communication and the rise in closed drug markets has led to a reconceptualization of the entire structure of drug distribution systems. Traditionally drug trafficking organisations have been depicted as large scale, hierarchical organisations forming a pyramid structure encompassing large-scale importers and traffickers, middle men or wholesalers, and retail level dealers (Pearson and Hobbs 2001). May and Hough (2004: 555) argue that changes to drug markets inspired by mobile phones and other new aspects of communication technology, have contributed to, at least at the lowest level, "a fragmented, non-hierarchical entrepreneurial market with little structure". Closed markets, often contrived between networks of friends and loose acquaintances in what has been termed 'social supply' (Potter 2009; Coomber and Moyle 2013), are usually conceived as less risky for all concerned as meetings and transactions can take place off the street and the suppliers of illegal substances do not have to tout for custom in public places. On the downside, however, drug suppliers are somewhat limited in terms of the range and geographical location of their potential customers, and would be customers may be hampered in their attempts to enter the market if they do not have pre-existing connections.

These changes in illicit drug markets were directly inspired by advances in technology that led to the development of mobile phones and other anonymous communications technology. The development of the internet and its potential as an anonymous communication tool, then, has led to even greater changes, the extent of which we are only recently beginning to realise. Just as in wider society the internet has transformed the way we communicate and interact, Seddon (2014) emphasises the internet as a driver of rapid change in drug markets which several researchers have described as being paradigm shifting (Mounteney et al. 2016a; Aldridge and Decary-Hetu 2014) in nature. As Aldridge and Decary-Hetu (2016a) elaborate, the internet transcends the previously noted time and space limitations usually associated with an open market, while maintaining the low risk environment provided by a closed market. More specifically, the internet gives drug suppliers access to a global market, allows them the opportunity to sell to strangers, facilitates anonymous trade, and provides a low-risk environment within which their transactions can occur. Martin (2014: 6) charts the rise of cryptomarkets where “goods and services are exchanged between parties who use digital encryption to conceal their identities”, and its significance in relation to illicit drug markets.

Although sustained academic focus on internet cryptomarkets in the drugs field has been relatively recent, they have actually been in existence as long as we have had an internet. The ARPANET (a precursor to the internet) was used by American university students to facilitate drug transactions (Walsh 2011) and internet chat room markets have long been used in a similar fashion (Aldridge and Decary-Hetu 2016a). In 2002 The Onion Router (TOR) was developed, with government input and support of the US military, out of a desire to create secure platforms to facilitate communication that could not be listened in on, even by national governments or global institutions (Buxton and Bingham 2015). The Onion Router technology allows access to what has widely become known as the ‘dark net’ where communication and business transactions can take place under the radar of official detection. Combined with the development of the encrypted e-currency BitCoin in 2009 and encrypted communication methods these technological advances attracted the interest of those involved in the buying and selling of illegal products and services, and the potential to create successful and undetectable cryptomarkets was greatly increased.

The first cryptomarket widely cited as having existed on the TOR network was The Drugstore, which was launched in 2009 (Buxton and Bingham 2015), but the phenomenon really captured global attention in 2011 with the launch of Silk Road. Silk Road quickly achieved a dominant cryptomarket share offering many illegal goods and services, including the opportunity to buy and sell a wide variety of illegal, semi-legal and prescription only substances. TOR provided an anonymous network within which suppliers could advertise their wares and potential purchasers could communicate with them; BitCoin provided a difficult to trace means of payment. Without ever meeting face to face or knowing any personal details about each other, buyers and sellers could thus operate efficiently and effectively. Barratt (2012), described Silk Road as an eBay for drugs based on the user-friendly nature of the site, the range of products available, the ease and speed of conducting business, and the important opportunity for buyers to leave feedback on the products they received as a result of their transactions. These rapid developments prompted more widespread academic investigation of cryptomarkets from an illicit drug markets perspective.

In October 2013 Silk Road was successfully taken down by the FBI and other law enforcement operatives, but was replaced only a few weeks later by Silk Road 2 and a proliferation of other cryptomarkets that became increasingly focused around the buying and selling of illicit drugs. Further cryptomarket closures have occurred at regular intervals, either as a result of successful law enforcement operations such as Operation Onymous in 2014, or due to exit scams whereby the cryptomarket owners take their own sites down, pocketing the proceeds of unprocessed transactions at the time of takedown. Nevertheless, cryptomarkets as a form of illegal trade, particularly in the area of illicit drugs, have prevailed. Soska and Chrispin (cited in Aldridge and Decary-Hetu 2016a) describe individual cryptomarkets as being short-lived, while the cryptomarket as a general concept remains resilient. Thus, in a similar manner to that observed in non-virtual drug markets, successful law enforcement operations lead to a 'displacement' (Youngers and Roisin 2005; Costa 2008) to new markets and an inspiration to develop even more innovative forms of technological security (Buxton and Bingham 2015; Mounteney et al. 2016a).

Many researchers in this area have highlighted the transformative nature of developing 'eBay style' markets within which users can purchase illicit drugs from the safety and ease of their own home (Mountenay et al. 2016b) and which may attract those who would not previously had the inclination or opportunity to purchase illicit drugs (Barratt and Maddox 2016). Others, however, have focused on the supply side of the phenomenon and the further changes that internet related technological advances may make to global systems of illicit drug distribution. Aldridge and Decary-Hetu (2016b) suggest that the advent of cryptomarkets has precipitated a reversal from closed to open drug markets, while maintaining the fragmented and networked characteristics that developed as part of the closed market scene. Opinion remains divided on the exact nature of further changes facilitated by cryptomarkets.

Martin (2014), for example, hypothesises that cryptomarkets could cut out the need for a 'wholesale' level, connecting large scale producers and suppliers with local level users directly. Aldridge and Decary-Hetu (2016b), meanwhile, find evidence in their research on the scale of transactions occurring within cryptomarkets, that it is not just users who purchase illicit drugs from cryptomarkets—it is also wholesalers. Thus, rather than cryptomarkets eliminating the need for wholesalers, they actually allow a greater number of people, without any existing connections or experience, to enter the market at this level. In turn, these new wholesalers could start supplying illegal drugs to street level dealers in areas that have not previously been connected to the global drugs market. Martin (2014) also notes the mundanity of the eBay style format for purchasing illicit substances which undermines our existing stereotypes about the danger and immorality of the drug market in general, and suggests that a further consequence of the proliferation of cryptomarkets could be an overall reduction in both organised crime level drug traffickers and street gang level drug market related violence.

Nor is the potential impact of internet and new media technology limited to the development of cryptomarkets. Although the United Nations was slow to recognise the importance of dark net drug markets, not featuring them in their World Drug Report until 2014 (UNODC 2014), international institutions are now exploring a range of transformative changes to the wider drugs field that have arisen as a result of technological change. For example, an EMCDDA and Europol joint report (2013) highlights the preferred use of the internet as a communication tool for high level drug suppliers predominantly operating off-line, for the provision of resources such as manuals and guides for those seeking to cultivate or produce substances, its role in facilitating the remote monitoring of drug production sites, and the use of social media sites such as Facebook to advertise products and recruit couriers. Much research has also focused on the ability of the internet to disseminate information on substances themselves, but also on methods for responsible use in line with the principle of harm reduction. Caudevilla (2016) documents the proliferation of internet forums such as Bluelight and Erowid facilitating "experiential discourse offering alternatives to the hegemonic narrative" (Walsh 2011: 55) around the irresponsibility of drug use. These forums often also provide drug checking or testing services with results widely shared and the exchange of specific harm reduction strategies which can be employed while using substances (O'Brien et al. 2015; Boothroyd and Lewis 2016).

Part of the impact of these forums is that they exist, not just on the dark web, hidden from official view and accessible only by those fully initiated in internet technology, but in plain sight on the clear web, as the everyday internet has sometimes become known. In fact, illegal drug markets are not restricted to the dark net, with Watters and Phair (2012) finding evidence of many people openly selling illegal substances on social media sites such as Facebook and Instagram. More recently, media headlines have focused on the use of sites like Craiglist to advertise the sale of illegal drugs (Rea 2017; Delibasic and Leader 2017) slightly more secretively, often under the code 420 which has become widely associated with cannabis culture. Finally, there has been an increase in the number of sites which openly facilitate the illegal drugs market—for example, We Be High which aims to connect travelling cannabis users unfamiliar with local markets with potential suppliers wherever in the world they happen to be. It should be noted, then, that both the clear web and the dark web provide a convenient and anonymous marketplace and also a means to disseminate information that normalises drug using culture.

It is also important to recognise the significant role the internet has played in promoting the use of semi-legal or legal substances. Interestingly, although the advent of NPS has often been labelled as the number one issue facing drug policy-makers of today (Chatwin 2017), a focus on the internet and technological advances in general reveals the instrumental role they have played at every stage of the NPS phenomenon (Potter and Chatwin 2018). It is widely acknowledged that the design and small-scale local sale of NPS has long existed, but it was not until developments were facilitated by the internet that the phenomenon really took off (Lavorgna 2016). With an anonymous advertising portal, and relatively secure methods of payment and delivery, the motivation for chemists to develop new substances hugely increased. Suddenly anyone with some chemistry background could set up a basic home laboratory and market the results on a global basis. The majority of NPS sales have usually occurred on the clear web rather than the dark web (EMCDDA and Europol 2016), advertised as research chemicals or legal highs, and have thus been highly observable to official audiences, hence the increasing concern this issue has caused with wide-ranging consequences for policies in general (see Chapter 2). The point here is that, without the facilitation of the internet, this significant change in the drugs market would probably not have occurred.

Similarly, although attracting much less attention, the internet has become an important factor in the proliferation of illegal online pharmacies selling counterfeit medicines, lifestyle drugs, HED, and/or prescription only medicines (Wilson 2016; Ghodse 2010). As outlined above, the internet provides a context within which a variety of products can be marketed and distributed on a global basis. As with NPS, the inconsistent legislative environment, which can differ significantly between different countries, has provided a further facilitation of these markets (Scammel and Bo 2016). Based on the information provided, we can thus chart the internet as contributing to a general blurring of traditional boundaries within illicit drug markets. This occurs in terms of substances—"the internet is a medium through which 'white', 'grey' and 'black' drug markets flourish, with the boundaries between them shifting and amorphous, fluid and arbitrary" (Walsh 2011: 56)—but also in terms of the benefits associated with open and closed markets, and of the clear and dark web communication tools. Lavorgna (2014: 85) thus describes the consequence as the development of a "hybrid market" that combines a range of substances with varying legislative status, sold under conditions combining the benefits of both open and closed markets, and utilising both clear and dark web communication tools.

Despite the significant changes outlined above, it is important to remember that internet drug markets currently represent only a tiny fraction of the global drug market (Aldridge and Decary-Hetu 2016a; Mountenay et al. 2016b). As Aldridge and Decary-Hetu (2016b) have suggested, poppy growers in Afghanistan are unlikely to switch over to internet markets in the near future—a certain level of technological infrastructure and a secure postal system (Martin 2014) are still essential to make full use of the opportunities offered by the internet—and thus other more traditional markets will still continue to thrive. Nevertheless, this should not be viewed as an entirely Western issue of impact and of interest only to those living in the global North. In relation to the HED, lifestyle and prescription only medicine market, for example, China and India (where technology is well integrated) have emerged as primary producers (Ghodse 2010). Walsh (2011) in particular highlights a "modern twist" on the old opium wars whereby pharmaceutical opiates (such as fentanyl which has recently made significant contribution to the number of drug-related deaths around the globe (Ciccarone 2017)) are being shipped to the West from India via online illegal pharmacies.

It is thus clear that technological advances have long played a significant role in the development of illicit drug markets, and that the advent of the internet and new media tools has facilitated an even wider set of drug-related developments that encompass, not only illicit drug markets, but also the dissemination of information and the development of harm reduction techniques. In recognition of this, Buxton and Bingham (2015: 1) suggested that UNGASS 2016 would provide a "timely opportunity" to discuss the new challenges of an increasingly complex and blurred drug market in the twenty-first century. The UNGASS Outcome Document (UNODC 2016) does demonstrate a commitment to develop guidelines for online illicit drug market law enforcement strategies, to increase the use of the internet for illicit drug prevention services, to increase the capacity for monitoring illicit behaviours, and to fund further research in this emerging area. It seems, however, to sidestep the issue of increasing complexity within the market as traditional boundaries blur. If we are to produce more effective global drug policies, we must recognise that technological change has facilitated a fluidity in the drug market between legal and illegal that will have far-reaching consequences for our general understandings of the kind of policies that will be successful. It is thus important that global drug policy debates do not become overly focused on particular areas (e.g. NPS) at the expense of fully considering wider drug scene developments.

Conclusion

Following the line of argument taken here, we thus need to broaden the horizons of the drug policy debate across a variety of spectrums in order to achieve more effective global drug policies. Bringing the perspective and experience of the global South into the debate will allow new approaches to emerge, will lead to a reframing of the overall global drug policy debate and will further emphasise the inappropriateness of seeking universal 'solutions' in this area. Applying a multi-level governance approach, with an important emphasis on the local level, will encourage the greater involvement of civil society and allow a proliferation of context specific strategies to develop and become widely known. Increasing the number of substances we consider within the debate will lead to a greater focus on public health and reduction of harm rather than criminalisation, and will lead to wider and more generally applicable understandings of the cultures and contexts of drug use. Finally, including the entire range of drug scene developments will increase the relevance and effectiveness of future policies.

References

Aas, K. F. (2011). Visions of global control: Cosmopolitan aspirations in a world of friction. In M. Bosworth & C. Hoyle (Eds.), *What is Criminology?* Oxford: Oxford University Press.

Aas, K. F. (2012). The Earth is one but the world is not: Criminological theory and its geopolitical divisions. *Theoretical Criminology, 16*(1), 5–20.

Aas, K. F. (2013). *Globalization and crime* (2nd ed.). London: Sage.

Aldridge, J., & Decary-Hetu, D. (2014). *Not an "eBay for drugs": The cryptomarket "silk road" as a paradigm shifting criminal innovation.* https://doi.org/10.2139/ssrn.2436643.

Aldridge, J., & Decary-Hetu, D. (2016a). Cryptomarkets and the future of illicit drug markets. In EMCDDA (Eds.), *The internet and drug markets* (EMCDDA Insights 21). Luxembourg: Publications Office of the European Union.

Aldridge, J., & Decary-Hetu, D. (2016b). Hidden wholesale: The drug diffusing capacity of online drug cryptomarkets. *International Journal of Drug Policy, 35*, 7–15.

Alexandrescu, L. (2017). *Spice is not the real problem, it's the way we look at poverty*. Volteface: www.volteface.me.
Babor, T., Caetano, R., Casswell, S., Edwards, G., Giesbrecht, N., Graham, K., et al. (2010). *Alcohol: No ordinary commodity: Research and public policy* (2nd ed.). Oxford: Oxford University Press.
Bache, I. (1998). *The politics of European Union regional policy: Multi-level governance or flexible gatekeeping?* Sheffield: Sheffield Academic Press.
Barratt, M. (2012). Silk road: eBay for drugs. *Addiction, 107*, 683.
Barratt, M., & Maddox, A. (2016). Active engagement with stigmatised communities through digital ethnography. *Qualitative Research, 16*(6), 701–719.
Barratt, M., Seear, K., & Lancaster, K. (2017). A critical examination of the definition of 'psychoactive effect' in Australian drug legislation. *International Journal of Drug Policy, 40*, 16–25.
Barrett, D., Bewley-Taylor, D., & Jelsma, M. (2014). *Fatal attraction: Brownfield's flexibility doctrine and global drug policy reform*. London: Huffington Post Politics.
Bauman, Z. (2000). *Liquid modernity*. Cambridge: Policy Press.
Blackman, S., & Bradley, R. (2017). From niche to stigma-Headshops to prison: Exploring the rise and fall of synthetic cannabinoid use amongst young adults. *International Journal of Drug Policy, 40*, 70–77.
Boothroyd, D., & Lewis, S. (2016). Rethinking evidence in online social drug use research. In A. O'Gorman, G. Potter, & J. Fountain (Eds.), *Evidence in European social drug research and drug policy*. Lengerich: Pabst.
Bourgain, C., Falissard, L. B., Benyamina, A., Karila, L., & Reynaud, M. (2012). A damage/benefit evaluation of addictive product use. *Addiction, 107*, 441–456.
Bowling, B. (2011). Transnational criminology and the globalisation of harm production. In M. Bosworth's & C. Hoyle's (Eds.), *What is criminology?* Oxford: Oxford University Press.
Buxton, J., & Bingham, T. (2015, January). *The rise and challenge of dark net drug markets*. Swansea: Global Drug Policy Observatory Policy Brief 7.
Caudevilla, F. (2016). The emergence of deep web marketplaces: A health perspective. In EMCDDA (Eds.), *The internet and drug markets* (EMCDDA Insights 21). Luxembourg: Publications Office of the European Union.
Caulkins, J., Reuter, P., & Coulson, C. (2011). Basing drug scheduling decisions on scientific ranking of harmfulness: False promise from false premise. *Addiction, 106*, 1886–1890.

Chan, J. (2005). Globalisation, reflexivity and the practice of criminology. In J. Sheptycki & A. Wardak (Eds.), *Transnational and comparative criminology*. London: Glasshouse Press.

Chatwin, C. (2017). Assessing the 'added value' of European policy on new psychoactive substances. *International Journal of Drug Policy, 40*, 111–116.

Chatwin, C., Blackman, S., & O'Brien, K. (2018, in print). Intersections in (new) drug research. *Drugs: Education, Prevention and Policy*.

Chatwin, C., Measham, F., O'Brien, K., & Sumnall, H. (2017). New drugs, new directions? Exploring critical and social research priorities in NPS and HED debates. *International Journal of Drug Policy, 40*, 1–5.

Ciccarone, D. (2017). Fentanyl in the US heroin supply: A rapidly changing risk environment. *International Journal of Drug Policy, 46*, 107–111.

CND. (2012). *Improving the participatory role of civil society in addressing the world drug problem*. Commission on Narcotic Drugs, Fifty-fifth session, Vienna 12–16 March, E/CN.7/2012/CRP.1.

Cohen, S. (1998). *Against criminology*. New Brunswick: Transaction.

Collins, J. (2017). Losing UNGASS? Lessons from civil society past and present. *Drugs and Alcohol Today, 17*(2), 88–97.

Connell, R. (2007). The Northern theory of globalization. *Sociological Theory, 25*(4), 368–385.

Coomber, R., & Moyle, L. (2013). Beyond drug dealing: Developing and extending the concept of "social supply" of illicit drugs to "minimally commercial supply". *Drugs: Education Prevention and Policy, 21*(2), 157–164.

Costa, A. (2008). *Making drug control 'fit for purpose': Building on the UNGASS decade*. Vienna: Commission on Narcotic Drugs.

Delibasic, S., & Leder, M. (2017, June 19). Craiglist ads: Drug dealers openly peddly ice, cannabis and cocaine. *Herald Sun*. www.heraldsun.com.au.

Doll, R., Peto, R., Boreham, J., & Sutherland, I. (2004). Mortality in relation to smoking: 50 years' observations on male British doctors. *British Medical Journal, 328*, 1519–1528.

EMCDDA, & Europol. (2013). *EU drug markets report: A strategic analysis*. Luxembourg: Publications Office of the European Union.

EMCDDA, & Europol. (2016). *EU drug markets report: In-depth analysis*. Luxembourg: Publications Office of the European Union.

Evans-Brown, M., McVeigh, J., Perkins, C., & Bellis, M. A. (2012). *Human enhancement drugs: The emerging challenges to public health*. Liverpool: North West Public Health Observatory.

Fischer, B., & Kendall, P. (2011). Nutt et al.'s harm scales for drugs—Room for improvement but better policy based on science with limitations than no science at all. *Addiction, 106*(11), 1891–1892.

Fox, E. (2015). *US sends mixed signals on UN drug convention flexibility*. https://www.talkingdrugs.org.

Gable, R. S. (2004). Comparison of acute lethal toxicity of commonly abused psychoactive substances. *Addiction, 99*, 686–696.

Garcia, M. (2006). Citizen practices and urban governance in European cities. *Urban Studies, 43*, 745–765.

Getimis, P., Parakevopoulos, C., & Rees, N. (2006). Domestic governance structures and policy learning East and West: The limits of Europeanisation. In C. Paraskevopoulos, P. Getimis, & N. Rees (Eds.), *Adapting to EU multi-level governance: Regional and environmental policies in cohesion and CEE countries*. Hampshire: Ashgate.

Ghodse, H. (2010). Watching internet pharmacies. *The British Journal of Psychiatry, 196*, 169–170.

Giddens, A. (1990). *The consequences of modernity*. Stanford: Stanford University Press.

Hall, W. (2016). Alcohol and cannabis: Comparing their adverse health effects and regulatory regimes. *International Journal of Drug Policy, 42*, 57–62.

Hall, W., Room, R., & Bondy, S. (1999). Comparing the health and psychological effects of alcohol, cannabis, nicotine and opiate use. In H. Kalant, W. Corrigall, W. Hall, & R. Smart (Eds.), *The health effects of cannabis*. Toronto: Centre for Addiction and Mental Health.

Hanley Santos, G., & Coomber, R. (2017). The risk environment of anabolic-androgenic steroid users in the UK: Examining motivations, practices and accounts of use. *International Journal of Drug Policy, 40*, 35–43.

Held, D. (2000). The changing contours of political community. In R. Ericson & N. Stehr (Eds.), *Governing modern societies*. Toronto: University of Toronto Press.

Hooghe, L., & Marks, G. (2001). *Multi-level governance and European integration*. Oxford: Rowman & Littlefield.

Kaul, I. (2010). The changing role of the United Nations: Lessons for multi-level governance. In H. Enderlein, S. Walti, & M. Zurn (Eds.), *Handbook on multi-level governance*. Cheltenham: Edward Elgar.

Lavorgna, A. (2014). Internet-mediated drug trafficking: Towards a better understanding of new criminal dynamics. *Trends in Organised Crime, 17*, 250–270.

Lavorgna, A. (2016). How the use of the internet is affecting drug trafficking practices. In EMCDDA (Eds.), *The internet and drug markets* (EMCDDA Insights 21). Luxembourg: Publications Office of the European Union.
Mackay, J., Eriksen, M., & Shafey, O. (2006). *The tobacco atlas* (2nd ed.). Atlanta, GA: American Cancer Society.
Martin, J. (2014). Lost on the Silk Road: Online drug distribution and the "cryptomarket". *Criminology & Criminal Justice, 14*(3), 351–367.
May, T., & Hough, M. (2004). Drug markets and distribution systems. *Addiction Research & Theory, 12*(6), 549–563.
Measham, F., & Newcombe, R. (2016). What's so new about new psychoactive substances? Definitions, prevalence, motivations, user groups and a proposed new taxonomy. In T. Kolind, B. Thom, & G. Hunt, *The Sage Handbook of Drug & Alcohol Studies*. London: Sage.
Morrison, W. (2005). Rethinking narratives of penal change in global context. In J. Pratt, et al. (Eds.), *The new punitiveness: Trends, theories, perspectives*. Cullompton: Willan.
Mounteney, J., Griffiths, P., & Vandam, L. (2016a). What is the future for internet drug markets. In EMCDDA (Eds.), *The internet and drug markets* (EMCDDA Insights 21). Luxembourg: Publications Office of the European Union.
Mounteney, J., Oteo, A., & Griffiths, P. (2016b). The internet and drug markets: Shining a light on these complex and dynamic systems. In EMCDDA (Eds.), *The internet and drug markets* (EMCDDA Insights 21). Luxembourg: Publications Office of the European Union.
Mulrooney, K. J. D., & van de Ven, K. (2015). *'Muscle profiling' Anti-doping policy and deviant leisure*. Deviant Leisure Research Group. https://deviantleisure.wordpress.com/2015/01/21/muscle-profiling-anti-doping-policy-and-deviantleisure.
Nelken, D. (2009). Comparative criminal justice: Beyond ethnocentrism and relativism. *European Journal of Criminology, 6*(4), 291–311.
Nutt, D., King, L. A., & Phillips, C. D. (2010). Drug harms in the UK: A multicriteria decision analysis. *The Lancet, 376*(9752), 6–12.
Nutt, D., King, L. A., Saulsbury, W., & Blakemore, C. (2007). Development of a rational scale to assess the harm of drugs of potential misuse. *The Lancet, 369*(9566), 1047–1053.
O'Brien, K., Chatwin, C., Jenkins, C., & Measham, F. (2015). New psychoactive substances and British drug policy: A view from the cyber-psychonauts. *Drugs: Education Prevention and Policy, 22*(3), 217–223.

Organisation of American States. (2013). *The drug problem in the Americas.* https://www.oas.org.

Parker, H., Aldridge, J., & Measham, F. (1998). *Illegal leisure: The normalization of adolescent recreational drug use.* London: Routledge.

Pearson, G., & Hobbs, D. (2001). *Middle market drug distribution.* Home Office Research Study 227. London: Home Office.

Pedersen, W., Fjaer, E. G., Gray, P., & von Soest, T. (2016). Perceptions of harms associated with tobacco, alcohol and cannabis in students from the UK and Norway. *Contemporary Drug Problems, 43*(1), 47–61.

Potter, G. R. (2009). Exploring retail-level drug distribution: Social supply, "real" dealers and the user/dealer interface. In Z. Demetrovics, J. Fountain, & L. Kraus (Eds.), *Old and new policies, theories, research methods and drug users across Europe.* Lengerich, Germany: Pabst Science Publishers.

Potter, G. R., & Chatwin, C. (2018). Not particularly special: Critiquing "NPS" as a category of drugs. *Drugs: Education, Prevention and Policy.* https://doi.org/10.1080/09687637.2017.1411885.

Pryce, S. (2012). *Fixing drugs: The politics of drug prohibition.* Basingstoke: Palgrave Macmillan.

Quintana, P., Ventura, M., Grifell, M., Palma, A., Galindo, L., Fornis, I., Gil, C., Carbon, X., Caudevilla, F., Farre, M., & Torrens, M. (2017). The hidden web and the fentanyl problem: Detection of ocfentanil as an adulterant in heroin. *International Journal of Drug Policy, 40*, 78–83.

Ralphs, R., Williams, Askew, R., & Ykhlef. (2017). Adding spice to the porridge: The development of a synthetic cannabinoid market in an English prison. *International Journal of Drug Policy, 40*, 57–69.

Rea, S. (2017). The Londoners who sell drugs online. *Londonist.* https://londonist.com.

Robertson, R. (1995). Glocalization: Time-space and homogeneity-heterogeneity? In M. Featherstone, S. Lash, & R. Robertson (Eds.), *Global modernities.* London: Sage.

Room, R. (2006). The dangerousness of drugs. *Addiction, 101*, 166–168.

Room, R. (2011). Scales and blinkers, modes and beams: Whose view is obstructed on drug scheduling? *Addiction, 106*(11), 1895–1896.

Rossow, I. (2011). Can harm ratings be useful? *Addiction, 106*, 1893–1894.

Scammell, L., & Bo, A. (2016). Online supply of medicines to illicit drug markets: Situation and responses. In EMCDDA (Eds.), *The internet and drug markets* (EMCDDA Insights 21). Luxembourg: Publications Office of the European Union.

Scholte, J. A. (2010). Civil society in multi-level governance. In H. Enderlein, S. Walti, & M. Zurn (Eds.), *Handbook on multi-level governance*. Cheltenham: Edward Elgar.
Seddon, T. (2014). Drug policy and global regulatory capitalism: The case of new psychoactive substances (NPS). *International Journal of Drug Policy*. https://doi.org/10.1016/j.drugpo.2014.03.009.
South, N. (1999). Debating drugs and everyday life: Normalisation, prohibition and "otherness". In N. South (Ed.), *Drugs: Cultures controls and everyday life*. London: Sage.
The Dialogue. (2016). *UNGASS 2016: Towards a new drug policy in the Americas?* https://www.thedialogue.org.
Toffler, A. (1970). *Future shock*. New York: Random House.
UNODC. (2013, March). *The challenge of new psychoactive substances*. Global Smart Programme.
UNODC. (2014). *World drug report 2014*. http://www.unodc.org/documents.
UNODC. (2016). *Outcome document of the 2016 United Nations General Assembly Special Session on the world drug problem. Our joint commitment to effectively addressing and countering the world drug problem*. New York: United Nations. http://www.unodc.org/documents.
van Amsterdam, J., Nutt, D., Phillips, L., & van den Brink, W. (2015). European rating of drug harms. *Journal of Psychopharmacology, 29*(6), 655–660.
van Amsterdam, J., Opperhuisen, A., Koeter, M., & van den Brink, W. (2010). Ranking the harm of alcohol, tobacco and illicit drugs for the individual and the population. *European Addiction Research, 16*, 202–207.
van de Ven, K., & Mulrooney, K. (2017). Social suppliers: Exploring the cultural contours of the Performance and Image Enhancing Drug (PIED) market amongst bodybuilders in the Netherlands and Belgium. *International Journal of Drug Policy, 40*, 6–15.
van Hout, M. C., & Hearne, H. (2017). New Psychoactive Substances (NPS) on cryptomarket fora: An exploratory study of characteristics of forum activity between NPS buyers and vendors. *International Journal of Drug Policy, 40*, 102–110.
van Swaaningen, R. (1999). Reclaiming critical criminology: Social justice and the European tradition. *Theoretical Criminology, 3*(1), 5–28.
Walsh, C. (2011). Drugs the internet and change. *Journal of Psychoactive Drugs, 43*(1), 55–63.

Watters, P. A., & Phair, N. (2012). Detecting illicit drugs on social media using automated social media intelligence analysis (ASMIA). In Y. Xiang, J. Lopez, C.-C. J. Kuo, & W. Zhou (Eds.), *Cyberspace safety and security*. Lecture Notes in Computer Science, 7672. Berlin and Heidelberg: Springer.

WHO. (2014). *Global status report on alcohol and health 2014*. http://apps.who.int.

Wilson, C. (2016). Addiction to prescription drugs is UK "public health disaster". *New Scientist*, Daily News, October 24, 2016.

Youngers, C. A. (2005). The collateral damage of the U.S. War on drugs: Conclusions and recommendations. In C. A. Youngers & E. Rosin (Eds.), *Drugs and democracy in Latin America*. London: Lynne Reiner Publishers.

Youngers, C. A., & Rosin, E. (2005). The U.S. "war on drugs". In C. A. Youngers & E. Rosin's (Eds.), *Drugs and democracy in Latin America*. London: Lynne Reiner Publishers.

Zurn, M., Walti, S., & Enderlein, H. (2010). Introduction. In H. Enderlein, S. Walti, & M. Zurn (Eds.), *Handbook on multi-level governance*. Cheltenham: Edward Elgar.

7 Conclusion

The intention of this book is to provide an outline of practical steps that could be taken towards achieving a more effective set of global drug policies. It strongly argues for the continuing need to acknowledge the failure of the war on drugs and the unintended and harmful consequences it has had around the globe. Alternative strategies should be explored, and this book advocates ones that do not primarily focus on reducing the prevalence of drug use, but rather try to reduce drug-related harm including human rights abuses and the harm that comes from societal and material inequality. In doing so, and in recognition of the current lack of effective options, it further recommends that flexibility is needed to encourage a diversity of approaches to flourish, regardless of whether they fit with dominant and Westernised conceptualisations of the issue. These policy innovations should be evaluated within their local context and discussed across international networks that facilitate the soft policy transfer process where appropriate. Finally, the horizons of the debate should be broadened along several lines. All voices in the debate should be included, particularly those that have been under-represented thus far such as the global South and the local-level. Equally, all potentially

C. Chatwin, *Towards More Effective Global Drug Policies*,
https://doi.org/10.1007/978-3-319-92072-6_7

harmful substances should be part of discussions, and the underlying influences of wider drug scene developments should be fully explored.

It is important to emphasise that none of these individual steps represents new ideas about how to improve global drug policies: the suggestions will come as no surprise to those familiar with the illegal drugs field. Many campaigners, experts, civil society representatives, service providers, drug users, and even some law enforcement agents have been calling for changes along one or more of these lines, virtually since the inception of the war on drugs approach. Writing in 1989, for example, Ethan Nadelmann (1989), founder of the Drug Policy Alliance and Professor of Politics and Public Affairs at Princeton University, drew attention to the limited effectiveness of strictly prohibition oriented drug policies, outlined the costs and consequences of these policies, and called for alternative approaches. Since then, analysis of a similar nature has remained consistent. Evidence strongly suggests, however, that despite sustained critique and increasingly open debate, not even the first of these steps has been taken. This point can be demonstrated by a brief exploration of emerging policy responses to the recent opioid crisis that has developed in the USA and which is spreading elsewhere.

In 2017, president Donald Trump declared a public health emergency within the US in respect of rising prevalence of opioid use, rising numbers of people becoming dependent on opioids, and rising cases of fatal overdose as a result of opioid use. Nearly 64,000 people died as a result of drug overdose in the US in 2016 (Hedegaard et al. 2017) with opioids (including heroin, synthetic opioids such as fentanyl, and prescription opioid painkillers such as OxyContin) playing the leading contributory factor, ahead of all other groups of substances. In a report for the health and medicine focused media organisation STAT (2017), leading public health experts forecast nearly 500,000 deaths over the next decade, surpassing the number of deaths over the same time period as a result of car accidents and gun deaths combined, and far outstripping the number of deaths at the peak of the HIV/AIDS epidemic. To a lesser extent, rises have also been seen in fatal opioid overdose statistics in Canada, Australia and some European countries, for example the UK. The latest European drug report (EMCDDA 2017) reports an overall 6% rise in overdose deaths mainly related to heroin and other opioids since 2014, with the UK accounting for 2655 or 31% of the estimated 8441 deaths.

Commentators attribute the current American crisis to a sharp rise in the prescription of opioid painkillers from the 1990s onwards. Kolodny et al. (2015) describe how an influential research study reported on in 1986 (now somewhat discredited) advised that opioid pain relievers could be safely prescribed for the long-term management of pain without significant risk of addiction. Over time, this led to a fundamental shift in the perception of opioid prescription related harm (Dhalla et al. 2011), and facilitated not only the development of new opioid pain relievers by leading pharmaceutical companies, but also their widespread prescription to the general public by doctors throughout the country. In fact, these substances proved to be highly addictive and led many users to develop an ongoing need for the prescription medicine, in some cases even when it was no longer available to them via official methods.

The International Narcotics Control Board (2007) report a marked acceleration of opioid use in the US since 1996. Many of these medical users became dependent on their prescription medicine: some turned to the black market to supplement or replace their use, and others sought out prescription medicine from illegal internet sites (Nixon 2018). Two defining features of the crisis have been that, in stark contrast to many previous epidemics, it is primarily the white, male, middle-aged demographic that has been affected (*The Economist* 2017), and that the illegal street market for heroin has become entangled with and contaminated by semi-legal prescription opioid and synthetic heroin markets (Dasgupta et al. 2017). Many of these prescription and synthetic opioids are much stronger than street heroin, leading existing street heroin users to take a much higher dose than they can tolerate and contributing significantly to instances of fatal overdose.

According to the National Institute of Drug Abuse (2018) the issue has had devastating consequences in terms of not only rising levels of opioid use and sharp increases in fatal overdose, but also rising incidence of neonates experiencing problems due to acute opioid withdrawal at birth, an increase in intravenous drug use, and an increase in related blood borne diseases such as HIV/AIDS and hepatitis C.

The responses to Trump's public health emergency that have been suggested thus far, however, fall almost entirely in the law enforcement camp and actually draw on existing war on drugs ideology. The opioid crisis has, for example, been styled a foreign, supply-side issue with emphasis on the many street opiates entering the country from Mexico and synthetic opiates such as fentanyl being widely available via the internet from China (Berenson 2017). The US department of State (Liu 2017), rather than focusing on demand for opioids within the US, has declared a strategy of increasing pressure on these countries as a primary method of improving the situation.

It has also focused on lobbying for fentanyl type synthetic opiates, relatively newly developed and therefore falling outside existing national and international legislation, to be added to the UN drug conventions: an ambition which was realised at the 61st session of the Commission on Narcotic Drugs in March 2018 (UNODC 2018). In further proposals, President Trump has called for significant budget increases in this area in line with many previous US presidents who have escalated the war on drugs, and has indicated the intention to revive a 'Just Say No' style national advertising campaign about the dangers inherent in drug taking in general (Collins 2018). Finally, in March 2018 Trump declared that "the only way to solve the drug problem is through toughness" (cited in Holpuch et al. 2018) and announced the intention to introduce harsher sentences for drug traffickers including, in the most serious cases, the death penalty.

Amongst these law enforcement approaches there have been some incidences of policies rooted in public health and aimed at reducing the harm of opioid use—for example, the provision of law enforcement and emergency service personnel with naloxone which can reverse opioid overdose if administered immediately, calls to increase funded treatment, and recognition of the fact that policies also need to include efforts to reduce opioid prescribing in the US and to help people recovering from addiction to find jobs and reintegrate into society. Rather than forming the centre-point of the response to the public health emergency, however, interventions such as naloxone provision have been implemented very much as an add-on to law enforcement strategies. Ideas in the area of treatment provision, prescription reduction and reintegration remain vague while the issues are complex and need significant attention to detail. In terms of opioid prescription, for example, it is of course important to recognise the role that over-prescribing has played in creating increased demand for opioids, but attempts to curtail prescription without putting a full range of public health interventions into place will mean that more people will turn to harmful illegal markets to obtain the substances on which they have become dependent.

The evidence presented in this book, and that is widely available elsewhere, suggests that war on drugs strategies have not been effective in previous iterations of the illicit drug problem, and it is thus difficult to imagine that they will be effective here. Furthermore, as extensively outlined in Chapter 2, the war on drugs style escalation of strict law enforcement approaches has wide ranging and harmful consequences. Again, in relation to the opioid crisis, this is already proving the case. Stricter prescribing laws have pushed many opioid users, originally able to access substances through legal means, into criminal markets such as either the street heroin market or the synthetic opiate market accessible via illegal online pharmacies and darknet sites. As a result, vulnerable people already suffering from dependence are at risk of stigmatisation and criminalisation, and their ability to use safely and responsibly is compromised by a lack of information about the strength and exact form of what they are taking. If they take the opportunity to purchase substances from the proliferating and potentially less harmful internet markets, then they are at further risk of being classed as importers and facing the most severe penalties. Furthermore, those people dependent on street heroin also experience increased harm via the contamination of existing markets with the stronger (and therefore more harmful) synthetic and prescription opioids.

Following the steps outlined in this book would lead to a very different approach to the case of the opioid crisis. The first—acknowledging a failure of the war on drugs approach and the unintended consequences it has caused—would lead many of the responses outlined above to be abandoned. Instead of seeking to intensify law enforcement approaches, blame producer countries and criminalise users, alternative approaches could be considered aiming to provide a public health response to a public health emergency. Strategies could include methods aimed at reducing the harm caused by existing drug policy, for example by extending the existing programme of substitution treatment currently available for dependent heroin users, or ensuring that, as in Portugal, anyone coming into contact with law enforcement agents because of their drug possession is offered appropriate treatment. Ideally, and in the long-term, they would also address harm related to material and societal inequality, working with vulnerable communities to improve opportunities and create an environment of resilience.

Flexibility to encourage diversity and innovation would allow more controversial methods already existing in some European countries to be implemented, such as the provision of legal opioid (rather than substitute) prescription programmes and safe consumption rooms where professionals could be on hand to offer advice about safe using practices. Importantly for this particular crisis, a variety of drug testing and checking programmes would have further potential to reduce incidence of fatal overdose. For example, recent research in response to Massachusetts's opioid crisis (Johns Hopkins 2018) demonstrates that a majority of opioid users are concerned about using responsibly and would welcome the widespread introduction of cheap drug testing strips which could be used to determine the form and purity of opioid prior to use. It would also allow the development of new measures not previously imagined: for example, Ric Curtis of John Jay College of Criminal Justice in New York (2017), has proposed that rescue dogs could be trained to detect whether a substance was street heroin, synthetic heroin or opioid prescription and deployed at known open drug scenes, so that even the most vulnerable and marginalised people who use drugs are able to rapidly assess the nature of their substances.

Once implemented, these new measures could be evaluated with results being disseminated so that those areas with emergent aspects of opioid crisis would have access to a range of interventions for potential soft policy transfer. In terms of broadening the horizons of the debate, ensuring the inclusion of the global South in discourse around this issue would help to frame the opioid crisis as one of demand as well as supply, and would encourage efforts to explore how Western policies impact on the global South. One example of this is provided by what has been termed 'the other opioid crisis' (Messac 2016): as international controls on opioids are tightened because of rising levels of dependent opioid use in the global North, so countries in the global South find it harder to access pain relief medicine that is genuinely needed for legitimate medical reasons. Ensuring the inclusion of the local level in international debates would provide important exposure for state funded research reports such as Massachusetts's investigation into drug testing, and for innovative ideas such as Curtis's dope dogs.

Furthermore, the opioid crisis is, by definition, one which would benefit from efforts to consider illegal (heroin), semi-legal (fentanyl) and legal via prescription (Oxycontin) forms of opioid alongside one another. The complex relationship between these markets, encompassing the movement of prescription users to street heroin markets and the contamination of street heroin markets with stronger legal and semi-legal opiates, is one which can only be understood by ignoring traditional legislative boundaries. Similarly, shifting drug scene landscapes are also relevant here as internet and new media technologies have become important drivers of synthetic and prescription opioid markets. This extended example demonstrates that the US remains unable to take the first step towards more effective national drug policies by acknowledging the failure of the war on drugs and its harmful consequences, and provides a sketch of what could ensue were it able to do so. Examples provided earlier in this book about increasingly stringent responses to New Psychoactive Substances (NPS) and failure to advocate moving away from war on drugs terminology at UNGASS 2016, suggest that the wider international community is also unable to take this first step. The next section will explore why it is so difficult to move forward in this area.

Obstacles to Implementing More Effective Global Drug Policies

Many drug policy experts have commented on the global drug policy deadlock: Reuter (2013) reports that while the drug scene has changed dramatically over the last 30 years, policies have hardly changed at all;

Pryce (2012: 125) accuses prohibition of becoming "a straightjacket that deters experiment"; Hartnoll (2000: 251) designates illegal drugs "a topic dominated by unthinking reaction based on moralistic rhetoric"; and Transform (2015: 26–27) suggests "the punitive enforcement approach has become entrenched, institutionalised, and largely immune from meaningful scrutiny". Furthermore, officials working in this field have often predicted that change will not happen, even in moments of great opportunity. For example, the OAS Scenarios document (2013), produced in 2013, predicted (correctly) that UNGASS 2016 would result in 'bland' agreement rather than significant change. Similarly, writing in 2003 ahead of a much anticipated UN drugs meeting where many countries hoped to refocus global drug policy on the demand side of the problem, Cindy Fazey, after 8 years of working within the United Nations International Drug Control Programme (UNDPC), accurately predicted that change would not be forthcoming (Fazey 2003). This section of the conclusion explores why changes in global drug policy are so difficult to bring about.

Pryce (2012) provides a comprehensive exploration of the reasons behind this failure to acknowledge the lack of success associated with the 'war on drugs' approach, and to move forward with new approaches. She provides five reasons behind the drug policy impasse. Ideological factors (i) mean that drugs are generally conceptualised as bad, subversive, foreign and evil. Drugs corrupt the individual, undermine societal values and capitalist economies, and to be on the side of the good is therefore to regard the use of drugs as morally reprehensible. Fear (ii) about drug policy change is a significant factor because no one really knows what it would be like if drugs were more freely available—would it result in significant increases in drug consumption, a world addiction epidemic, unforeseen unintended consequences of regulated markets, and/or unforeseen public health impacts? Fear of drug policy change impacts on the general public who have long been bombarded with the dangers of drug use but is also of great importance to politicians who fear implementing risky strategies that could result in negative opinion ratings, for both individuals and political parties or institutions. Ultimately, fear is compounded by ignorance about alternative strategies which have thus far failed to find political or public support.

Issues of political expediency (iii) mean that it can be difficult for individual countries to drive forward drug policy change, for example if they are dependent on the US for aid. Furthermore, many long-standing and embedded industries now exist with a vested interest (iv) in drug control (e.g. drug testing programmes, police and security agents, prison officers looking after those incarcerated for drugs offences, substitution treatment providers), further contributing to resistance to change as these, often powerful, groups lobby in favour of maintaining the status quo. Finally, and perhaps most importantly to the arguments put forward in this book, bureaucratic inertia (v) which describes a national and international drug control apparatus that is so complex and slow moving that effecting change becomes virtually impossible. It is so difficult to reach agreement about something like changing the international drug conventions that it isn't worth the political risk involved for those in powerful positions who might otherwise be motivated to advocate change.

Cutting through all the factors raised by Pryce (2012) is the lack of motivation for political leaders, either national or international, to abandon the war on drugs. In an exploration of the continuation of a 'war on drugs' approach under the Obama regime, despite official indications that it was to be abandoned as a term, Youngers (2011: 341), concluded that a 'tough on drugs' approach remained popular with constituents and encouraged leaders to play "on public fears, turning a public health issue into an all-out war on addictive substances and those who supply them". Telling people what really needs to be done in terms of the alleviation of poverty, the treatment of people who are dependent on drugs, and the nurturing of global regions that are susceptible to drug trade related corruption, is a strategy much less likely to win support and would require courageous leadership indeed (Isacson 2005). Politicians are predisposed to choose strategies that are likely to win the public vote and thus tend to favour the status quo. In a situation about which great uncertainty exists, it is likely to be both less risky and more popular to stick with existing strategies (MacCoun and Reuter 2001). Given the fear associated with the unknown outcomes of any relaxation of the global drug policy regime, to take even the first step towards such a position could very easily amount to political suicide in the media outcry that would sure to follow (Reuter 2011).

Finally, as some of the examples from earlier in this book have illustrated, it really is difficult to implement effective alternative approaches. Uruguay, for example, has experienced difficulty in implementing a fully operational regulated cannabis market, with only the domestic cultivation strand of the strategy really taking off so far. Sales via pharmacies were long delayed and access to cannabis as part of social clubs has remained limited due to teething problems surrounding interaction with financial institutions and poor distribution infrastructure (Hudak et al. 2018). Elsewhere, in Jamaica, concerns remain about the potential for the proposed regulated market to curtail the existing criminal market effectively (Davenport and Pardo 2016), and in the US anxiety is growing about the highly commercialised nature of many developing markets (Room 2013). A final example of these practical difficulties is provided by New Zealand's attempts to create a regulated market for NPS when they first began to emerge at a significantly increased rate.

New Zealand's 2013 Psychoactive Substances Act (PSA) represented a radical and ambitious attempt to create a regulated market for NPS, and was widely described at the time as innovative, world-leading and game changing (Brown 2014). Essentially, the legislation stipulated that psychoactive substances would become illegal *unless* drug companies and other potential vendors were willing to undertake extensive and expensive trials to determine an acceptable level of risk. Key here is that it allowed the possibility that some psychoactive substances might be found to be of such minimal harm that a regulated market could be created for them and aimed to lay out the conditions (restricted outlets, constrictions on age of purchase and advertising) under which they would have been licensed for sale. The Act, however, hit a stumbling block when an outcry emerged about the use of animal testing to ascertain the safety of a substance that would largely be used for pleasure and, as a direct result, a government amendment cut off the licensing phase and halted the legal sale of all psychoactive substances.

Brown (2014) thus suggested that an impasse had been reached with the accurate determination of risk impossible without the provision to include tests on animals, making the likelihood of future approval of an NPS virtually non-existent. Despite the intention to introduce an alternative approach to drug policy, without being able to approve any NPS for regulation, The New Zealand PSA became another incidence of 'blanket ban' legislation (Barratt et al. 2017), doing nothing more than criminalising the supply of all psychoactive substances indiscriminately. In fact, Wilkins (2017) suggests that, somewhat ironically, New Zealand legislation now represents one of the harshest in the world with respect to NPS as it also criminalises the possession of all psychoactive substances, while some countries such as the UJK have only criminalised supply. This brief exploration of New Zealand's efforts to create a regulated market for some NPS thus demonstrates that even where the political will for change does exist, the practical problems of implementing alternative approaches can be insurmountable. Collectively, the evidence presented in this section suggests significant difficulties in effecting global drug policy change.

Nature of Global Drug Policy Change

The prospects for global drug policy change thus appear limited. According to Fazey's (2003) account of working on drug policy related issues for the UN, windows of opportunity (Kingdon 1984), whereby problem, policy and politics streams align to create periods of rapid and significant change, are rather unlikely to occur. In addition to the many obstacles outlined above—ideological beliefs and values about the immorality of illegal drug use, fear of the unknown, drug policy dependent international aid, the vested interests of drug related industries, bureaucratic inertia, political preference for the status quo, and the complexity of designing and implementing new approaches—international institutions such as the UN are actually not well placed to effect change of this nature. The UN drug control apparatus is well-established with a long history. It is particularly resilient to change (Bewley-Taylor 2003) for a number of reasons: there is no global agreement about either the need for change or the appropriate direction that change should take; any significant change (under current rules) would necessitate the agreement of a two thirds majority of existing member states; and there is a widespread perception that enough flexibility already exists within the treaties.

Fazey's (2003) work is illuminative here, reporting on the complex structure of UN decision making processes in this field. She describes how UN high level meetings and conferences are often perceived as providing opportunities for open and transparent debate that could lead to significant policy change. In contrast, however, she maintains that events are not internally viewed as arenas for discussion, but rather as opportunities to demonstrate continued consensus in a formal manner. In reality, discussions and debates take a long time and occur away from the global stage. They are subject to approval of the main drugs programme funders and usually result in the lowest possible denominator that can be agreed on—whatever is "least offensive to the largest number" (Fazey 2003: 159). The net result is institutions that are "reactive and unlikely to initiate change" (Hartnoll 2000: 243). The validity of Fazey's (2003) arguments have been borne out, firstly by the failure of the 2003 high level meeting she was writing in advance of to result in significant change, and again, more recently, with the events that unfolded around UNGASS 2016, the focus of hope for many invested in drug policy change that resulted in further disappointment.

Change that comes about via the UN apparatus of drug control, as a result of top-down and high level agreements, is therefore likely to remain incremental, and be introduced only in the most gradual way and at the pace of the most conservative members. Incremental change holds some benefits as it allows the necessary supportive infrastructure to develop in preparation for progress to occur (Harding 2000). For example, important lessons can be drawn from the difficulties pioneering member states have experienced in implementing regulated drug markets, either for cannabis or NPS, and very slowly progress can be made towards 'best practice' approaches and international standards. Until experience and evidence grows exponentially, these approaches will not win the endorsement of international institutions of drug control. Furthermore, Pryce (2012) suggests that perhaps the difficulties with achieving consensus about drug policy strategies that are less palatable to a global audience can be overcome by instead agreeing that any change that does take place, should do so on a very cautious and gradual basis.

Those seeking more significant change should perhaps look outside the UN structures of drug control. This is evidenced by, arguably, the HIV/AIDS crisis experienced across the globe in the 1980s which acted as a spur for substantial change in global drug policy, but not as a result of international institutional intervention. In response to this crisis, the goal of reducing the harm caused by drug policies received a significant boost in terms of public and political support as concerns grew about the public health threat to vulnerable drug using populations and to the wider population. As discussed in Chapter 3, the lobbying and implementation of specific harm reduction measures such as substitution treatment and needle exchange programmes, emerged as an alternative response. In the beginning such initiatives tended to be supported at the grass-roots level, primarily by drug users themselves, those living in the neighbourhoods visibly affected by drug use, and those involved in providing services directly to drug users. They attracted the attention of individual political leaders, such as Margaret Thatcher in the UK, and, as they became more established and evidence began to emerge about their effectiveness in containing levels of HIV/AIDS, they spread to many (but crucially not all) areas of the world.

Once many countries had begun to offer such initiatives and with the growth of harm reduction related NGOs, changes started to be reflected in international drug policy. It is notable, however, how slow this has been. For many years the European Union limited the use of the phrase 'harm reduction' in its official documentation, while elsewhere encouraging the proliferation of substitution treatment programmes and needle exchanges within Europe. Similarly, United Nations publications—such as, for example, the UNGASS 2016 Outcome Document—continue to avoid the term 'harm reduction' completely, while incorporating a growing number of its principal features under the more palatable umbrella of public health priorities. Based on this example, significant change in the direction of global drug policy is perhaps more likely as a result of grass-roots efforts in response to new critical developments. These are likely to be pioneered by a few particularly affected countries and, if successful, are slowly reflected in global practice and official international policy documentation.

It is difficult, however, to find further examples of grass-roots policy change in response to drug related issues. One important development within the global drug scene has been the rapid expansion of the market for NPS and other new drugs. As outlined in Chapter 2, this issue has been widely perceived as the latest global challenge facing drug policy and inspired some anticipation of renewed interest in alternative approaches better suited to their control. Despite the harm that comes from using NPS and from their criminalisation being disproportionately experienced by vulnerable populations such as those who are imprisoned, the homeless, those experiencing acute mental health issues, and/or the very young, responses have been overwhelmingly prohibition oriented. In fact, in many cases governments have increased legislative and law enforcement powers in response to this issue, and in some cases have actually abandoned the justification of drug laws based on harm in favour of laws that are based on the effect a substance *might* have. Public health and harm reduction strategies, developed in response to widespread NPS use among vulnerable populations, in contrast, remain severely limited.

The opioid crisis described more thoroughly above could perhaps provide an alternative impetus for grass-roots and local-level responses aimed at reducing the harm caused by substances and the policies that control them. The sharply rising death toll, affecting not just vulnerable populations, but also some high profile celebrities and many members of the affluent middle-class, could provide an important stimulus for the more widespread introduction of new harm reduction strategies. Trump's recent calls for harsher sentences and tougher enforcement messages suggest otherwise, but there are also encouraging developments, for example around low threshold drug checking services, that could provide an alternative way forward. The point of these examples is, that any significant change in global drug policy is likely to begin at the local level, in response to a harmful new development in the drug scene, to gather more widespread support without ever becoming universally accepted, and to gradually infiltrate the official international apparatus of drug control.

This line of reasoning about the development of global drug policy has much in common with the 'Pathways' scenario outlined in the influential OAS (2013) report on alternative drug policy approaches that provides different stories about how global drug policy could develop over the next few years. The pathways scenario essentially imagines that the need for international agreement in the area of drug policy becomes less important over time. In line with the arguments presented in this book, the lack of universal solutions to issues posed by illegal drugs means that countries and regions should have more flexibility to experiment with innovative approaches within a system that also values and prioritises the evaluation and dissemination of local-level strategies on a global basis. Within such a scenario, international institutions could develop over time to become less about maintaining and enforcing control methods, and more about the facilitation of information exchange (Hartnoll 2000). The result would not be an end to global prohibition—many countries would choose to retain the status quo—but it would provide the opportunity for "hundreds of local experiments in drug policy" (Levine 2003: 151), some of which would be considered appropriate for more widespread adoption.

The recent emergence of several experiments in creating regulated cannabis markets provides a developing example of the imagined pathways scenario. Several countries are finding the criminalisation of cannabis harmful and counter-productive and have made moves to implement alternative and innovative approaches. Thus far, those responsible for implementing the changes have not sought to use them to challenge the international conventions directly, but rather have tried to push the boundaries of existing flexibility. There is no consensus about the best way to implement a regulated drugs market and the varied systems offered by the countries and regions leading the way will provide much valuable information about future developments. Governments responsible for implementing regulated markets are not trying to put pressure on others to do the same, but rather focusing on the serious and ongoing evaluation of their own systems. Over time, robust data will be collected about the consequences, positive and negative, of ending criminalisation of an illicit substance. Based on this data, other areas will be able to make informed judgements about the more widespread suitability of regulated markets, as well as the particular parameters that would suit the nature of their context specific drug scene.

To conclude, global drug policy development is highly likely to remain incremental in nature. Changes that do occur will emerge at the local-level and will be driven by grass-roots support in response to specific and critical issues in the wider drug scene, which may not be experienced on a global basis. If an increasing number of individual governments, or a future group of likeminded countries, continue to push the boundaries of international apparatus of drug control, then global norms in this area will gradually develop, but are extremely unlikely to result in consensus. The best way out of a political impasse around global drug policy change is therefore to accept that future global drug policies will be increasingly divergent. Different geographical and cultural populations do not experience the impact of harmful substances in the same way, and should be granted the flexibility to develop an array of approaches. Importantly, there is still a vital role for the international level of drug control in facilitating the creation and exchange of new information, establishing guidelines around identified areas of 'best practice', and providing a forum for documenting and promoting the growing body of existing knowledge that can be drawn upon in this area.

References

Barratt, M., Seear, K., & Lancaster, K. (2017). A critical examination of the definition of 'psychoactive effect in Australian drug legislation'. *International Journal of Drug Policy, 40,* 16–25.

Berenson, T. (2017, October 26). President Trump blamed criminals, drug companies, Mexico and China for the opioid crisis. *Time Magazine.*

Bewley-Taylor, D. (2003). Challenging the UN drug control conventions: Problems and possibilities. *International Journal of Drug Policy, 14,* 171–179.

Brown, R. (2014, November). Our "psycho" psychoactive substances legislation. *Matters of Substance, 25*(4).

Collins, M. (2018). *Just say no to Trump's drug war budget.* Drug Policy Alliance. www.drugpolicy.org.

Curtis, R. (2017). '*Dope Dogs*'. Conference presentation at the Common Sessions in Critical Criminology, May 3–5 2017, New York.

Dasgupta, N., Beletsky, L., & Ciccarone, D. (2017). Opioid crisis: No easy fix to its social and economic determinants. *American Journal of Public Health, 108,* 182–186.

Davenport, S., & Pardo, B. (2016). The dangerous drugs act amendment in Jamaica: Reviewing goals, implementation, and challenges. *International Journal of Drug Policy, 37,* 60–69.

Dhalla, I. A., Pesaud, N., & Juurlink, D. N. (2011). Facing up to the prescription opioid crisis. *British Medical Journal, 33,* d5142.

EMCDDA. (2017). *Netherlands country drug report 2017.* www.emcdda.europa.eu.

Fazey, C. (2003). The commission on narcotic drugs and the United Nations International Drug Control Programme: Politics, policies and prospect for change. *International Journal of Drug Policy, 14,* 155–169.

Harding, W. M. (2000). Informal social controls and the liberalization of drug laws and policies. In R. Coomber's (Ed.), *The control of drugs and drug users* (2nd ed.). Amsterdam: Harwood Academic Publishers.

Hartnoll, R. (2000). International trends in drug policy. In R. Coomber's (Ed.), *The control of drugs and drug users* (2nd ed.). Amsterdam: Harwood Academic Publishers.

Hedegaard, M. D., Warner, M., & Minino, A. M. (2017, December). *Drug overdose deaths in the United States, 1999–2016.* National Center for Health Statistics Data Brief No. 294.

Holpuch, A., Glenza, J., & Jacobs, B. (2018, Monday, March 19). Trump calls for death penalties for drug dealers as focus of opioids plan. *The Guardian,* Washington.

Hudak, J., Ramsey, G., & Walsh, J. (2018). Uruguay's cannabis law: Pioneering a new paradigm. *Brookings.* https://www.brookings.edu.

INCB. (2007). *The report of the International Narcotics Control Board.* Vienna: INCB.

Isacson, A. (2005). The U.S. Military in the War on Drugs. In C. A. Youngers & E. Rosin's (Eds.), *Drugs and democracy in Latin America. The impact of U.S. policy.* London: Lynne Rienner Publishers.

Johns Hopkins. (2018, February 6). *Fentanyl overdose reduction checking analysis study.* Johns Hopkins Bloomberg School of Public Health: Forecast.

Kingdon, J. (1984). *Agendas, alternatives, and public policies*. Boston, MA: Little Brown.

Kolodny, A., Courtwright, D. T., Hwang, C. S., Kreiner, P., Eadie, J. L., Clark, T. W., & Alexander, G. C. (2015). The prescription opioid and heroin crisis: A public health approach to an epidemic of addiction. *Annual Review of Public Health, 36,* 559–574.

Levine, H. G. (2003). Global drug prohibition: Its uses and crises. *International Journal of Drug Policy, 14,* 145–153.

Liu, E. (2017). *Fighting opioids—International solutions to an American epidemic*. US Department of State Official Blog. https://blogs.state.gov.

MacCoun, R., & Reuter, P. (2001). *Drug war heresies*. Cambridge: Cambridge University Press.

Messac, L. (2016). The other opioid crisis—People in poor countries can't get the pain medication they need. *The Conversation*, March 25, 2018. https://theconversation.com.

Nadelmann, E. (1989). Drug prohibition in the US: Costs, consequences and alternatives. *Science, 245,* 939–947.

National Institute on Drug Abuse. (2018). *Opioid overdose crisis*. https://www.drugabuse.gov.

Nixon, R. (2018, January 24). Online sales of illegal opioids from China surge in U.S. *The New York Times*.

Organisation of American States. (2013). *Scenarios for the drug problem in the Americas 2013–2025*. https://www.oas.org.

Pryce, S. (2012). *Fixing drugs: The politics of drug prohibition*. Basingstoke: Palgrave Macmillan.

Reuter, P. (2011). *Options for regulating new psychoactive drugs: A review of recent experiences*. UK Drug Policy Commission.

Reuter, P. (2013). Why has US drug policy changed so little over 20 years? *Crime and Justice, 42*(1), 75–140.

Room, R. (2013). Legalizing a market for cannabis for pleasure: Colorado, Washington, Uruguay and beyond. *Addiction, 109,* 345–351.

STAT. (2017). *STAT forecast: Opioids could kill nearly 500,000 Americans in the next decade*. https://www.statnews.com.

The Economist. (2017). A selective scourge: Inside the opioid epidemic. https://www.economist.com.

Transform. (2015). *Ending the war on drugs. How to win the global drug policy debate*. https://www.tdpf.org.uk.

UNODC. (2018). *Twelve substances 'scheduled' at the 61st session of the Commission on Narcotic Drugs*. UNODC Early Warning Advisory on New Psychoactive Substances. https://www.unodc.org.

Wilkins, C. (2017). Recent developments with the New Zealand regulated market approach to "low-risk" psychoactive products. *Addiction, 112,* 32–39.

Youngers, C. A. (2011, April). *The Obama administration's drug control policy on auto-pilot*. IDPC Briefing Paper. http://www.idpc.net.

References

Aas, K. F. (2011). Visions of global control: Cosmopolitan aspirations in a world of friction. In M. Bosworth & C. Hoyle (Eds.), *What is criminology?* Oxford: Oxford University Press.

Aas, K. F. (2012). The Earth is one but the world is not: Criminological theory and its geopolitical divisions. *Theoretical Criminology, 16*(1), 5–20.

Aas, K. F. (2013). *Globalization and crime* (2nd ed.). London: Sage.

ACMD. (2002). *The classification of cannabis under the Misuse of Drugs Act 1971*. Home office: https://www.gov.uk.

Akgul, A., & Gurer, C. (2014). The European Union and emergence of a drug policy institution in Turkey. *Drugs: Education, Prevention and Policy, 21*(6), 460–469.

Aldridge, J., & Decary-Hetu, D. (2014). *Not an "eBay for drugs": The cryptomarket "silk road" as a paradigm shifting criminal innovation*. https://doi.org/10.2139/ssrn.2436643.

Aldridge, J., & Decary-Hetu, D. (2016a). Cryptomarkets and the future of illicit drug markets. In EMCDDA (Eds.), *The internet and drug markets* (EMCDDA Insights 21). Luxembourg: Publications Office of the European Union.

Aldridge, J., & Decary-Hetu, D. (2016b). Hidden wholesale: The drug diffusing capacity of online drug cryptomarkets. *International Journal of Drug Policy, 35*, 7–15.

C. Chatwin, *Towards More Effective Global Drug Policies*,
https://doi.org/10.1007/978-3-319-92072-6

Alexander, M. (2010). *The new jim crow: Mass incarceration in the age of colorblindness*. New York: The New Press.
Alexandrescu, L. (2017). *Spice is not the real problem, it's the way we look at poverty*. Volteface: www.volteface.me.
Allen, L., Trace, M., & Klein, A. (2004). *Decriminalisation of drugs in Portugal: A current overview*. London: DrugScope and The Beckley Foundation.
Alonso, B. (2011, January). *Cannabis social clubs in Spain: A normalising alternative underway* (Series on Legislative Reform of Drug Policies Nr 9). Spain: Transnational Institute. https://www.tni.org.
Amnesty International. (2011). *Addicted to death: Executions for drug offenses in Iran*. London: Amnesty International. https://www.amnesty.org.uk.
Anderson, D., & Jarvinen, M. (2007). Harm reduction—Ideals and paradoxes. *Nordic Studies on Alcohol and Drugs, 24*, 235–252.
Babor, T., Caetano, R., Casswell, S., Edwards, G., Giesbrecht, N., Graham, K., et al. (2010). *Alcohol: No ordinary commodity: Research and public policy* (2nd ed.). Oxford: Oxford University Press.
Bacchi, C. (2009). *Analysing policy: What's the problem represented to be*. Sydney: Pearson Education.
Bache, I. (1998). *The politics of European Union regional policy: Multi-level governance or flexible gatekeeping*? Sheffield: Sheffield Academic Press.
Backstrand, K. (2004). Civic science for sustainability: Reframing the role of experts, policy-makers and citizens in environmental governance. *Global Environmental Politics, 3*(4), 24–41.
Barratt, M. (2012). Silk road: eBay for drugs. *Addiction, 107*, 683.
Barratt, M., & Maddox, A. (2016). Active engagement with stigmatised communities through digital ethnography. *Qualitative Research, 16*(6), 701–719.
Barratt, M., Seear, K., & Lancaster, K. (2017). A critical examination of the definition of 'psychoactive effect' in Australian drug legislation. *International Journal of Drug Policy, 40*, 16–25.
Barrett, D., Bewley-Taylor, D., & Jelsma, M. (2014). *Fatal attraction: Brownfield's flexibility doctrine and global drug policy reform*. London: Huffington Post Politics.
Barrett, D., Lines, R., Schleifer, R., Elliott, R., & Bewley-Taylor, D. (2008). *Recalibrating the regime. The need for a human-rights based approach to international drug policy*. The Beckley Foundation Drug Policy Programme: https://www.internationaldrugpolicy.net.

Bastos, F., & Strathdee, S. (2000). Evaluating effectiveness of syringe exchange programmes: Current issues and future projects'. *Social Science and Medicine, 51*, 1771–1782.

Bauman, Z. (2000). *Liquid modernity*. Cambridge: Policy Press.

Baumgartner, F. R., & Jones, B. D. (1993). *Agendas and instability in American politics*. Chicago: University of Chicago Press.

Beaumont, P., Townsend, M., & Helm, T. (2010, September 5, Sunday). Britain looks at Portugal's success story over decriminalising personal drug use. *Observer*.

Bennett, C. J. (1991). Review article: What is policy convergence and what causes it? *British Journal of Political Science, 21*, 215–233.

Benson, D., & Jordan, A. (2011). What have we learned from policy transfer research? Dolowitz and Marsh revisited. *Political Studies Review, 9*, 366–378.

Berenson, T. (2017, October 26). President Trump blamed criminals, drug companies, Mexico and China for the opioid crisis. *Time Magazine*.

Berridge, V., & Thom, B. (1996). Research and policy: What determines the relationship? *Policy Studies, 17*(1), 23–34.

Bewley-Taylor, D. (2003). Challenging the UN drug control conventions: Problems and possibilities. *International Journal of Drug Policy, 14*, 171–179.

Bewley-Taylor, D. (2012a). The contemporary international drug control system: A history of the UNGASS decade. In J. Collins & N. Kitchen (Eds.), *Governing the global drug wars*. LSE Special Report SR014: https://www.eprints.lse.ac.uk.

Bewley-Taylor, D. (2012b). *International drug control: Consensus fractured*. Cambridge: Cambridge University Press.

Bewley-Taylor, D. (2013). Towards revision of the UN drug conventions: Harnessing like-mindedness. *International Journal of Drug Policy, 24*(1), 60–68.

Bewley-Taylor, D. (2016, April). *Towards metrics that measure outcomes that matter* (Policy Brief 10). Swansea, UK: Global Drug Policy Observatory. https://www.swansea.ac.uk/gdpo.

Bewley-Taylor, D., & Jelsma, M. (2011). *Fifty years of the 1961 single convention on narcotic drugs: A reinterpretation* (Series on Legislative Reform of Drug Policies). Transnational Institute: http://www.tni.org.

Bewley-Taylor, D., & Jelsma, M. (2012). *The UN drug control conventions: Limits of latitude*. Transnational Institute: https://www.tni.org.

Bewley-Taylor, D., & Jelsma, M. (2016, June). *UNGASS 2016: A broken or B-r-o-a-d consensus? UN summit cannot hide growing divergence in the global drug policy landscape* (Drug Policy Briefing 45). Amsterdam: Transnational Institute. https://www.tni.org.

Bewley-Taylor, D., & Trace, M. (2006). *The INCB: Watchdog or guardian of the UN drug control conventions*? The Beckley Foundation Drug Policy Programme.

Bewley-Taylor, D., Jelsma, M., & Blickman, T. (2014). *The rise and decline of cannabis prohibition*. Transnational Institute: http://www.tni.org.

Beyers, J., Toumbourou, J., Catalano, R., Arthur, M., & Hawkins, J. (2004). A cross-national comparison of risk and protective factors for adolescent substance use: The United States and Australia. *Journal of Adolescent Health, 35*, 3–16.

Birdwell, J., Chapman, J., & Singleton, N. (2011). *Taking drugs seriously: Aa demos and UK drug policy commission report on legal highs*. http://www.ukdpc.org.uk.

Black, N. (2001). Evidence based policy: Proceed with care. *British Medical Journal, 323*, 275–279.

Blackman, S., & Bradley, R. (2017). From niche to stigma—Headshops to prison; Exploring the rise and fall of synthetic cannabinoid use amongst young adults. *International Journal of Drug Policy, 40*, 70–77.

Boekhout van Solinge, T. (1999). Dutch drug policy in a European context. *Journal of Drug Issues, 29*, 511–528.

Boothroyd, D. (2016, September 6). *Roundtable: New drugs and the "bigger picture*" (Unpublished conference paper delivered at the ESRC Seminar Series on New Drugs). Canterbury: University of Kent.

Boothroyd, D., & Lewis, S. (2016). Rethinking evidence in online social drug use research. In A. O'Gorman, G. Potter, & J. Fountain (Eds.), *Evidence in European social drug research and drug policy*. Lengerich: Pabst Science Publishers.

Bourgain, C., Falissard, L. B., Benyamina, A., Karila, L., & Reynaud, M. (2012). A damage/benefit evaluation of addictive product use. *Addiction, 107*, 441–456.

Bourgois, P., & Schonberg, J. (2009). *Righteous Dopefiend*. London: University of California Press.

Bowling, B. (2011). Transnational criminology and the globalisation of harm production. In M. Bosworth & C. Hoyle (Eds.), *What is Criminology?* Oxford: Oxford University Press.

Brown, R. (2014, November 22). Our "psycho" psychoactive substances legislation. *Matters of Substance, 25*(4), 22–25.

Bruun, K., Pan, L., & Rexed, I. (1975). *The gentleman's club*. Chicago and London: University of Chicago Press.

Bullington, B. (2000). America's drug war: Fact or fiction. In Coomber (Ed.), *The control of drug use and drug users*. Amsterdam: Harwood Academic Publishers.

Bulmer, S., & Padgett, S. (2004). Policy transfer in the European Union: An institutionalist perspective. *British Journal of Political Science, 35*(1), 103–126.

Burawoy, M. (2004). Public sociologies: Contradictions, dilemmas, and possibilities. *Social Forces, 82*, 1603–1618.

Burawoy, M. (2005). 2004 presidential address: For public sociology. *American Sociological Review, 70*, 4–28.

Burawoy, M., Gamson, W., Ryan, C., Pfohl, S., Vaughan, D., Derber, C., & Schor, J. (2004). Public sociologies: A symposium from Boston college. *Social Problems, 51*, 103–130.

Burris, S., & Strathdee, S. (2006). To serve and protect? Towards a better relationship between drug control policy and public health. *AIDS, 20*, 117–118.

Buxton, J., & Bingham, T. (2015, January). *The rise and challenge of dark net drug markets* (Policy Brief 7). Swansea: Global Drug Policy Observatory.

Canas, V. (2002). *The policy for the fight against drugs and drug addiction in Portugal: Recent developments*. London: Speech Given to DrugScope.

Capoccia, G. (2016). Critical junctures. In O. Fioretos, G. Tulia, & A. Sheingate (Eds.), *The Oxford handbook of historical institutionalism*. Oxford: Oxford University Press.

Carrier, N. (2014). On some limits and paradoxes of academic orations on public criminology. *Radical Criminology, 4*, 85–115.

Caudevilla, F. (2016). The emergence of deep web marketplaces: A health perspective. In EMCDDA (Eds.), *The internet and drug markets* (EMCDDA Insights 21). Luxembourg: Publications Office of the European Union.

Caulkins, J., & Kilmer, B. (2015). Considering marijuana legalization carefully: Insight for other jurisdictions from analysis in Vermont. *Addiction, 111*, 2082–2089.

Caulkins, J., Reuter, P., & Coulson, C. (2011). Basing drug scheduling decisions on scientific ranking of harmfulness: False promise from false premise. *Addiction, 106*, 1886–1890.

Cerda, M., & Kilmer, B. (2017). Uruguay's middle ground approach to cannabis legalization. *International Journal of Drug Policy, 42*, 118–120.

Chan, J. (2005). Globalisation, reflexivity and the practice of criminology. In J. Sheptycki & A. Wardak (Eds.), *Transnational and comparative criminology*. London: Glasshouse Press.

Chatwin, C. (2003). Drug policy developments within the European Union. The destabilizing effects of Dutch and Swedish drug policies. *British Journal of Criminology, 43*, 567–582.

Chatwin, C. (2010). User involvement in the illegal drugs field: What can Britain learn from European experiences? *Safer Communities, 9*, 51–60.

Chatwin, C. (2011). *Drug policy harmonization and the European Union*. Basingstoke: Palgrave Macmillan.

Chatwin, C. (2014). New psychoactive substances: New European policy landscapes. In G. R. Potter, M. Wouters, & J. Fountain (Eds.), *Change and continuity: Researching evolving drug landscapes in Europe*. Lengerich: PABST Science Publishers.

Chatwin, C. (2015). *Mixed messages from Europe on drug policy reform: The cases of Sweden and The Netherlands*. Brookings: https://www.brookings.edu.

Chatwin, C. (2017). Assessing the 'added value' of European policy on new psychoactive substances. *International Journal of Drug Policy, 40*, 111–116.

Chatwin, C., & Potter, G. (2011). Blurred boundaries: The artificial distinction between 'use' and 'supply' in the UK cannabis market. *Contemporary Drug Problems, 41*(4), 536–550.

Chatwin, C., Blackman, S., & O'Brien, K. (2018, in print). Intersections in (new) drug research. *Drugs: Education, Prevention and Policy*.

Chatwin, C., Measham, F., O'Brien, K., & Sumnall, H. (2017). New drugs, new directions? Exploring critical and social research priorities in NPS and HED debates. *International Journal of Drug Policy, 40*, 1–5.

Ciccarone, D. (2017). Fentanyl in the US heroin supply: A rapidly changing risk environment. *International Journal of Drug Policy, 46*, 107–111.

CND. (2012). *Improving the participatory role of civil society in addressing the world drug problem*. Commission on Narcotic Drugs, Fifty-Fifth Session, Vienna 12–16 March, E/CN.7/2012/CRP.1.

CND. (2014). *Proposed strategic framework on 2016–2017 for the United Nations Office on Drugs and Crime*. Commission on Narcotic Drugs, Fifty-Seventh Session, Vienna, 13–21 March 2014, E/CN.7/2014/CRP.4.

Cohen, S. (1998). *Against criminology*. New Brunswick: Transaction.

Cohen, P. (2010). Looking at the UN, smelling a rat: A comment on "Sweden's successful drugs policy: A review of the evidence". *Amsterdam Law Forum, 2*(4), 10.

Collins, J. (2017a). Rethinking "flexibilities" in the international drug control system—Potential, precedents and models for reform. *International Journal of Drug Policy*. https://doi.org/10.1016.12.014.

Collins, J. (2017b). Losing UNGASS? Lessons from civil society past and present. *Drugs and Alcohol Today, 17*(2), 88–97.

Collins, M. (2018). *Just say no to Trump's drug war budget*. Drug Policy Alliance: www.drugpolicy.org.

Commission of the European Communities. (2004). *Communication from the Commission to the Council and the European Parliament on the results of the Final EU Drugs Strategy and Action Plan on Drugs (2000–2004)*. http://www.emcdda.europa.eu.

Connell, R. (2007). The northern theory of globalization. *Sociological Theory, 25*(4), 368–385.

Cook, C., Bridge, J., & Stimson, G. (2010). The diffusion of harm reduction in Europe and beyond. In European Monitoring Centre for Drugs and Drug Addiction (Ed.), *Harm reduction: Evidence, impacts and challenges*. https://www.emcdda.europa.eu.

Coomber, R., & Moyle, L. (2013). Beyond drug dealing: Developing and extending the concept of "social supply" of illicit drugs to "minimally commercial supply". *Drugs: Education Prevention and Policy, 21*(2), 157–164.

Costa, A. (2008). *Making drug control 'fit for purpose': Building on the UNGASS decade*. Vienna: Commission on Narcotic Drugs.

Coulson, C., & Caulkins, J. P. (2011). Scheduling of newly emerging drugs: A critical review of decisions over 40 years. *Addiction, 107*, 766–773.

Council of Ministers. (1999). *National drug strategy* (Resolution of the Council of Ministers No. 46/99). http://www.drugtext.org.

Council of the European Union. (2012, December 29). EU drugs strategy (2013–2020). *Official Journal of the European Union*.

Crepault, D. (2016). The rise of partisan pedagogy: How stakeholders outside of the academy are answering the call to public criminology. *British Journal of Criminology, 57*, 789–807.

Crick, E., Haase, H. J., & Bewley Taylor, D. (2013, November). *Legally regulated cannabis markets in the US: Implications and possibilities* (Policy Report 1). Swansea, UK: Global Drug Policy Observatory.

Csete, J. Y., & Wolfe, D. (2007). *Closed to reason: The international narcotics control board and HIV/AIDS*. Toronto and New York: Canadian HIV/AIDS Legal Network and The International Harm Reduction Development (IHERD) Programme of the Open Society Institute.

Cullen, F. T. (2011). Beyond adolescence-limited criminology. Choosing our future—The American Society of Criminology 2010 Sutherland address. *Criminology, 49*(2), 287–330.

Currie, E. (1993). *Reckoning: Drugs, the cities and the American future*. New York: Hill and Wang.

Currie, E. (2007). Against marginality: Arguments for a public criminology. *Theoretical Criminology, 11*, 175–190.

Curtis, R. (2017). '*Dope dogs*'. Conference presentation at the Common Sessions in Critical Criminology, May 3–5, New York.

Dasgupta, N., Beletsky, L., & Ciccarone, D. (2017). Opioid crisis: No easy fix to its social and economic determinants. *American Journal of Public Health, 108*, 182–186.

Davenport, S., & Pardo, B. (2016). The dangerous drugs act amendment in Jamaica: Reviewing goals, implementation, and challenges. *International Journal of Drug Policy, 37*, 60–69.

Decorte, T. (2015). Cannabis social clubs in Belgium: Organizational strengths and weaknesses, and threats to the model. *International Journal of Drug Policy, 26*(1), 122–130.

Decorte, T., Pardal, M., Queirolo, R., Boidi, M. F., Sánchez Avilés, C., & Parés, O. (2017). Regulating cannabis social clubs: A comparative analysis of legal and self-regulatory practices in Spain, Belgium and Uruguay. *International Journal of Drug Policy, 43*, 44–56.

de Jarlais, D. C. (1995). Editorial: Harm reduction—A framework for incorporating science into drug polic. *American Journal of Public Health, 85*(1), 10–12.

de Kort, M., & Cramer, T. (1999). Pragmatism versus ideology: Dutch drug policy continued. *Journal of Drug Issues, 29*, 473–492.

Delibasic, S., & Leder, M. (2017, June 19). Craiglist ads: Drug dealers openly peddly ice, cannabis and cocaine. *Herald Sun*. www.heraldsun.com.au.

Dhalla, I. A., Pesaud, N., & Juurlink, D. N. (2011). Facing up to the prescription opioid crisis. *British Medical Journal, 33*, d5142.

Doll, R., Peto, R., Boreham, J., & Sutherland, I. (2004). Mortality in relation to smoking: 50 years' observations on male British doctors. *British Medical Journal, 328*, 1519–1528.

Dolowitz, D. P., & Marsh, D. (1996). Who learns what from whom? A review of the policy transfer literature. *Political Studies, 44*(2), 343–357.

Dolowitz, D. P., & Marsh, D. (2000). Learning from abroad: The role of policy transfer in contemporary policy making. *Governance, 13*(1), 5–24.

Dorn, N., & Jamieson, A. (2000). *Room for manoeuvre: Overview of comparative legal research into national drug laws of France, Germany, Italy, Spain, The Netherlands and Sweden and their relation to three international drugs conventions.* A Study of DrugScope for the Independent Inquiry on the Misuse of Drugs Act 1971, London.

Duke, K., & Thom, B. (2014). The role of evidence and the expert in contemporary processes of governance: The case of opioid substitution treatment policy in England. *International Journal of Drug Policy, 25*, 964–971.

Duke, S. B., & Gross, A. (1982). *America's longest war.* New York: Putnam and Sons.

Eastwood, N., Fox, E., & Rosmarin, A. (2012). *A quiet revolution: Drug decriminalisation policies in practice across the globe.* Release: http://www.release.org.uk.

EMCDDA. (2010). *Annual report 2010: The state of the drugs problem in Europe.* http://www.emcdda.europa.eu.

EMCDDA. (2011). *European drug report 2011.* http://www.emcdda.europa.eu.

EMCDDA. (2015). *European drug report 2015.* http://www.emcdda.europa.eu.

EMCDDA. (2017a). *Cannabis legislation in Europe: An overview.* www.emcdda.europa.eu.

EMCDDA. (2017b). *Statistical bulletin 2017.* http://www.emcdda.europa.eu.

EMCDDA. (2017c). *European drug report 2017.* http://www.emcdda.europa.eu.

EMCDDA. (2017d). *The Netherlands country drug report 2017.* www.emcdda.europa.eu.

EMCDDA. (2018). *Mission.* http://www.emcdda.europa.eu/mission-en.

EMCDDA, & Europol. (2013). *EU drug markets report: A strategic analysis.* Luxembourg: Publications Office of the European Union.

EMCDDA, & Europol. (2016). *EU drug markets report: In-depth analysis.* Luxembourg: Publications Office of the European Union.

ENCOD. (2007). *Common press release of Giusto Catania MP and ENCOD.* http://www.encod.org.

ENCOD. (2014). *What is a cannabis social club*? ENCOD: http://www.cannabis-social-clubs.org.

Erickson, P. G. (1997). Reducing the harm of adolescent substance use. *Canadian Medical Association Journal, 156*(10), 1397–1399.

European Monitoring Centre for Drugs and Drug Addiction. (2016). *Legal approaches to controlling new psychoactive substances*. Luxembourg: Publications Office of the European Union.

European Parliament. (2016). *A review and assessment of EU drug policy*. Directorate General for Internal Policies, Policy Department C: Citizens' Rights and Constitutional Affairs, Civil Liberties, Justice and Home Affairs, PE 571.400.

European Union. (2016). *European Union common position on UNGASS 2016*. www.unodc.org.

Evans-Brown, M., McVeigh, J., Perkins, C., & Bellis, M. A. (2012). *Human enhancement drugs: The emerging challenges to public health*. Liverpool: North West Public Health Observatory.

Ezard, N. (2001). Public health, human rights and the harm reduction paradigm: From risk reduction to vulnerability reduction. *International Journal of Drug Policy, 12*, 207–219.

Farthing, L., & Kohl, B. (2012). Supply-side harm reduction strategies: Bolivia's experiment with social control. *International Journal of Drug Policy, 23*, 488–494.

Fazey, C. (2003). The commission on narcotic drugs and the United Nations international drug control programme: Politics, policies and prospect for change. *International Journal of Drug Policy, 14*, 155–169.

Felbab-Brown, V. (2008). *Counternarcotics policy overview: Global trends & strategies*. Brookings: https://www.brookings.edu.

Felbab-Brown, V. (2015). *No easy exit: Drugs and counternarcotics policies in Afghanistan*. https://www.brookings.edu.

Felbab-Brown, V., & Trinkunas, H. (2015). *UNGASS 2016 in comparative perspective: Improving the prospects for success*. https://www.brookings.edu.

Ferreira, S. (2010). Portugal's drug laws draw new scrutiny. *Wall Street Journal*. European Coalition for Just and Effective Drug Policies: http://www.encod.org.

Fischer, B., & Kendall, P. (2011). Nutt et al. harm scales for drugs—Room for improvement but better policy based on science with limitations than no science at all. *Addiction, 106*(11), 1891–1892.

Flynn, P. (2001). *Social consequences of and responses to drug misuse in member states*. Social, Health and Family Affairs Committee, Parliamentary Assembly. Luxembourg: Office for Official Publications of the European Communities.

Fordham, A. (2016, May 3). The drugs consensus is not pretty—It's been ripped apart at the seams. *Huffington Post*. http://www.huffingtonpost.co.uk.

Fordham, A., & Jelsma, M. (2016). *Will UNGASS 2016 be the beginning of the end for the 'war on drugs*? Transnational Institute: https://www.tni.org.
Foucault, M. (1979). *The birth of biopolitics: Lectures at the College de France 1978–1979*. New York: Palgrave Macmillan.
Foucault, M. (1991). Governmentality. In G. Burchell, C. Gordon, & P. Miller (Eds.), *The foucault effect: Studies in governmentality*. Chicago: The University of Chicago Press.
Fox, E. (2015). *US sends mixed signals on UN drug convention flexibility*. https://www.talkingdrugs.org.
Freeman, L., & Sierra, J. L. (2005). Mexico: The militarization trap. In C. A. Youngers & E. Rosin (Eds.), *Drugs and democracy in Latin America: The impact of U.S. policy*. Boulder, CO: Lynne Rienner Publishers Inc.
Freisthler, B., & Gruenewald, P. J. (2014). Examining the relationship between the physical availability of medical marijuana and marijuana use across fifty Californian cities. *Drug and Alcohol Dependence, 143*, 244–250.
Gable, R. S. (2004). Comparison of acute lethal toxicity of commonly abused psychoactive substances. *Addiction, 99*, 686–696.
Galeotti, M. (2015). *Narcotics and nationalism: Russian drug policies and futures*. Brookings: https://www.brookings.edu.
Gallahue, P., & Lines, R. (2015). *The death penalty for drug offences: Global overview 2015*. London: Harm Reduction International.
Galtung, J. (1990). Theory formation in social research: A plea for pluralism. In E. Oyen (Ed.), *Comparative methodology*. London: Sage.
Garcia, M. (2006). Citizen practices and urban governance in European cities. *Urban Studies, 43*, 745–765.
Gberie, L. (2015). *Crime, violence and politics: Drug trafficking and counter narcotics policies in Mali and Guinea*. https://www.brookings.edu.
Getimis, P., Parakevopoulos, C., & Rees, N. (2006). Domestic governance structures and policy learning East and West: The limits of Europeanisation. In C. Paraskevopoulos, P. Getimis, & N. Rees (Eds.), *Adapting to EU multi-level governance: Regional and environmental policies in cohesion and CEE countries*. Hampshire: Ashgate.
Ghodse, H. (2010). Watching internet pharmacies. *The British Journal of Psychiatry, 196*, 169–170.
Giddens, A. (1990). *The consequences of modernity*. Stanford: Stanford University Press.
Global Commission on Drug Policy. (2011). *War on drugs: Report of the Global Commission on Drug Policy*. http://www.globalcommissionondrugs.org.

Global Commission on Drug Policy. (2014). *Taking control: Pathways to drug policies that work*. http://www.globalcommissionondrugs.org.
Global Commission on Drug Policy. (2016, April 21). *Public statement by the Global Commission on Drug Policy on UNGASS 2016*. New York: Global Commission on Drug Policy. http://www.globalcommissionondrugs.org.
Goldberg, T. (2005). Will Swedish and Dutch drug policy converge? The role of theory. *International Journal of Social Welfare, 14*, 44–54.
Goldstein, P. J. (1985). The drugs-violence nexus: A tripartite conceptual framework. *Journal of Drug Issues, 15*, 493–506.
Gomis, B. (2016, October). *US drug policy; Clinton vs. Trump*. Global Drug Policy Observatory Situation Analysis.
Greene, J. (1999). Zero tolerance: A case study of policies and practices in New York City. *Crime and Delinquency, 45*, 171–187.
Greenfield, V. A., & Paoli, L. (2012). If supply-oriented drug policy is broken, can harm reduction help fix it? Melding disciplines and methods to advance international drug-control policy. *International Journal of Drug Policy, 23*(1), 6–15.
Greenwald, G. (2009). *Drug decriminalization in Portugal: Lessons for creating fair and successful drug policies*. The Cato Institute: http://www.cato.org.
Grund, J. P., & Breeksema, J. (2013). *Coffeeshops and compromise: Separated illicit drug markets in The Netherlands*. Open Society Foundations: http://www.opensocietyfoundations.org.
Haken, J. (2011). *Transnational crime in the developing world*. Global Financial Integrity: http://www.gfintegrity.org.
Hakim, C. (2000). *Research design: Successful designs for social and economic research* (2nd ed.). London: Routledge.
Hakim, P. (2011). *Rethinking US drug policy*. Inter-American Dialogue: https://www.thedialogue.org.
Hall, W. (2016). Alcohol and cannabis: Comparing their adverse health effects and regulatory regimes. *International Journal of Drug Policy, 42*, 57–62.
Hall, W., Room, R., & Bondy, S. (1999). Comparing the health and psychological effects of alcohol, cannabis, nicotine and opiate use. In H. Kalant, W. Corrigall, W. Hall, & R. Smart (Eds.), *The health effects of cannabis*. Toronto: Centre for Addiction and Mental Health.
Hanley Santos, G., & Coomber, R. (2017). The risk environment of anabolic-androgenic steroid users in the UK: Examining motivations, practices and accounts of use. *International Journal of Drug Policy, 40*, 35–43.
Harding, W. M. (2000). Informal social controls and the liberalization of drug laws and policies. In R. Coomber (Ed.), *The control of drugs and drug users* (2nd ed.). Amsterdam: Harwood Academic Publishers.

Harm Reduction International. (2016a). *The global state of harm reduction 2016*. https://www.hri.global.

Harm Reduction International. (2016b, January 23). *Harm reduction international has serious concerns with draft UNGASS outcome document*. https://www.hri.global.

Hartnoll, R. (2000). International trends in drug policy. In R. Coomber (Ed.), *The control of drugs and drug users* (2nd ed.). Amsterdam: Harwood Academic Publishers.

Hathaway, A. (2001). Shortcomings of harm reduction: Toward a morally invested drug reform strategy. *International Journal of Drug Policy, 12*, 125–137.

Head, B. W. (2008). Three lenses of evidence-based policy. *The Australian Journal of Public Administration, 67*(1), 1–11.

Hedegaard, M. D., Warner, M., & Minino, A. M. (2017, December). *Drug overdose deaths in the United States, 1999–2016* (National Center for Health Statistics Data Brief No. 294).

Held, D. (2000). The changing contours of political community. In R. Ericson & N. Stehr (Eds.), *Governing modern societies*. Toronto: University of Toronto Press.

Hetzer, H. (2016). *UNGASS outcome: Missed opportunity for UN, but global reform movement grows & continues to push for better drug policies*. Drug Policy Alliance: www.drugpolicy.org/blog.

Holpuch, A., Glenza, J., & Jacobs, B. (2018, March 19, Monday). *Trump calls for death penalties for drug dealers as focus of opioids plan. The Guardian*. Washington.

Hooghe, L., & Marks, G. (2001). *Multi-level governance and European integration*. Oxford: Rowman & Littlefield.

Hope, A. (2015). *Plus ca change: Structural continuities in Mexican counternarcotics policy*. https://www.brookings.edu.

Hudak, J., Ramsey, G., & Walsh, J. (2018). *Uruguay's cannabis law: Pioneering a new paradigm*. Brookings: https://www.brookings.edu.

Hughes, B., & Winstock, A. R. (2011). Controlling new drugs under marketing regulations. *Addiction, 107*, 1894–1899.

Hughes, C. (2006). *Overcoming obstacles to reform?: Making and shaping drug policy in contemporary Portugal and Australia*. PhD thesis, Department of Criminology, University of Melbourne.

Hughes, C., & Stevens, A. (2010). What can we learn from the Portuguese decriminalisation of illicit drugs? *British Journal of Criminology, 50*, 999–1022.

Hulme, R. (2005). Policy transfer and the internationalisation of social policy. *Social Policy and Sociology, 4*(4), 417–425.

Hunt, N. (2003). *A review of the evidence-base for harm reduction approaches to drug use*. Release: http://www.forward-thinking-on-drugs.org/review2.

Hunt, N., & Stevens, A. (2004). Whose harm? Harm reduction and the shift to coercion in UK drug policy. *Social Policy and Society, 3*(4), 333–342.

Hylton, A. (2016, April 23, Saturday). Setting the record straight on the Ganja law. *Jamaica Observer*. http://www.jamaicaobserver.com.

IDPC. (2016). The United Nations General Assembly Special Session (UNGASS) on the world drug problem. *Report of Proceedings*. http://www.idpc.net.

INCB. (2007). *The report of the international narcotics control board 2007*. Vienna: INCB.

INCB. (2012). *International narcotics control board 2012 report*. www.incb.org.

Inciardi, J. (Ed.). (1999). *The drug legalisation debate* (2nd ed.). Thousand Oaks, London, and New Delhi: Sage.

International Harm Reduction Development Programme. (2010). *Detention as treatment: Detention of methamphetamine users in Cambodia, Laos and Thailand*. Open Society Institute. https://www.opensocietyfoundations.org.

Intraval. (2007). *Coffeeshops in Nederland* (English Summary). http://www.wodc.nl.

Isacson, A. (2005). The U.S. military in the war on drugs. In C. A. Youngers & E. Rosin (Eds.), *Drugs and democracy in Latin America. The impact of U.S. policy*. London: Lynne Reinner Publishers.

Jelsma, M. (2011, January). *The development of international drug control: Lessons learned and strategic challenges for the future* (Working Paper). Geneva: Global Commission on Drug Policies.

Jelsma, M. (2015). *UNGASS 2016: Prospects for treaty reform and UN system-wide coherence on drug policy*. Brookings: http://www.brookings.edu.

Johns, H. (2018, February 6). *Fentanyl overdose reduction checking analysis study*. Johns Hopkins Bloomberg School of Public Health: Forecast.

Johnson, B. (2006). The development of user influence on Swedish drug policy, 1965–2004. In J. Anker, V. Asmussen, P. Kouvonen, & D. Tops (Eds.), *Drug users and spaces for legitimate action* (NAD Monograph No. 49). Helsinki: Nordic Alcohol and Drug Council.

Jones, S. (2016). Farming medical Ganja in Jamaica. *International Journal of Drug Policy, 36*, 151–155.

Jones, S., Porter, R., & Bishop, C. (2017). The implementation of medical Ganja in Jamaica. *International Journal of Drug Policy, 42*, 115–117.

Kaplan, C., & Leuw, E. (1996). A tale of two cities: Drug policy instruments and city networks in the European Union. *European Journal on Criminal Policy and Research, 4*, 74–89.

Kaul, I. (2010). The changing role of the United Nations: Lessons for multi-level governance. In H. Enderlein, S. Walti, & M. Zurn (Eds.), *Handbook on multi-level governance*. Cheltenham: Edward Elgar.

Keane, H. (2002). Critiques of harm reduction, morality and the promise of human rights. *International Journal of Drug Policy, 14*, 227–232.

Kebjaj, S., Shahidinia, N., Testa, A., & Williams, J. (2013). Collateral damage & the war on drugs: Estimating the effect of zero tolerance policies on drug arrest rates, 1975–2002. *The Public Purpose, XI*, 1–25.

Kellogg, S. H. (2003). On "gradualism" and the building of the harm reduction—Abstinence continuum. *Journal of Substance Abuse Treatment, 25*, 241–247.

Kilmer, B., & Pacula, R. L. (2016). Understanding and learning from the diversification of cannabis supply laws. *Addiction, 12*, 1128–1135.

Kilmer, B., Midgette, G., & Saloga, C. (2015). *Back in the national spotlight: An assessment of recent changes in drug use and drug policies in the United States*. Brookings: https://www.brookings.edu.

Ki-moon, B. (2013). *Statement: Secretary-general's remarks at special event on the international day against drug abuse and illicit trafficking*. United Nations: http://www.un.org.

Kingdon, J. (1984). *Agendas, alternatives, and public policies*. Boston, MA: Little Brown.

Klein, A. (2011). Written evidence to the house of lords' enquiry into the European drug strategy' in House of Lords. *The EU drugs strategy, oral and written evidence*. Home Affairs Subcommittee of the European Select Committee: http://www.parliament.co.uk.

Klein, K. (2016). Entrepreneurship, identity and the transformation of marketing systems: Medical cannabis in California. *Journal of Macromarketing, 57*(1), 85–101.

Kleinman, M. A. R., Ziskind, J. A., & Collins, J. (2014). *Lawful access to cannabis: Gains, losses and design criteria. Ending the drug wars: Report of the LSE expert group on the economics of drug policy*. London, UK: The London School of Economics and Political Science.

Knoepfel, P., & Kissling-Naf, I. (1998). Social learning in policy networks. *Policy and Politics, 26*(3), 343–367.

Kolodny, A., Courtwright, D. T., Hwang, C. S., Kreiner, P., Eadie, J. L., Clark, T. W., & Alexander, G. C. (2015). The prescription opioid and heroin crisis: A public health approach to an epidemic of addiction. *Annual Review of Public Health, 36*, 559–574.

Korf, D. J. (2008). An open front door: The coffeeshop phenomenon in The Netherlands. In S. Rodner, B. Sznitman, B. Olsson, & R. Room (Eds.), *A cannabis reader: Global issues and local experiences—Perspectives on cannabis controversies, treatment and regulation in Europe* (EMCDDA Monograph No. 8). Luxembourg: Office for Official Publications of the European Communities.

Lancaster, K. (2016). Performing the evidence-based drug policy. *Contemporary Drug Problems, 43*(2), 142–153.

Lavorgna, A. (2014). Internet-mediated drug trafficking: Towards a better understanding of new criminal dynamics'. *Trends in Organised Crime, 17*, 250–270.

Lavorgna, A. (2016). How the use of the internet is affecting drug trafficking practices. In EMCDDA (Eds.), *The internet and drug markets* (EMCDDA Insights 21). Luxembourg: Publications Office of the European Union.

Lemmens, P. H. (2003). Dutch government backs down on heroin prescription, despite successful trial. *Addiction, 98*, 247–249.

Lenton, S. (2004). P'ot, politics and the press—Reflections on cannabis law reform in Western Australia. *Drug and Alcohol Review, 23*, 223–233.

Lenton, S., & Single, E. (1998). The definition of harm reduction. *Drug and Alcohol Review, 17*, 213–220.

Leroy, B. (1995). Assessing the legalisation debate. In G. Estievenart (Ed.), *Policies and strategies to combat drugs in Europe: Framework for a new European strategies to combat drugs*. Dordrecht: Martinus Nijhoff Publishers.

Levine, H. G. (2003). Global drug prohibition: Its uses and crises. *International Journal of Drug Policy, 14*, 145–153.

Liu, E. (2017). *Fighting opioids—International solutions to an American epidemic*. US Department of State Official Blog: https://blogs.state.gov.

Loader, I., & Sparks, R. (2010). What is to be done with public criminology? *Criminology and Public Policy, 9*, 771–781.

Lopez, G. (2017). *How Obama quietly reshaped America's war on drugs*. Vox media: https://www.vox.com.

MacCoun, R., & Reuter, P. (2001). *Drug war heresies*. Cambridge: Cambridge University Press.

MacGregor, S. (2011a). Written evidence to the house of lords' enquiry into the European drug strategy in house of lords. *The EU drugs strategy: Oral and written evidence*. Home Affairs Subcommittee of the European Select Committee: http://www.parliament.co.uk.

MacGregor, S. (2011b). The impact of research on policy in the drugs field. *Methodological Innovations Online, 6*(1), 41–57.

Mackay, J., Eriksen, M., & Shafey, O. (2006). *The tobacco atlas* (2nd ed.). Atlanta, GA: American Cancer Society.

Maher, L., & Dixon, D. (1999). Policing and public health: Law enforcement and harm minimisation in a street-level drug market. *British Journal of Criminology, 39*, 488–512.

Marks, A. (2015, February). *The legal landscape for cannabis social clubs in Spain*. Observatorio Civil de Drogos and Transnational Institute.

Marlatt, G. A. (1996). Harm reduction: Come as you are. *Addictive Behaviours, 21*(6), 779–788.

Martin, J. (2014). Lost on the silk road: Online drug distribution and the "cryptomarket". *Criminology & Criminal Justice, 14*(3), 351–367.

Matthews, R. (2009). Beyond 'so-what?' criminology: Rediscovering realism. *Theoretical Criminology, 13*(3), 341–362.

Matthews, R. (Ed.). (2016). *What is to be done about crime and punishment? Towards a 'Public criminology'*. London: Palgrave Macmillan.

May, T., & Hough, M. (2004). Drug markets and distribution systems. *Addiction Research and Theory, 12*(6), 549–563.

McGrath, M. (2016, March 8, Tuesday). Nancy Reagan and the negative impact of the 'just say no' anti-drug campaign. *The Guardian.*

Measham, F. (2013). Social issues in the use of novel psychoactive substances: Differentiated demand and ideological supply. In P. Dargan & D. Wood (Eds.), *Novel psychoactive substances: Classification, pharmacology and toxicology*. London: Elsevier.

Measham, F., & Newcombe, R. (2016). What's so new about new psychoactive substances? Definitions, prevalence, motivations, user groups and a proposed new taxonomy. In T. Kolind, B. Thom, & G. Hunt. *The Sage handbook of drug & alcohol studies*. London: Sage.

Measham, F., Wood, D., Dargan, P., & Moore, K. (2011). The rise in legal highs: Prevalence and patterns in the use of illegal drugs and first and second generation 'legal highs' in south London gay dance clubs. *Journal of Substance Use, 16*(4), 263–272.

Mejia, D. (2015). *Plan Colombia: An analysis of effectiveness and costs*. https://www.brookings.edu.

Mena, F., & Hobbs, R. (2010). Narcophobia: Drugs prohibition and the generation of human rights abuses. *Trends in Organised Crime, 13*(1), 6–74.

Mendes, S. (2000). Property crime and drug enforcement in Portugal. *Criminal Justice Policy Review, 11*, 195–216.

Messac, L. (2016). The other opioid crisis—People in poor countries can't get the pain medication they need. *The Conversation*, March 25, 2018. https://theconversation.com.

Miller, P. (2001). A critical review of the harm minimization ideology in Australia. *Critical Public Health, 11*(2), 167–178.

Mintrom, M. (1997). Policy entrepreneurs and the diffusion of innovations. *American Journal of Political Science, 41*(3), 738–770.

Miraglia, P. (2015). *Drugs and drug trafficking in Brazil: Trends and policies*. Brookings: http://www.brookings.edu.

Monaghan, M. (2008). Appreciating cannabis: The paradox of evidence in evidence-based policy making. *Evidence and Policy, 4*(2), 209–231.

Moore, D., & Dietze, P. (2005). Enabling environments and the reduction of drug-related harm: Re-framing Australian policy and practice. *Drug and Alcohol Review, 24*, 275–284.

Moore, D., & Fraser, S. (2006). Putting at risk what we know: Reflecting on the drug-using subject in harm reduction and its political implications. *Social Sciences and Medicine, 62*, 3035–3067.

Morrison, W. (2005). Rethinking narratives of penal change in global context. In J. Pratt et al. (Eds.), *The new punitiveness: Trends, theories, perspectives*. Cullompton: Willan.

Mounteney, J., Griffiths, P., & Vandam, L. (2016a). What is the future for internet drug markets. In EMCDDA (Eds.), *The internet and drug markets* (EMCDDA Insights 21). Luxembourg: Publications Office of the European Union.

Mounteney, J., Oteo, A., & Griffiths, P. (2016). The internet and drug markets: Shining a light on these complex and dynamic systems. In EMCDDA (Eds.), *The internet and drug markets* (EMCDDA Insights 21). Luxembourg: Publications Office of the European Union.

Muggah, R., & de Carvalho, S. (2015). How new metrics can reset global drug policy. *World Politics Review*. https://www.worldpoliticsreview.com.

Muggah, R., Aguirre, K., & de Carvalho, S. (2015, January). *Measurement matters: Designing new metrics for a drug policy that works* (Strategic Paper 12). Brazil: Instituto Igarape.

Mulgan, G. (2004). Government, knowledge and the business of policy making: The potential and limits of evidence-based policy. *Evidence and Policy, 1*(2), 215–226.

Mullen, E. J. (2016). Reconsidering the "idea" of evidence in evidence-based policy and practice. *European Journal of Social Work, 19*(3–4), 310–335.

Mulrooney, K. J. D., & van de Ven, K. (2015). *'Muscle profiling' anti-doping policy and deviant leisure*. Deviant Leisure Research Group: https://deviantleisure.wordpress.com/2015/01/21/muscle-profiling-anti-doping-policy-and-deviantleisure.

Murkin, G. (2015). *Cannabis social clubs in Spain: Legalisation without commercialisation*. Transform: https://www.tdpf.org.uk.

Musto, C. (2017). *Regulating cannabis markets: The construction of an innovative drug policy in Uruguay*. Unpublished thesis, University of Kent, Canterbury, UK.

Nadelmann, E. (1989). Drug prohibition in the US: Costs, consequences and alternatives. *Science, 245*, 939–947.

Nadelmann, E. (1993). Progressive legalizers, progressive prohibitionists and the reduction of drug-related harm. In N. Heather, A. Wodak, & E. Nadelmann (Eds.), *Psychoactive drugs and harm reduction: From faith to science*. London: Whurr Publishers.

National Institute on Drug Abuse. (2018). *Opioid overdose crisis*. https://www.drugabuse.gov.

Naughton, M. (2005). "Evidence-based policy" and the government of the criminal justice system—Only if the evidence fits! *Critical Social Policy, 25*(1), 47–69.

Nelken, D. (2009). Comparative criminal justice: Beyond ethnocentrism and relativism. *European Journal of Criminology, 6*(4), 291–311.

Newcombe, R. (1992). The reduction of drug related harm: A conceptual framework for theory, practice and research. In O'Hare et al. (Eds.), *The reduction of drug related harm*. London: Routledge.

Nixon, R. (2018, January 24). Online sales of illegal opioids from China surge in U.S. *The New York Times*.

Nutt, D., King, L. A., & Phillips, C. D. (2010). Drug harms in the UK: A multicriteria decision analysis. *The Lancet, 376*(9752), 6–12.

Nutt, D., King, L. A., Saulsbury, W., & Blakemore, C. (2007). Development of a rational scale to assess the harm of drugs of potential misuse. *The Lancet, 369*(9566), 1047–1053.

O'Brien, K., Chatwin, C., Jenkins, C., & Measham, F. (2015). New psychoactive substances and British drug policy: A view from the cyber-psychonauts. *Drugs: Education, Prevention and Policy, 22*(3), 217–223.

O'Hare, P. (2007). Merseyside, the first harm reduction conferences, and the early history of harm reduction. *International Journal of Drug Policy, 18*, 141–144.

O'Malley, P. (2009). *Drugs, risks and freedoms: Illicit drug "use" and "misuse" under neo-liberal governance* (Legal Studies Research Paper No. 09/120). Sydney Law School.

Organisation of American States. (2013a). *Scenarios for the drug problem in the Americas 2013–2025*. https://www.oas.org.

Organisation of American States. (2013b). *The drug problem in the Americas.* https://www.oas.org.

Owen, T. (2016, March 6). Just say no: How Nancy Reagan helped America lose the war on drugs. *Vice News.*

Page, E. (2000). *Future governance and the literature on policy transfer and lesson drawing* (Future Governance Papers). Swindon, UK: ESRC.

Pardo, B. (2014). Cannabis policy reforms in the Americas: A comparison of Colorado, Washington and Uruguay. *International Journal of Drug Policy, 25*, 727–735.

Parker, H., Aldridge, J., & Measham, F. (1998). *Illegal leisure: The normalization of adolescent recreational drug use.* London: Routledge.

Pearce, W., Wasselink, A., & Colebatch, H. (2014). Evidence and meaning in policy making. *Evidence and Policy, 10*(2), 161–165.

Pearson, G., & Hobbs, D. (2001). *Middle market drug distribution* (Home Office Research Study 227). London: Home Office.

Pedersen, W., Fjaer, E. G., Gray, P., & von Soest, T. (2016). Perceptions of harms associated with tobacco, alcohol and cannabis in students from the UK and Norway. *Contemporary Drug Problems, 43*(1), 47–61.

Perrone, D. (2016). Designer drugs. In H. H. Brownstein (Ed.), *The handbook of drugs and society*. Chichester, UK: Wiley Blackwell.

Philippines Daily Inquirer. (2016, October 16). *Story in numbers war on drugs.* https://www.newsinfo.inquirer.net.

Pinto Coelho, M. (2010, February 2). *Decriminalization of drugs in Portugal—The real facts*! World Federation Against Drugs: http://www.wfad.se/latest-news/1articles/123-decriminalization-of-drugs-in-portugal–the-real-facts.

Portuguese Institute for Drugs and Drug Addiction. (2005). *National plan against drugs and drug addiction 2005–2012: Executive Summary*. http://www.idt.pt.

Portuguese Institute for Drugs and Drug Addiction. (2008). *'Portugal': New development, trends and in-depth information on selected issues.* 2008 National Report (2007 data) to the EMCDDA by the Reitox Focal Point. https://idt.pt.

Potter, G. R. (2009). Exploring retail-level drug distribution: Social supply, "real" dealers and the user/dealer interface. In Z. Demetrovics, J. Fountain, & L. Kraus (Eds.), *Old and new policies, theories, research methods and drug users across Europe.* Lengerich, Germany: Pabst Science Publishers.

Potter, G. R., & Chatwin, C. (2018). Not particularly special: Critiquing "NPS" as a category of drugs. *Drugs: Education, Prevention and Policy.* https://doi.org/10.1080/09687637.2017.1411885.

Provine, D. M. (2007). *Unequal under law: Race in the war on drugs.* Chicago and London: University of Chicago Press.

Pryce, S. (2012). *Fixing drugs: The politics of drug prohibition.* Basingstoke: Palgrave Macmillan.

Queirolo, R., Boidi, M. F., & Cruz, J. (2016). Cannabis clubs in Uruguay: The challenges of regulation. *International Journal of Drug Policy, 34*, 41–48.

Quintana, P., Ventura, M., Grifell, M., Palma, A, Galindo, L., Fornis, I., Gil, C., Carbon, X., Caudevilla, F., Farre, M. and Torrens, M. (2017). The hidden web and the fentanyl problem: Detection of ocfentanil as an adulterant in heroin. *International Journal of Drug Policy, 40*, 78–83.

Race, K. (2008). The use of pleasure in harm reduction: Perspectives from the history of sexuality. *International Journal of Drug Policy, 19*, 417–423.

Ralphs, R., Williams, L., Askew, R., & Norton A. (2017). Adding spice to the porridge: The development of a synthetic cannabinoid market in an English prison. *International Journal of Drug Policy, 40*, 57–69.

Rea, S. (2017). The Londoners who sell drugs online. *Londonist*: https://londonist.com.

Reinarman, C., Cohen, P., & Kaal, H. (2004). The limited relevance of drug policy: Cannabis in Amsterdam and San Francisco. *American Journal of Public Health, 94*, 836–842.

Reuter, P. (2011). *Options for regulating new psychoactive drugs: A review of recent experiences.* London: UK Drug Policy Commission.

Reuter, P. (2013). Why has US drug policy changed so little over 20 years? *Crime and Justice, 42*(1), 75–140.

Reuter, P., & Pardo, B. (2016). Can new psychoactive substances be regulated effectively? An assessment of the British psychoactive substances bill. *Addiction.* https://doi.org/10.1111/add.13439.

Reuter, P., & Pardo, B. (2017). New psychoactive substances: Are there any good options for regulating new psychoactive substances? *International Journal of Drug Policy, 40*, 113–118.

Rhodes, T. (2002). The risk environment: A framework for understanding and reducing drug related harm. *International Journal of Drug Policy, 13*, 85–94.

Rhodes, T. (2009). Risk environments and drug harms: A social sciences for harm reduction. *International Journal of Drug Policy, 20*, 193–201.

Rhodes, T., & Hedrich, D. (2010). Harm reduction and the mainstream. In European Monitoring Centre for Drugs and Drug Addiction (Eds.), *Harm reduction: Evidence, impacts and challenges*. https://www.emcdda.europa.eu.

Rhodes, T., Singer, M., Bourgois, P., Friedman, S., & Strathdee, A. (2005). The social production of HIV risk among injecting drug users. *Social Science and Medicine, 61*, 1026–1044.

Rittel, H. W. J., & Webber, M. M. (1973). Dilemmas in a general theory of planning. *Policy Sciences, 4*, 155–169.

Ritter, A. (2009). How do drug policy makers access research evidence? *International Journal of Drug Policy, 20*, 70–75.

Ritter, A., & Bammer, G. (2010). Models of policy-making and their relevance for drug research. *Drug and Alcohol Review, 29*, 352–357.

Robelo, D. (2013). *Breaking the Taboo: Why the OAS report on alternatives to drug prohibition is such a big deal*. Drug Policy Alliance: www.drugpolicy.org.

Roberts, M. (2014). Making drug policy together: Reflections on evidence, engagement and participation. *International Journal of Drug Policy, 25*, 952–956.

Robertson, R. (1995). Glocalization: Time-space and homogeneity-heterogeneity? In M. Featherstone, S. Lash, & R. Robertson (Eds.), *Global modernities*. London: Sage.

Roe, G. (2006). Harm reduction as paradigm: Is better than bad good enough? The origins of harm reduction. *Critical Public Health, 15*(3), 243–250.

Rolles, S. (2014). *Cannabis policy in The Netherlands: Moving forwards not backwards*. https://www.tdpf.org.uk.

Rolleston Report. (1926). *Departmental committee on Morphine and heroin addiction*. London: HMSO.

Room, R. (2006). The dangerousness of drugs. *Addiction, 101*, 166–168.

Room, R. (2011). Scales and blinkers, modes and beams: Whose view is obstructed on drug scheduling? *Addiction, 106*(11), 1895–1896.

Room, R. (2012). Reform by subtraction: The path of denunciation of international drug treaties and reaccession with reservations. *International Journal of Drug Policy, 23*, 401–406.

Room, R. (2013). Legalizing a market for cannabis for pleasure: Colorado, Washington, Uruguay and beyond. *Addiction, 109*, 345–351.

Room, R., & MacKay, S. (2012). *Roadmaps to reforming the UN drug convention.* A Beckley Foundation Report: http://www.beckleyfoundation.org.

Room, R., & Reuter, P. (2012). How well do international drug conventions protect public health? *The Lancet, 379*, 84–91.

Room, R., Fischer, B., Hall, W., Lenton, S., & Reuter, P. (2010). *Cannabis policy: Moving beyond stalemate*. Oxford: Oxford University Press and The Beckley Foundation.

Rose, R. (1991). What is lesson-drawing? *Journal of Public Policy, 11*(1), 3–30.

Rossow, I. (2011). Can harm ratings be useful? *Addiction, 106*, 1893–1894.

Roumeliotis, F. (2015). Politics of prevention: The emergence of prevention science. *International Journal of Drug Policy, 26*, 746–754.

Ruane, D. (2015). Harm reduction of psychedelic support? Caring for drug-related crises at transformational festivals. *Dancecult: Journal of Electronic Dancemusic Culture, 7*(1), 55–75.

Sanderson, I. (2009). Intelligent policy making for a complex world: Pragmatism, evidence and learning. *Political Studies, 57*, 699–719.

Scammell, L., & Bo, A. (2016). Online supply of medicines to illicit drug markets: Situation and responses. In EMCDDA (Eds.), *The internet and drug markets* (EMCDDA Insights 21). Luxembourg: Publications Office of the European Union.

Scholte, J. A. (2010). Civil society in multi-level governance. In H. Enderlein, S. Walti, & M. Zurn (Eds.), *Handbook on multi-level governance*. Cheltenham: Edward Elgar.

Seddon, T. (2014). Drug policy and global regulatory capitalism: The case of new psychoactive substances (NPS). *International Journal of Drug Policy*. https://doi.org/10.1016/j.drugpo.2014.03.009.

Shiner, M. (2003). Out of harm's way? Illicit drug use, medicalisation and the law. *British Journal of Criminology, 43*, 772–796.

Small, W., Wood, E., Jurgens, R., & Kerr, T. (2005). Injection drug use HIV/AIDS and incarceration: Evidence from the Vancouver injection drug users study. *HIV AIDS Policy Law Review, 10*, 5–10.

Snap, Z. (2016). Drug policy innovations in Latin America. *Latin America Policy Journal*. Harvard Kennedy School Student Publication: www.hkslapj.com.

Souleymanov, R., & Allman, D. (2016). Articulating connections between the harm reduction paradigm and the marginalisation of people who use illicit drugs. *British Journal of Social Work, 46*, 1429–1445.

South, N. (1999). Debating drugs and everyday life: Normalisation, prohibition and "otherness". In N. South (Ed.), *Drugs: cultures, controls and everyday life*. London: Sage.

Standring, A. (2012). An ever closer union—Towards the "soft" convergence of European drug policies. *Drugs and Alcohol Today, 12*(1), 12–19.

STAT. (2017). *STAT forecast: Opioids could kill nearly 500,000 Americans in the next decade*. https://www.statnews.com.

Stevens, A. (2007). Survival of the ideas that fit: An evolutionary analogy for the use of evidence. *Social Policy and Society, 6*(1), 25–35.

Stevens, A. (2011a). *Drugs, crime and public health: The political economy of drug policy*. London: Routledge-Cavendish.

Stevens, A. (2011b). Telling policy stories: An ethnographic study of the use of evidence in policy-making in the UK. *Journal of Social Policy, 40*, 237–255.

Stevens, A., & Hughes, C. (2016). Decriminalisation and public health: The Portuguese approach to drug policy (translation). *Mouvement, 86*, 22–33.

Stevens, A., & Measham, F. (2014). The 'drug policy ratchet': Why do sanctions for new psychoactive substances typically only go up? *Addiction, 109*(8), 1226–1232.

Stevens, A., Fortson, R., Measham, F., & Sumnall, H. (2015). Legally flawed, scientifically problematic, potentially harmful: The UK psychoactive substance bill. *International Journal of Drug Policy, 26*, 1167–1170.

Stimson, G. V. (1995). AIDS and injecting drug use in the United Kingdom, 1987–1993: The policy response and the prevention of the epidemic. *Social Science Medicine, 41*(5), 699–716.

Stone, D. (2001a). Think tanks, global lesson-drawing and networking social policy ideas. *Global Social Policy, 1*(3), 338–360.

Stone, D. (2001b, April). *Learning lessons, policy transfer and the international diffusion of policy ideas* (Working Paper No. 69.01). Centre for the Study of Globalisation and Regionalisation.

Strang, J., Babor, T., Caulkins, J., Fischer, B., Foxcroft, D., & Humphreys, K. (2012). Drug policy and the public good: Evidence for effective interventions. *The Lancet, 379*, 71–83.

Sumnall, H. R., Evans-Brown, M., McVeigh J. (2011). Social, policy, and public health perspectives on new psychoactive substances. *Drug Testing and Analysis, 3*, 515–523.

Szalavitz, M. (2009). Drugs in Portugal: Did decriminalisation work? *Time*. http://www.time.com.

The Dialogue. (2016). *UNGASS 2016: Towards a new drug policy in the Americas?* https://www.thedialogue.org.

The Economist. (2017). *A selective scourge: Inside the opioid epidemic.* https://www.economist.com.

Transnational Institute. (2015). *Canadian company to tap into Jamaica for medicinal cannabis supply.* https://www.tni.org.

Transnational Institute. (2016a). *UNGASS 2016: Watershed event or wasted opportunity?* https://www.tni.org.

Transnational Institute. (2016b). *The UNGASS outcome document: Diplomacy or denialism?* https://www.tni.org.

Transnational Institute. (2018). *Mission.* https://www.tni.org/en/page/mission.

Toffler, A. (1970). *Future shock.* New York: Random House.

Tops, D. (2001). *A society with or without drugs? Continuity and change in drug policies in Sweden and The Netherlands.* Lunds Dissertations in Social Work 5, Lund University, Lund.

Transform. (2014). *Drug decriminalisation in Portugal: Setting the record straight.* https://www.tdpf.org.uk.

Transform. (2015). *Ending the war on drugs. How to win the global drug policy debate.* https://www.tdpf.org.uk.

Transform. (2016). *Diplomacy or denialism? The language that the UNGASS outcome document overlooked.* www.tdpf.org.uk.

Transnational Institute. (2015). *UNGASS 2016: Background memo on the proposal to establish an expert advisory group.* https://www.tni.org.

Transnational Institute. (2016). *Cannabis regulation and the UN drug treaties: Strategies for reform.* https://www.tni.org.

Travis, A. (2014, January 13, Monday). Legal highs: UK to opt out of new EU regulations regime. *The Guardian.*

True, J. L., Jones, B. D., & Baumgartner, F. R. (2007). Punctuated-equilibrium theory: Explaining stability and change in public policymaking. In P. A. Sabatier (Ed.), *Theories of the policy process.* Boulder, CO: Westview Press.

Uchtenhagen, A. (2014). Some critical issues in cannabis policy reform. *Addiction, 109*(3), 356–358.

Uggen, C., & Inderbitzen, M. (2010). Public criminologies. *Criminology and Public Policy, 9*, 725–749.

Uitermark, J. (2004). The origins and future of the Dutch approach towards drugs. *Journal of Drug Issues, 34*, 511–532.

United Nations. (1961). *Single convention on narcotic drugs, 1961*. http://www.druglibrary.org/schaffer/legal.
United Nations Development Programme. (2015). *Perspectives on the development dimensions of drug control policy*. www.undp.org.
UNODC. (2007). *Sweden's successful drug policy: A review of the evidence*. http://www.unodc.org.
UNODC. (2008). *World drug report 2008*. http://www.unodc.org/documents.
UNODC. (2010). *World drug report 2010*. http://www.unodc.org/documents.
UNODC. (2011). *World drug report 2011*. http://www.unodc.org/documents.
UNODC. (2013, March). *The challenge of new psychoactive substances*. Global Smart Programme.
UNODC. (2014). *World drug report 2014*. http://www.unodc.org/documents.
UNODC. (2016). *Outcome document of the 2016 United Nations General Assembly Special Session on the world drug problem. Our joint commitment to effectively addressing and countering the world drug problem*. New York: United Nations. http://www.unodc.org/documents.
UNODC. (2017). *World drug report 2017*. http://www.unodc.org/documents.
UNODC. (2018). *Twelve substances 'scheduled' at the 61st session of the commission on narcotic drugs*. UNODC Early Warning Advisory on New Psychoactive Substances: https://www.unodc.org.
Valentine, K. (2009). Evidence, values and drug treatment policy. *Critical Social Policy, 29*(3), 443–464.
van Amsterdam, J., Nutt, D., & van den Brink, W. (2013). Generic legislation of new psychoactive drugs. *Journal of Psychopharmacology, 27*(3), 317–324.
van Amsterdam, J., Nutt, D., Phillips, L., & van den Brink, W. (2015). European rating of drug harms. *Journal of Psychopharmacology, 29*(6), 655–660.
van Amsterdam, J., Opperhuisen, A., Koeter, M., & van den Brink, W. (2010). Ranking the harm of alcohol, tobacco and illicit drugs for the individual and the population. *European Addiction Research, 16*, 202–207.
van de Ven, K., & Mulrooney, K. (2017). Social suppliers: Exploring the cultural contours of the Performance and Image Enhancing Drug (PIED) market amongst bodybuilders in The Netherlands and Belgium. *International Journal of Drug Policy, 40*, 6–15.
van het Loo, M., van Beusekom, I., & Kahan, J. (2002). Decriminalisation of drug use in Portugal: The development of a policy. *Annals of the American Academy of Political and Social Science, 582*, 49–63.

van Hout, M. C., & Hearne, H. (2017). New Psychoactive Substances (NPS) on cryptomarket fora: An exploratory study of characteristics of forum activity between NPS buyers and vendors. *International Journal of Drug Policy, 40*, 102–110.

van Swaaningen, R. (1999). Reclaiming critical criminology: Social justice and the European tradition. *Theoretical Criminology, 3*(1), 5–28.

Vasconi, C. (2013). *Where next for Europe on drug policy reform?* Expert Seminar 20–21 June, Lisbon, Portugal, Transnational Institute.

Vastag, B. (2009, April). 5 year's after: Portugal's decriminalization policy shows positive results. *Scientific American 7*. http://www.scientificamerican.com.

Walker, J. (1969). The diffusion of innovations among the American States. *American Political Review, 33*(3), 880–899.

Walsh, C. (2011). Drugs the internet and change. *Journal of Psychoactive Drugs, 43*(1), 55–63.

Walsh, J., & Ramsey, G. (2016). *Uruguay's drug policy: Major innovations, major challenges*. Brookings: https://www.brookings.edu.

Watters, P. A., & Phair, N. (2012). Detecting illicit drugs on social media using automated social media intelligence analysis (ASMIA). In Y. Xiang, J. Lopez, CC. J. Kuo, & W. Zhou (Eds.), *Cyberspace safety and security* (Lecturenotes in Computer Science, 7672). Berlin, Heidelberg: Springer.

Weiss, C. H. (1977). The enlightenment function of social science research. *Policy Analysis, 3*(4), 531–545.

Weiss, C. H. (1986). The many meanings of research utilisation. In M. Bulmer (Ed.), *Social science and social policy*. London: Allen Unwin.

Werb, D., Kazatchkine, M., Kerr, T., Nutt, D., Strathdee, S., Hankins, C., et al. (2016). A call to reprioritise metrics to evaluate illicit drugs policy. *The Lancet, 387*, 1371.

Werb, D., Kerr, T., Nosyk, B., Strathdee, S., Montaner, J., & Wood, E. (2013). The temporal relationship between drug supply indicators: An audit of international government surveillance systems. *BMJ Open, 3*, 1–8.

Werb, D., Rowell, G., Guyatt, G., Kerr, T., Montaner, J., & Wood, E. (2011). Effect of drug law enforcement on drug market violence: A systematic review. *International Journal of Drug Policy, 22*(2), 87–94.

Werb, D., Wood, E., Strathdee, S., Kazatchkine, M., des Jarlais, D., Hankins, C., et al. (2016). *Open letter to the United Nations: A call for a reprioritisation of metrics to evaluate illicit drug policy*. International Centre for Science in Drugs Policy: https://www.icsdp.org.

West Africa Commission on Drugs. (2014). *Not just in transit. Drugs, the state and society in West Africa*. http://www.wacommissiondrugs.org.

WHO. (2014). *Global status report on alcohol and health 2014*. http://apps.who.int.

Wilkins, C. (2017). Recent developments with the New Zealand regulated market approach to "low-risk" psychoactive products. *Addiction, 112*, 32–39.

Wilson, C. (2016, October 24). Addiction to prescription drugs is UK "public health disaster". *New Scientist Daily News*.

Winstock, A., & Ramsey, J. (2010). Legal highs and the challenges for policy makers. *Addiction, 105*(10), 1685–1687.

Wolfe, D., & Malinowska-SEmpruch, K. (2004). *Illicit drug policies and the global HIV epidemic. Effects on UN and national government approaches*. New York: Open Society Institute, International Harm Reduction Development.

Wood, E., Werb, D., Kazatchkine, M., Kerr, T., Hankins, C., Gorna, R., et al. (2010). Vienna declaration: A call for evidence-based drug policies. *The Lancet, 376*, 310–312.

Woodiwiss, M. (1988). *Crime, crusades and corruption: Prohibitions in the United States, 1900–1987*. London: Pinter.

Woodiwiss, M., & Bewley-Taylor, D. (2005). *The global fix: The construction of a global enforcement regime*. Amsterdam: Transnational Institute, Crime and Globalisation Programme.

Wouters, M., Benschop, A., van Laar, M., & Korf, D. J. (2012). Cannabis use and proximity to coffeeshops in The Netherlands. *European Journal of Criminology, 9*(4), 337–353.

Young, J. (1971). *The drugtakers: The social meaning of drug use*. London: McGibbon & Kee.

Young, K., Ashby, D., Boaz, A., & Grayson, L. (2002). Social science and the evidence-based policy movement. *Social Policy and Society, 1*(3), 215–224.

Youngers, C. A. (2005). The collateral damage of the U.S. war on drugs: Conclusions and recommendations. In C. A. Youngers & E. Rosin (Eds.), *Drugs and democracy in Latin America*. London: Lynne Reiner Publishers.

Youngers, C. A. (2011, April). *The Obama administration's drug control policy on auto-pilot* (IDPC Briefing Paper). http://www.idpc.net.

Youngers, C. A., & Rosin, E. (2005). The U.S. "war on drugs". In C. A. Youngers & E. Rosin (Eds.), *Drugs and democracy in Latin America*. London: Lynne Reiner Publishers.

Zahariadis, N. (2007). The multiple streams framework: Structure, limitations, prospects. In P. A. Sabatier (Ed.), *Theories of the policy process.* Boulder, CO: Westview Press.

Zhang, S., & Chin, K. -L. (2015). *A people's war: China's struggle to contain its illicit drug problem*. Brookings: https://www.brookings.edu.

Zurn, M., Walti, S., & Enderlein, H. (2010). Introduction. In H. Enderlein, S. Walti, & M. Zurn (Eds.), *Handbook on multi-level governance.* Cheltenham: Edward Elgar.

Index

C. Chatwin, *Towards More Effective Global Drug Policies*,
https://doi.org/10.1007/978-3-319-92072-6

The manufacturer's authorised representative in the EU is Springer
Nature Customer Service Centre GmbH, Europaplatz 3, 69115 Heidelberg,
Germany. If you have any concerns regarding our products, please
contact ProductSafety@springernature.com

Printed and bound by CPI Group (UK) Ltd, Croydon, CR0 4YY
30/09/2026
02225653-0007